Wanderland

Living the Traveling Life

Kate Evans

Wanderland: Living the Traveling Life

ISBN: 978-1-960326-28-7

Tehom Center Publishing is a 501c3 non-profit imprint of Parson's Porch Books. Tehom Center Publishing celebrates feminist and queer authors, with a commitment that at least half our authors are people of color. Its face and voice is Rev. Dr. Angela Yarber.

Wanderland

For Dave

traveling companion, life companion

and in memory of Mark Phinney

What is home anyway, but what we cobble together
out of our changing selves?
— Abigail Thomas

Author's Note:

I wrote this book to take you along on a real journey. In addition to relying on my memory, I referenced my social media posts, blog entries, and photographs. I also sent sections to people who were involved as a check on my facts. Any errors are mine and mine alone. Most human and pet names are real, although a few were changed or omitted.

Also by Kate Evans:

Call It Wonder: An Odyssey of Love, Sex, Spirit, and Travel
For the May Queen
Complementary Colors
Target
Like All We Love
Negotiating the Self
Revolutionary Kiss (co-authored with Mary Janelle Melvin as Mary-Kate Summers)

Contents

Prologue

A Stranger's House

Thanksgiving, 2019

On Thanksgiving, we enter a stranger's house. At the end of the deep hallway lined with atmospheric oil paintings, a stylish kitchen emerges: antique gas stove, butcher block island, and cast-iron pans dangling from gleaming racks. The adjoining dining room features an oak table long enough to seat ten guests. But tonight we need only two chairs: one for my husband and one for me.

The living room's creamy sectional couch is draped with woolly throws, and the built-in shelves are crammed with enticing books. I scrutinize titles. Lots of choice, but I'll have to pick wisely because we'll be here only four days. We peek into the bathroom: pedestal sink and curvy clawfoot tub. The lemony, lavender scent of bath products, and a silk robe draped from a hook, cast such a sensual spell I feel like a voyeur. In the adjoining bedroom, a painting of a woman's nude back—wisps of chestnut hair escaping her bun—presides over the bed. I press my hand into the mattress, and its plushness invites me in. But we have a lot to do before we can rest.

A rattling noise draws us toward the closet, pocket door ajar. Silks and velvets overflow the rod, and hatboxes slouch on the top shelf above crowded shoe racks. I think about how I used to own dozens of shoes but now have five pair. As my eyes adjust to the haze, I hear a vocalization, like the squeal of a newborn—and a furry blur springs from the closet.

"Hey there." Dave greets a striped cat with pondwater-green eyes. He bends to stroke her head, and she threads her narrow body around Dave's ankles.

"This must be Stella." I hold out my hand and she sniffs at my knuckles. "I wonder where Santana is?" I remember the cats' names because we have a friend named Stella and as children of the 70's, who can forget Santana?

"He'll show up," Dave says. "Let's get our stuff."

And so begins the ritual of making a stranger's house our home. After having eaten Thanksgiving brunch with my sister in a nearby town, we'd grocery shopped—so we have those bags to haul in, plus our suitcases,

15

my ukulele, and my blue fuzzy blanket. I don't care how many comfy throws a house has, if we are traveling by car, my blankie has to come.

Dave's priority is arranging his toiletries and clothes in an empty closet or drawer, if the homeowner thought to clear space for us. If not, he'll prop his open suitcase on a chair or extra bed so wandering bugs or animals don't invade his things. He'll locate a spot for my suitcase, too. Although he was never in the military, he's Army barracks clean-and-organized. And he likes to perform one task at a time. Whereas me, I might scatter my shoes in the entryway and shove on my slippers, stash the cold food in the fridge, claim my side of the bed by draping my nightgown on the pillow, then circle back to the kitchen.

In the bedroom, I pull out my Kindle to place on the side stand and, noting the pillows propped side-by-side, I recall the homeowner had mentioned on the housesitting website that she is a recent widow. Although she hadn't referred to her husband's death during our phone conversation, she'd said "they" had owned this home for many years. She was sorry we couldn't meet in person since she'd have to leave in the early morning—but she hid the key for us.

I wonder if she is the artist, or was he? Or were they both not art makers but collectors, art lovers? How many of the hundreds of books in this house had he held in his hands, reading glasses resting on the bridge of his nose? When was the last time they curled together in this bed?

The sense of absence makes my knees soft.

"Hey, let's go on a walk." Dave comes up from behind and nuzzles my neck, as though my thoughts have drawn him to me.

Before we leave, we locate Santana, the shy cat, a larger version of his sister. The two felines are now pretzeled together on a living room chair. While Dave—living up to his nickname Dr. Doolittle—gives them rubs and chats with them, I make sure they have clean water and dry food in their bowls.

The morning fog has melted away to unveil an aqua sky smeared with silvery clouds. We've bundled up in gloves, hats, and jackets. The air feels delicate and frosty, especially after having spent six months in balmy Hawai'i. We've come to California to visit friends and family before heading south to Mexico.

We traipse up the hill through a neighborhood of Victorian architecture, houses frosted with spirals and turrets and gingerbread flair. We pass stately Marina Middle School, the names of renowned thinkers chiseled on the roofline: Euclid, Emerson, Darwin. Winding our way over to the Palace of Fine Arts, we stroll around the rotunda, along the colonnades that echo Ancient Roman and Greek ruins but that were built for the 1915 Panama-Pacific Exposition. Dave—whose primary accoutrement is not a smartphone but a real camera with telephoto lens—takes a shot of an ornamental pillar, a swan slipping across the mirrored lagoon and, when we've ventured further into the Marina District, a selfie of us with the iconic Golden Gate Bridge hovering behind our heads.

We're playing tourists in an area we know well. Twenty years ago, when Dave was in his early forties, he lived a few blocks from where we now stand. Before that, growing up in a nearby town, he worked in his parents' San Francisco-based optical business. My mother was born and raised in the city's Mission District. Her brother, my Uncle Bob, walked with his buddies across the Golden Gate Bridge the day it opened. When we'd first met, Dave and I discovered we were both native Californians for several generations, and we'd lived in the Bay Area for years.

But now, where was home?

For the past nine years we've been living in other people's houses. We have done nearly fifty housesits in the States and abroad, caring for people's pets and gardens. When we're not housesitting, we might rent an Airbnb (or, rarely, a hotel room). We've stayed with friends from Massachusetts to Oregon, from India to Australia. The longest we've been in one location was nearly a year in China.

What started as an experiment of living on the road has morphed into a way of life. A wandering life, residing in not one place but many. A life of travel, not as vacation but vocation.

Over the years, we meet more and more people who embrace versions of the itinerant life. From retired full-time travelers to digital nomads to those deemed "location independent" to world-schoolers who take their kids along, people are seizing the flexibility of making a living online and using websites and social media to find free or inexpensive places to perch. We hadn't realized we'd be part of a movement.

I wonder what my parents would have thought of my unconventional life. They loved to travel but the notion of housing stability was vital to them. Experimental wayfaring would have been unrecognizable for children of the Depression who bought their first home with the help of the G.I. bill. As their careers developed and salaries increased they moved our family into nicer and nicer suburban houses and finally built their split-level dream home, designed by my dad. I remember tracing my finger over the squeaky blueprints as he let my two sisters and me choose our rooms. Our first night there we had no electricity so we went to bed early in the dark, engulfed in the exotic scent of new wood, glue, and shag wall-to-wall carpet. I'd excitedly kept my eyes open in the dark as long as I could, feeling like a girl in an adventure novel.

Dave—also a child of California rural suburbia—has a strikingly similar memory. Like me, he was the middle of three kids and was also twelve when his parents built a new house. For the first time, he wouldn't have to share a room with his brother. Dave's bedroom furniture was delivered a day early. Eagerly he asked his parents if he could spend one night alone in the new house, which was down the road. What had been enticing morphed into fear of alien noises and unfamiliar smells. Yet soon, that house became home.

Five years later, though, he lost that family dwelling when his parents divorced and sold it. His father relocated to a city apartment and his mother moved in with her new boyfriend. In his last semester of high school, Dave and his brother leased an apartment, paying rent by doing the books for his dad's optical office. It was surreal, he said, to be uprooted, his previously stable nuclear family torn asunder. And yet part of him had been excited about being on the cusp of change, preparing to go to college, being an adult moving out into the world. However, due to their new circumstances, his parents said they could no longer afford to pay tuition. He had to abandon his plans to attend a private university and focused instead on U.C. Berkeley, a public institution which was actually affordable in the 1970s. He'd missed the application deadline for the dorms, so he rushed a fraternity in hopes one would take him in.

While waiting, he loaded his car with all his possessions and stayed in a camper in a friend's yard. Fortunately, Sigma Chi signed him on, and he moved into the fraternity house. While he might go to his mom's for holiday dinners, or visit his grandmother in nearby Menlo Park, he didn't have a room with family. He was one of a handful of fraternity brothers who didn't go home for breaks or summer. This clique jokingly dubbed themselves the "Holiday Losers." Dave loved that they weren't under their families' thumbs. Berkeley was theirs. They'd run the hills, kick soccer balls, and get drunk together on Golden Gate Field—exulting in their freedom.

"Home" as shifting sands was a theme in both of our lives. Before we met, Dave and I had each lived in many houses and apartments, sometimes alone, other times with lovers or roommates or spouses. Dave had a nine-year marriage under his belt. I had two: five years to a man and fifteen to a woman.

Dave and I met in the twenty-first century singles' bar: a dating website. At that point we were both renters. He lived in a spacious Sausalito apartment atop a hill with a sparkling bay vista—with two stunning female roommates. I wasn't sure what *that* was about until I got to know him better. Dave has lots of friends, women and men. And, having been unmarried for nearly a decade, he'd lived in lots of alternative situations. When we met, he was newly working for a tech startup in San Jose, more than an hour commute, so several nights a week he crashed on a friend's couch.

I, too, was in a transitional time, living alone in San Jose in a sixth-floor, one-bedroom apartment across the street from the university where I was teaching. I was entangled in a dreadful, drawn-out divorce from my wife, who was claiming I had no stake in the house we'd owned for three years. It was her mother's former domicile, after all, a third of which she'd inherited—the only reason we could afford to buy a house in the insanity that is California real estate. Stupidly, I'd allowed my name to be left off the title. I don't recall the reasoning, but we were going to be together forever, so who cared? During the split, she claimed my contribution to the mortgage had been "rent." As two women we were a new breed of married couple, but our divorce was the archetypal shattering of home and vows. (Ironically, we had wed during the brief window of time same-sex marriage was legalized in California before voters overturned it in a referendum. So we had the piece of paper, but the legality was in limbo. Nevertheless, we had to engage lawyers for a dissolution.)

Three months after Dave and I met, he dismantled his Sausalito life and moved in with me. It made sense; his office was only a few miles away. Besides, we were in love. We discovered we were of the same tribe: we liked to lift anchor, to explore and travel—and we tended to relish change. After a year in the apartment, we traded the city for the seaside, moving to a rental townhome in beachside Santa Cruz.

Our friends nicknamed our place The Love Nest. Small and architecturally stylish, its staircase spiraled up to the loft bedroom. Our first summer there, we flew to Mexico City to visit friends and buy our wedding outfits then traveled to Hawai'i to get married on 'Anaeho'omalu Bay Beach with forty guests, a sea turtle at our feet the best man. The next spring, we were informed our Love Nest had gone up for sale. It was as though a big finger in the sky tipped the first domino. I took an early retirement from the university. With no debt and some savings, with no rent or mortgage, what was possible?

And now, here we are, nine years into an experiment that has become our life.

Eight years earlier

"What's it like to live without a house?"

We'd been nomadic for a year and were gathered with a group one warm night on the deck of a sprawling house near Zion National Park. Now that the sun had set in a flare of purple and orange, gaudy stars draped the

19

sky like Liberace's cape. What a show-off Mother Nature was in Southwest Utah.

Our friend Mark had rented the house over Fourth of July week and invited Dave and me. After traveling in Australia, Hong Kong, India, and Sri Lanka, we were back in California on a road trip. Our bikes strapped to the top of our car, we drove south through the Golden State and at Big Bear Mountain Resort, we'd hauled our bikes up on the ski lift and ridden them down the fire trails. In L.A., we'd stayed with friends, danced to Michael Franti's ebullient tunes at the Hollywood Bowl—then on our way to Zion, stayed at Airbnbs in Palm Springs and Sedona, Arizona.

When we arrived at Mark's vacation rental house, we hadn't realized we were walking into a family reunion: twenty people spread over three generations, featuring communal meals, group hikes, and living room dances to Mark's DJing and laser light machine. Mark's Aunt Jackie, wineglass in hand, posed the question about living house-free. She stressed that she loved traveling but eventually looked forward to going home, to be in her familiar surroundings and involved in her rituals.

I understood what she meant. I'd felt that way most of my life, the interplay between being rooted and flying, how one seems to rely on the other. You go on a trip, spread your wings. When they tire, you return to the nest, settle in, watch the sky.

Was Jackie uncomfortable with the idea of being untethered? Was I? I once read the literal translation for *where are you from?* in Haitian is *where are you a person?* Was there something fundamental missing in me without *home?* I loved the quirkiness and freedom of our life. The inventive nature of being a different person in new places. The jostling of an identity that can solidify in one spot. We didn't even have a grand plan to confirm our purpose, no scheme, for example, to circumnavigate the globe and see eighteen countries in a year. We merely wanted to wander where opportunity invited.

Yet every so often, I'd hear someone refer to their house and town, and I'd imagine a shady backyard garden abloom with lilies and asters, or a living room with stuffed bookshelves, and a homesick ache would threaten to congeal in my bones. A nebulous desire. The closest word I could pin to that feeling was *comfort*. I no longer had a favorite chair. A reliably snug mattress. My own dog. A friend down the street to borrow our lawn mower or invite us over for brunch.

But was comfort crucial? Could it deaden the soul, stale and numb the spirit? Before that homesick sensation tsunamied me, I'd *been fine*. Comfortable…or comfortable enough. No place or pillow or pet could fill this peculiar void. Funny how "wanting" means both desiring and missing. I often remind myself nothing is truly missing *in this moment*. Discomfort is my mind clinging to some idea of solidity. I may occasionally romanticize "home", but the reality of being fastened to one spot, surrounded by a lot of *stuff*, makes me want to fly away.

I turned to Dave. "What do you think?"

His face was half-lit by a slice of Utah moon. "We didn't leave with an idea that we'd go back to somewhere." His precise diction had a relaxed quality, like a newscaster on holiday. "There is no looking forward to returning. Wherever we are, that's where we're living."

A chill pricked my arms. It was existential. Not return? Were we astronauts floating in a no-gravity zone? Did we belong nowhere, or everywhere? My DNA felt on the verge of redistributing, like I was becoming another kind of creature that didn't rely on habitats. Or habits.

I said something to Jackie about home being a mindset, and how we nest on longer housesits, but as the words tumbled from my mouth they sounded pat. I couldn't capture the complexity of what I was feeling. I didn't want to come to conclusions, to live life by a slogan. I wanted to stay open, to not make up my mind. To witness, not explain. To live in the unfolding. To, as Rilke says, learn to love the questions themselves.

But how long can we stay open before our guts and brains fall out? Don't we need some sort of skin that holds it all together? Isn't home a major point on the hierarchy of needs, four walls to hold us and a carpet for warmth? Maybe Dave and I were being too literal. Yes, life was a journey…but could the journey really have no end point except the grave? Or was it vital to eventually plant ourselves in one place we'd call forever home?

Chapter One

The Farmer's Wife

Summer 2014

Flies crept on pans in the sink, crawled across the countertop, and scurried around bowls of overripe fruit. Laundry lay heaped on the table and chairs, and all the screenless windows and doors were open to the summer day, an invitation to insects.

The homeowner, a friendly, gangly guy with chaotic hair, gave us each a hug and thanked us for coming a day early so he could orient us. He had been alone for a week, his wife and kids having departed to Europe before him. Through a friend, we'd been invited to do this housesit for two weeks. We'd never done anything like it before, taking care of someone else's home. But when we'd heard "beautiful property in the Santa Cruz mountains" and "free place to stay," we'd gleefully agreed. We hadn't thought to ask certain questions, such as, "Can we see pictures?" and "What are the tasks?"

He opened the fridge and reached into a jumble to pull out a blender jar containing a smoothie made, he said, from his homegrown berries. As he sipped his drink, he talked about how we'd need to get up at six every morning to let out the chickens, ducks, turkeys, and geese, feed the rabbits, haul hay, and water the extensive garden. We followed him outside. Against the sapphire sky, laundry hung crooked on the line. My nostrils rebelled at the farm-ripe scent of poop. He led us to the animal enclosure, forty squawking, hooting, jostling fowl and rabbits. As a kid, I'd been in 4-H and had two show ducks, but this was intimidating.

"I can walk you through the feeding routine later. You'll have more eggs than you'll know what to do with."

Okay, well, that's a bonus, I thought. *Free organic food.*

I didn't yet realize the half of it. Beyond the cages, a candy store of a garden exploded with orange and purple dahlias, heavy-headed sunflowers, and a mass of greens: kale, spinach, lettuces. Raspberry and blueberry vines bulged with fruit. Beyond that, a stand of trees swelled with peaches, nectarines, apricots, and plums. He told us the cat was around somewhere and showed us how to put her food and water in bowls in the shed.

Back inside, he toured us through the house. The living room couches looked comfortable, except they were piled with kids' toys and clothes. A partially-packed suitcase was splayed open on a chair. Next, he showed us to our room, a patchouli-scented mother-in-law unit, complete with a mattress on the floor covered in a velvet quilt. A lump hitched my breath. We'd be sleeping on the *floor* for two weeks?

That night in bed, a thin dread ran through my blood. What the hell were we doing living such a crazy life? I started to cry. Dave held me but didn't offer up his thoughts or verbal reassurances. That was his way, using touch to comfort. It was possible he was a little irritated with me, given his mantra: *Why freak out about things? It doesn't help.* In the midst of my sniveling, I had to admit the setup was kind of cozy. The mattress cupped my body, and some kind of night bird pipped in the distance. We weren't exactly sleeping on a cracked sidewalk with a cardboard blanket. I wondered where my enlightenment went.

The previous year, two months into our full-time travels, I'd had a seizure in the middle of the night. A wild force hardened my muscles and thrust a roar through my brain, waking me from a dream. Unable to pry open my eyes, I was terrified, certain I was dying. But then a memory came to me of the dream. Gabriele, a beloved friend who'd recently died—more than a friend, actually; she was my mentor and other-mother—had come to me glowing and healthy and said: *Don't be afraid of dying; the veil between the worlds is thinner and more beautiful than you can imagine.* An electric current had run through me. At the time of the seizure, Gabriele's assuring words transformed my fear into surrender. I stopped fighting and thought if it was my time to go, it was okay because everyone dies, and I'd been living the life I wanted. I relaxed and released, like raising my hands as the roller coaster plummeted—and excitement ran through me about plunging into the mysteries.

But instead of dying, I woke up, and Dave hustled me to the emergency room, where a brain scan revealed I had a tumor. The doctor prescribed anti-seizure medications and told me I'd need surgery. We flew to California to meet with a surgeon. At that point we were staying with a friend, but I knew in order to heal we'd need a quiet place to ourselves. We figured we could rent an Airbnb or stay in a hotel, but another friend who turned out to be going on vacation offered us her home. The timing was perfect and, although streaks of fear jolted me, for the most part I was grateful: for the fact that the doctor had said the tumor was likely benign; that I had medical insurance; and that I felt deeply loved by the deluge of support from friends and family. Fortunately, post-surgical pathology confirmed the tumor was not cancer, and even after having my skull cracked open, I spent merely one night in the hospital. Two months later, we stepped on an international flight.

After living through that near-disaster, I thought I'd be forever thankful to be alive, and that nothing trivial would throw me ever again. I believed I'd never lose sight of the big picture: that everything is temporary, that this fleeting life is to be cherished. And now, really? I was distraught by insects and lack of a bed frame?

I focused on my breath. *I'm okay. Right here, right now. Don't close down.* I recalled Byron Katie's words, "Serenity is an open door." Over the years, I listened to a lot of dharma talks and did yoga and meditated and read soul-expansion books galore. Maybe it was a lot of work, but it was less taxing than believing every destructive thought I had.

Burrowing into Dave's arms, I tried to think about something good: how fortunate I was to have a partner in life, how lucky we were to have traveled together to Australia, Hong Kong, India, and Sri Lanka—as well as through the States, spending time with friends in Boston, New Hampshire, Cape Cod. And how a brain tumor, which could have been deadly, was merely a footnote to my year.

We awoke to the 6 a.m. alarm. Dave went out with the homeowner to feed the animals while I organized our room. Once our host left for the airport, we scrambled to shut every window and door and started killing flies. Dave was relentless. *Bang, bang, bang.* I scrubbed the kitchen counters and refrigerator shelves. We tossed mushy produce into the compost, swept the floors, ran a rag over the dusty furniture, redistributed clutter into manageable piles. I was starting to feel better. Meanwhile, I tried not to be judgmental. After all, they had a farm and two young children—and he had been trying to handle the place's demands on his own for a week. Besides, everyone's sense of livable space is different.

Later, while Dave gathered eggs, I picked blackberries and raspberries, my fingers staining amethyst. I plucked plums from the overladen tree and filled two buckets. I pulled lettuce from the dirt and cut kale from the stalk. In the deep kitchen sink, I ran cool water over the veggies to prepare for a stir fry and found sugar and flour in the cabinets to make a pie. *Look at me, being a farmer's wife. That's a new one.*

"Wow, check this out," Dave said, walking in carrying a basket brimming with eggs of all sizes and colors. A single goose egg filled his hand.

It was sweet but strange to be back in Santa Cruz, the sea-and-redwoods town we'd left the year before when we'd decided to take to the road. The thought did cross my mind: Should we never have left? I felt a pang when, in town to shop, we drove past the Love Nest, with its redwood façade and swooping, wave-patterned roof. I remembered the sounds that the breeze brought to us through our open windows: sea lions squawking, roller coaster riders shrieking, a summertime band's guitars pulsating. We'd regularly strolled Seabright Beach, where sandpipers scurried, pelicans swooped and, beyond the crashing break, shiny backs of dolphins slid by. I remembered how on our last walk through those sands, my eyes had teared.

"Think of all the beautiful beaches in the world we'll walk on," Dave had said.

He was right. I reminded myself that while letting go had been bittersweet, a more forceful part of me had felt compelled to plunge into living home-free.

It wasn't quite accurate, however, to say we didn't have a house. We just hadn't seen it yet. It was being built in Baja California Sur, Mexico. After six months of traveling, we'd learned from my sister Ann that a one-bedroom townhouse was being constructed next to hers in a small resort near the beach in the pueblo of El Pescadero. For years she'd driven down with her family from their home in San Diego and talked about how she wanted to retire there. I was intrigued by her stories of secluded shorelines, bumpy dirt roads, and sweet-smelling basil fields. Dave and I had been to Mexico but never to that spot where the desert meets the sea. When Ann told us the price—less than the cost of a nice car in the U.S.—we wired down the first of three payments. We figured if we didn't dig it, we could rent it out or sell it.

While at the farmhouse in Santa Cruz, we sent the second payment. We were assured it was "almost completely finished." Via email we'd chosen paint colors and the style of Talavera sink. Every so often we received updates—*the patio is almost done, the toilet installed*—supplemented by pictures from my sister. She had been urging us to come down, but we had other plans. We figured the developer was overseeing the build and we'd arrive when it was *totally* finished.

Maybe we were being foolish, too trusting. Part of me didn't even believe we owned a house. I was fifty-one and never had—unless you counted the three years in the house my ex-wife gaslit away from me. Except for the loss of money, I later understood she did me a favor. I'd felt claustrophobic there, in a dying relationship, drenched in her late mother's memory. Even though we refinished the floors and painted the walls, a mustiness pervaded, like mushrooms growing in the shadows. Dozens of her mother's unopened classic hardbound books, the kind with bible-thin pages bought on subscription, lined the bookshelves that spanned the living room. As much as I loved books, those unread tomes echoed the stagnation of our marriage. And her mother had been a sore spot with us. When I'd wanted to travel, she'd said her mother—who had been ill for many years—might die, so she couldn't leave town. After her mother eventually passed on, our lives became centered around fixing up the house. I would have preferred spending our time and money traveling. In my deeply buried fantasies, I imagined fleeing: secretly boarding a sailboat or plane and disappearing.

Yet I wasn't willing to relinquish the story that we were soulmates. After fourteen years together, we married—less a romantic act, it seemed, than of nailing down loose boards. Shortly before our wedding, our bodies rebelled: shingles painfully raked her skin, and I developed a vicious head cold. Hardly a year later, my wife started an affair with a neighbor, a woman supposedly my friend too. Shocked and devastated by the betrayal, I clung to her, begging her not to leave. Who would I be without her, without us, without our devotion? When I left that house for the last time, I was shattered. Fifteen years had been ripped away, and I had to create a new home for myself from the void.

At the farmhouse, Dave soon got into the groove of waking up at dawn to feed the animals, and water and let out the fowl. He did the same at sundown, herding them into their enclosure. I enjoyed watching him take to something completely different. While he wasn't happy about the early alarm's assault— we'd thought as retirees those days were over—he didn't complain, he just went for it. *Became* it.

Our hours filled with chores and sunshine and games of Yahtzee and reading and cooking. I made plum pie and potato salad with hard-boiled duck eggs. I baked cobbler and relentlessly stir-fried veggies. Dave used dinner leftovers for breakfast, cracking a fresh egg over the hash, and I blended smoothies. When I cut the tops off strawberries or rooted out a rotten nectarine, I set them aside for the animals. Eggshells, banana peels, and peach pits went to the worms that made fortified dirt. Dave brought in flowers from the garden and set them in a vase on the coffee table.

One day while in the kitchen with my laptop, I came across an article about something new people were doing: Housesitting. I discovered there was a new movement afoot with websites connecting homeowners to sitters. No money changed hands. The hosts got someone to take care of their home, pets, and property—and the sitters got a free place to stay in a location they wanted to explore. We had stumbled into housesitting the farm, but now I learned we could do this all over the world.

Immediately I signed up on two sites. We had a few months before our casita would be ready. Where did we want to go? I applied for a gig in the Pacific Northwest, knowing fall was a great time to be there and hoping to see our friends in the Seattle area. In the pictures, the house looked spacious and uncluttered, and the two golden retrievers were beauties. The tasks were listed as: *Feeding and exercising the dogs, yard maintenance, keeping the house picked up and clean, and maintaining a presence.* Sounded doable. A few days later I got a message from the homeowners: They wanted to talk. After we Skype chatted, they chose us. We'd be striding into new territory, caring for a home of people we'd never met in person.

Soon, our last day on the farm arrived. While we cleaned and packed, I thought about leaving our routine of berry picking and animal feeding and pie baking. I thought about saying goodbye to the fragrant redwood trees and the comfy couch where I read each morning. In two short weeks the farm had morphed from foreign to familiar. From a problem to our dwelling. From unknown to home. I was feeling clingy, a bit sad about relinquishing this farm, as though part of me had forgotten it wasn't mine. Yet another part welled with anticipation about what lay ahead. Movement juiced me. In this lifestyle, nothing remained settled. We embodied the truth that life is change.

Chapter Two

Synchronicity

Fall 2014

"Here are the keys to the house, and to the pickup truck. Please use the truck to take the dogs to the beach so you don't get your car dirty. Also, these are the keys to the RV, if you feel like going on a camping trip with the dogs."

Dave and I looked at each other. Was this real? Had we just been handed keys to two vehicles and a custom home by virtual strangers?

When we'd arrived at the Pacific Northwest town of Port Townsend, Washington, we'd parked our Subaru and crunched along a leaf-strewn path, past a buddha statue with pink flowers nestled at the base, and let ourselves in through a red gate. Two big boy golden retrievers—Max and Levi—had trotted up to meet us. We'd set down our bags and dug our hands into their luxurious fur and made instant friends.

The pictures of the house hadn't honored its beauty: the August sun sculpted the rooms through plate-glass windows, softening the honeyed hardwood floors and leather furniture, and warming the kitchen filled with high-end appliances. Charlie and Jessica were headed to India for two months to be with Amma, the hugging saint, in her ashram. I'd read about Amma, a Hindu guru, who like most worshipped sages wasn't without controversy. Some claimed her organization to be a money-making cult. Others said she deserved sainthood for the massive charity for the poor she founded in Kerala, India—and for traveling the world and hugging 37 million people over the years to spread healing, peace, and love. According to *The Guardian*, "she's hugged everyone from Sting to lepers, sucking pus from their contagious wounds."

The essence of Jessica and Charlie's spiritual tendencies came through in the house's Zen feeling: an uncluttered space dotted with small statues and wall hangings from various religious traditions, and a bookshelf neatly filled with tomes by spiritual teachers. Their deck looked out to a garden and a wood-fired sauna, with towering pines edging the yard. Green and blue Adirondack chairs were set up to enjoy the view, including the array of birds clustered at feeders around the yard.

On the deck, Charlie told us to watch for pileated woodpeckers, and as though it heard the invitation a quirky Woody Woodpecker look-alike landed and began pecking at a block of seeds. After Charlie explained how to fill the feeders, he took us on a stroll through the garden.

Like the farmhouse in the Santa Cruz mountains, the variety of fresh produce could stock a grocery store. Herbs, lettuce, carrots, raspberries, blueberries—and a first for me, potatoes. He instructed me to dip my hand into the soil. I wrapped my fingers around a cool node and pulled up buried treasure.

We brought our stuff into the guest room set up with an air bed. I was relieved when they told us we could move to their room the next day because blow-up mattresses, no matter the technology, are never comfortable to me. Thinking about the floor mattress at the farm and the air mattress here, I made a mental note to ask about the size and type of bed in future housesitting applications. After our long drive from California, I was ready for a solid night's sleep. In fact, I was so tired I could have climbed between the sheets right then. But Jessica and Charlie had more to tell us about the house and routines, and they were fixing us dinner.

That evening while we dined, Charlie told us he liked to run the dogs on the trails when he didn't take them to the beach. The boys—four-year-old brothers—thrived on exercise. He invited us to join him on a trail run in the morning before they left, to show us the route.

And so after a night of Dave sleeping soundly and my squirming on the air mattress to seek elusive comfort, we laced up our running shoes and headed out the door. The dogs lovingly pushed their strong bodies into our legs. We walked them down the road lined with pines and madrones, breathing in the rich, rotting forest cologne. When we reached the trail, which was shaded by lush jade foliage, Charlie let the boys off leash and they bolted like horses from a paddock. Dave and I struggled to keep up with Charlie's strides. Tall and rangy, he had legs ropy with muscles, fitting the stereotype of owners looking like their dogs.

Soon, my lungs and legs were burning and I was on high alert, constantly in danger of tripping over roots. I liked to run—I'd done a marathon once—but I preferred to go slow. I glanced at Dave and he mind-beamed to me he was feeling the same, that this was too much. Later he told me that going so fast wasn't allowing him to do his usual Boy Scout orienteering, identifying landmarks to help us recall the route. But if we asked Charlie to slow down, would he think we were a terrible choice for this housesit? Getting a good review on the website was crucial if we wanted to be picked in the future. I felt like I was performing the talent portion of Miss America, sweating under the lights, hoping the world would love me.

At a fork in the trail, Charlie stopped moving forward but kept jogging in place. Dave and I dead-stopped. Casually gasping for breath, we labored to stay upright. Charlie told us one way looped around and the other, shorter path headed back. He asked us what we'd like to do.

SHORT! my mind screamed.

Dave suggested the quicker way would be good today.

Charlie bounded away like a grasshopper, and we straggled after him. The dogs sprinted ahead; from time to time we'd lose sight of them, but they'd eventually stop and wait for us to catch up, their pink-and-black tongues lolling. I tried to focus on the beauty around me rather than the pain in my body. Inhaling the forest's loamy essence, I hoped, would serve as a tonic to keep me upright. My reward that night, I decided, would be a soak in their deep tub.

When Charlie and Jessica left for the airport, we wanted to collapse. But we couldn't relax until we moved to the main bedroom and set up our things. Fortunately, we didn't have a lot of stuff. Long before we'd ever heard of Marie Kondo, downsizing, or decluttering, we'd both been drawn to living light.

When we'd decided to live without a house, we got rid of truckloads of belongings. But that wasn't the first time Dave and I had "divested ourselves of the holds that would hold us" to paraphrase Walt Whitman's "Song of the Open Road." Perhaps there's a direct line from my reading that poem as a grad student to living the life I am now. After finishing a master's degree in my late twenties, I was restless and impulsively applied for a job I circled in the Want Ads to teach in Japan. I'd fantasized about traveling and living in another country but had roped myself into a high school teaching career and a young marriage (which had dissolved after five years). When I was offered the job and had a short time to get to Yokohama, I held a yard sale where I sold my possessions, including my old Honda Civic. I reveled in the intoxicating sensation of owning merely two suitcases and two boxes of books and papers stored at my parents' house.

Years later, when Dave decided to join me in my one-bedroom city apartment, he had to pare down his three-bedroom house. He told me to pick out what we should keep, and he got rid of the rest. Later, when we moved to the Love Nest, we had just enough furniture to fill its tight space.

The following year, in our mindset of flight, we hadn't wanted to be weighed down. And yet we weren't sure about the future—would travel be merely a migration?—so we stored a stack of furniture and clothes in our friend Chambliss' garage. At times, perhaps while flying across the ocean in a dark airplane while most passengers dozed, I'd try to remember what we'd stored. But the only thing I could picture was our purple couch, its curved back and scrolled arms.

30

A year into our nomadic lives, we held a yard sale at Chambliss', knowing we wouldn't be setting up house again in California. The one thing I couldn't sell, though, were my journals. After reading *The Diary of Anne Frank* in third grade, I'd started keeping my own diary. Forty years later I had accumulated a world of words on thousands of pages. Other than being stored in my parents' dirt room in plastic tubs while I lived in Japan, my journals had been lugged from place to place as I moved around for decades. Years had passed when I hadn't cracked open the mildewing pages. I had recently finished writing a memoir, and during the process had glimpsed into only two or three journals. They didn't serve a purpose anymore, except as nostalgia. Although I sometimes long for the disappeared past, I mostly subscribe to Bill Kenower's assertion to "go only forward; that is the direction of life."

So one afternoon in Chambliss' living room, I pulled journal after journal from the boxes, flipped through the pages, lingered on certain passages, and occasionally snapped pictures on my phone of lines I wanted to "keep." One by one, I thanked each diary for all the life experiences, even as I time-traveled through scribbles that flared up shame or regret—especially as I thumbed through ink wasted obsessing over guys or the shape of my body when I could have been learning a new language or climbing a mountain. Finally I hauled the stacks of notebooks to the chasm of Chambliss's blue recycle bin.

Other than a few random items at Chambliss's, all we owned now was Chitty Chitty Bang Bang (our blue Subaru), a couple of suitcases of clothes, skis and boots, cards and Yahtzee, two bikes, my blue blankie, a laptop, our phones, toiletries, and a partially-built casita in Mexico.

We soon discovered Port Townsend was a jewel of forest and beaches, the air salt-fresh. After our struggle-run on the trails, we preferred to take the dogs to North Beach, a few minutes' drive away. As a Californian from the crowded and expensive Bay Area, I was astonished at the plentiful and free parking spaces.

We had to put the dogs on leashes before they jumped out from the truck, and it wasn't easy to hold them back, they were fervent to run. The dogs weren't mean, but they were so rambunctious they might jump on someone bending down to comb the sand for sea glass. We had to lead them to the more isolated part of the beach before we could let them run free. It was like wrangling rhinos. Early on, one yanked Dave's arm and he tweaked his foot, an injury that stayed with him for years. We'd be walking on the beach in Mexico or Thailand and he'd say, "Ouch, there's Port Townsend again."

Once, one of the dogs romped up to another dog and started humping. He wouldn't respond when we called him, and we had to yank him off. When we texted Charlie for pointers, he admitted his goldens weren't neutered. I'd never thought to ask. I'd have to add that to my list of questions when interviewing for a housesit because animals who aren't fixed have different needs and behaviors. No wonder those boys were so strong; they had the full force of testosterone storming through their veins.

Mostly, though, the dogs stayed with us on the beach, chasing sticks into the icy Puget Sound waters. As we walked, we discovered otters bobbing on their backs, choirs of squawking sea birds, and occasionally a great blue heron uncoiling its elegant neck. The sand and sky spread out so far it seemed we were alight at the edge of the world.

Port Townsend had the laid-back vibe of many beach communities, with lots of artsy and outdoorsy people marching to the rhythm of their own bongos. Downtown featured abundant restaurants, retail shops, bookstores, and a Food Co-op with a loudspeaker playing the Indigo Girls. Every Wednesday and Saturday a farmer's market offered lush produce, locally made foods, and a bearded guy noodling on the guitar.

One night we sat on the outdoor patio of The Pourhouse overlooking the Puget Sound and sipping craft beer. On the beach, two women dipped oversized wands into a soapy bucket and let loose fantastical bubbles that undulated like anemones. A smoky charcoal scent wafted our way as a guy grilled salmon atop his double kayak.

We'd come to see a band we'd heard about from a local guy we'd chatted with in town. When he asked us where we lived, we'd said we're originally from California but now were traveling. That had become our standard answer, but we'd long stumbled over how to respond to that question.

When we mentioned Santa Cruz and that we loved live music, he told us his band was playing at the Pourhouse. He mentioned he knew the founders of a bluegrass festival we'd recently attended, and that he developed a mandolin symposium with one of Dave's favorite musicians, David Grisman (who played with The Grateful Dead's Jerry Garcia) which takes place in Santa Cruz. His 99-year-old mother, he went on, lived in Santa Cruz—and his father served as mayor of San Jose, the city where I taught for many years. We were a thousand miles away from our former home but, somehow, it was following us around.

Such a coincidence, but it felt meaningful, as though reminding us we carry home with us wherever we go. Swiss psychologist Carl Jung called meaningful coincidences "synchronicity." During a therapy session with a serious and rational woman who was describing a dream about a piece of jewelry called a golden scarab, he heard a tapping at the windowpane. Jung

32

opened the window to discover a goldish-green scarab beetle, not native to the area, and handed it to the client. That event helped break her from her overly rationalistic view and to see how meaning can be derived not only from thinking but from dreaming. Living a rich life, Jung said, meant one informed not only by the rational mind but by the unconscious and intuition. He believed many occurrences labeled as "coincidences" are not merely chance but serve to provide powerful insight, direction, and guidance.

More synchronicity seemed to happen in our lives these days, perhaps due to the innovative, unconventional way we were living. We couldn't repose in the "sensible" mindset that we were doing life the way we were "supposed" to. Our improvisational lifestyle broke us out of rationality, allowing us to be more in touch with our intuitions. Or maybe our lifestyle *required* us to tap into our instincts in order to be safe and happy. Being in a state of frequent change, we'd attuned ourselves to being open to possibilities, opportunities, and synchronicities. I like to think they are reminders to keep moving forward on what Carlos Casteneda calls "the path with heart."

Another synchronicity soon occurred when our friends Jennifer and Dwight, who lived a ferry ride away in north Seattle, came to visit. When we poured wine, assembled snacks, and gathered on the deck to enjoy the fall afternoon, Dwight beelined to the Adirondack chairs and said, "These are mine." By this he meant, those were chairs he'd designed and his company had built. He sat and smiled for a picture Dave took of the maker and his chair reunited.

Later, Dave and I piled into the truck with the dogs and followed Dwight's motorcycle, with Jen perched on back, through winding roads lined with Douglas firs and red alders through Olympic National Park. We stopped at Lake Crescent, a glacier-carved sapphire nestled in the foothills of the Olympic mountains. The hills glistened so green the day felt like a Kodachrome dream. The dogs rushed around, Max chasing sticks and Levi splattering into the water pursuing uncatchable birds. As we hiked, nature sandpapered smooth the sharp expectations of civilization.

I'd known Jennifer since high school—and my time in Port Townsend became a kind of inadvertent high school reunion. Two others from my small-town Auburn, California class of 1980 also lived in the area. We didn't have to travel far to get to Laurie and her husband Lou who lived across town. One afternoon we played Cards Against Humanity with them and their teenagers who had friends over, all talented young people who did things like play the cello and perform in plays. Laughing and eating and talking about our lives, I was awash with affection for this family; I hadn't seen Laurie in nearly thirty-five years, but she'd unhesitatingly opened her home and invited us in.

Another day, Dave and I took the ferry to Whidbey Island where we met up with Mike and Kim. We'd brought the dogs and released them to romp on a wild beach strewn with strands of bull kelp so that afterward they'd be content to nap in the truck while at a restaurant we ate fresh mussels, a Whidbey delicacy. I was flung into wistfulness sitting across from the former boy who'd been in my Journalism class in the 1970s. And now here we were, both writers.

One of my biggest worries about being a nomad had been missing out on time with family and friends. But as the years unfolded, we ended up spending *more* time with some than ever before. When we were in their area, we knew it was temporary so everyone would make an effort to connect. Sometimes they planned a trip to join us wherever we were. Instead of a quick coffee or a calendar-planned lunch, we'd share lingering days together.

I also hadn't known we'd soon join online groups of nomads—and that "meet ups" of travelers would become a thing. I hadn't thought about all the people we'd meet in cafes, on buses, and in neighbors' homes while housesitting. For instance, the Port Townsend neighbors invited us over to their hand-built custom home. He was a ferry engineer who recently quit after twenty-eight years, and she was a nurse. They planned to sail around the world when she retired. Behind their house they'd constructed a two-story room reminiscent of an airplane hangar where they showed us their project: re-building a 48-foot sailboat. When they finished, they said, they'd demolish the room to pull the boat free.

We'd been in Port Townsend a month when we sent in our final payment for our casita, having been assured it was *completely* finished. In the small resort, our place was Unit Eleven, which happened to be our favorite number, so we named it Casita Once (pronounced *own-say*), a double entendre of English "once" and the word for eleven in Spanish. Soon we would drive down to the tip of Baja to see it for the first time, our own little house. Pictures my sister had sent shuffled around in my mind like playing cards, so elusive I couldn't land on a solid image. Casita Once loomed like an enigmatic hologram.

The next day, one of the biggest hurricanes to ever hit southern Baja swooped down. We watched the news in horror: 125-mile-per-hour winds had ripped off roofs and toppled trees; cars were swept away by rushing waters. A number of deaths and injuries were reported. The airport was closed, and early accounts announced looting and loss of electricity and lack of drinking water. Hurricane Odile was being dubbed Baja's Katrina.

I worried about my sister Ann who was down there. Anxiously we awaited news. Finally she was able to grab a cell signal and called us. She recounted that the night of the storm, she'd been at a friend's house in town, away from our beach casitas. She'd hunkered in the shower with three other people and two dogs while the house's windows shattered. The road to our casitas was impassable through the arroyo's violently rushing waters. There was no way to know what shape our casitas were in. We'd paid for a home that might no longer be standing.

Chapter Three

There is No Try

October-November 2014

Sitting in Chambliss' back yard in San Jose, California—his Fuyu persimmon tree bedecked with glowing lanterns of fruit—we talked about Baja. A category three hurricane, the storm had killed eighteen people. Reports of the tragedies glutted social media, as did heartening stories about people helping each other. My sister Ann had finally gotten to our casitas and was amazed to find no problems bigger than water splashed on the polished cement floors. However, the resort's massive woven palapa by the pool had crashed down, and a neighbor's motorhome had blown over. The RV had been stocked with food, so the owner was feeding everyone she could. There was no electricity to run air-conditioners and fans for relief in the hot sticky climate. After days of flushing her toilet with buckets of pool water, Ann planned the tricky drive back to the States with a friend, hoping they could make it through. They did, but along the way, they encountered ravished roads and overturned vehicles and destroyed homes. Road crews were already working—and within two weeks of the storm, most electricity and water services had been restored.

Dave and I were stunned about this staggering turn of events, as well as our good fortune. As dusk set in, our conversation with Chambliss segued to the 1989 Loma Prieta earthquake that killed sixty-three people. We'd all been in the Bay Area at the time and remembered buckled roads, power outages, the collapse of the upper deck of the Bay Bridge and the Cypress Freeway, and the blazing fires in the Marina District. Safety had nothing to do with staying home.

Ever since we began living a traveling life, whenever we came through the Bay Area, we spent a few days with Chambliss. We cooked, watched *Jeopardy*, and hung out in the backyard with a neighborhood couple who swung by on their walks with their golden retriever. In an unfinished room at the rear of his house, he let us store some things we hadn't sold at the yard sale: skis and bikes, a few boxes of clothes, and the last vestiges of our memorabilia, stuff we knew we'd one day toss or take with us on a drive to Mexico.

Every time we arrived, it felt good to drive up his street, flanked by monumental sycamores, to his Tudor-style house with its high-pitched gables and spread of lawn. He always came out and gave us hugs, said "Welcome back!", and helped us bring a load inside. I felt like Dorothy who had gone to Oz and experienced flying monkeys, talking scarecrows, narcotic poppy fields, witches good and bad—then returned to Kansas where nothing had changed.

When we'd divested ourselves of most of our belongings, some had ended up in Chambliss' house: our coffee table and cherry wood dining set, Dave's antique steamer trunk, and his two framed New Orleans Jazz Fest posters. Mugs and bowls that used to be ours were stacked in his cabinets, and Dave's old flip-flops were parked at the backdoor. It was oddly funny, and a little disorienting, to encounter remnants of our lives in someone else's home. On paper, it was our home, too. Chambliss let us use his address as our California home base in order to maintain a U.S. address for our driver's licenses, medical insurance, vehicle registration, and banking.

As welcoming as our friend was, we didn't want to overstay—and given that it might be a month or more before we could safely traverse Baja, Dave and I decided to drive to Southern California to spend time with friends. I logged on to a housesitting website and scanned the listings where hosts included photos of their milieu and pets, a description of the house and neighborhood, and the animals' needs, which ranged from "throw dry food in the bowl for the outdoor cat" to "walk Misty the labradoodle five times a day, cut up raw food into eighteen bite-sized chunks, brush her regularly, and snuggle with her under the covers at night." We avoided the latter—but would possibly reconsider if the abode was, say, a castle in the South of France or a beach-front property in the Caribbean. The hosts also indicated what else they wanted sitters to attend to: water plants, bring in the mail, use coasters so their antiques don't get stained.

We, too, had a profile page as sitters. I'd worked diligently on it, making sure we sounded mature but not feeble, responsible but not boring. Dave said my being a writer was our magic juice. I'd included pictures of us nuzzling dogs and cats, and of Dave feeding the farm brood, to highlight how much we love the little beasts. I also mentioned that Dave used to volunteer for the Humane Society. We paid extra for the optional background check and asked friends to write references.

Drawn to a gig in West Hollywood that fit our dates, I immediately applied. After a brief phone call with the couple, whose Australian accents intrigued me, we secured our next housesit—actually, an apartment-sit, caring for a pug named Duke. We hugged Chambliss goodbye and hit the road for the six-hour drive.

In L.A., we spent only about an hour with the couple, who were in their twenties, before they yanked their suitcases into the trunk of the car and headed for the airport. This sit couldn't have been more different than the Santa Cruz mountain farm with a slew of animals, or the Washington custom

37

home in the woods with two hulking dogs. Duke weighed at most ten pounds. On our walks, he'd comically whip into a handstand and continue moving forward on his front legs…while arcing his pee as high as he could. Clearly his goal was to spray his scent to great heights so other dogs would be in awe of the colossal canine who'd passed by.

The four-unit complex was tucked amongst an eclectic mix of shabby and elegant houses in West Hollywood. The apartment, circa 1940s, had a closet-sized kitchen, a light-drenched living room with one love seat, and a loft bedroom lined with racks for hanging clothes to compensate for lack of closets. The hosts had been living in California for about a year and were returning to Australia for a wedding. Perhaps the fact they were recent transplants explained their minimalistic style of only the one couch, no extra chairs, and not a single book on the lone, low-slung bookshelf. Or perhaps living with less was a personal preference, or a budget-based necessity. I suspected, though, it had to do with youth. The apartments of my second decade had a similar nearly-vacant aesthetic. Rummaging through the kitchen, I discovered three plates, two cereal bowls, a smattering of bent and mismatched utensils, and a few dull knives. They probably ate out all the time—after all, there were fifty restaurants within walking distance and another thousand that would deposit meals at your door with the swift touch of an app.

In addition to a free place to stay, housesitting meant saving money by being able to cook. I have a love-hate relationship with cooking, so I was glad for the excuse to avoid it for ten days. Longer and I'd start to crave my own creations. Truly, though, the apartment had the basics we needed: a roomy floor for yoga, a comfortable bed, and a cute dog—much better than paying to sleep in a stale hotel or overstaying at friends' homes.

After having lived the slow life in Port Townsend, we were both a bit rattled by the L.A. traffic and noise. But a few days in, and we were buzzing around town, checking out quirky stores and restaurants, and letting everyone from children to homeless guys pet adorable Duke, a people-magnet.

Normally we don't care if a house doesn't have a TV, but we wanted to watch the final game of the World Series because our San Francisco Giants were contenders. We walked a couple of blocks to a local sports bar, Barney's Beanery, an L.A. institution stuffed with nostalgic sports and entertainment memorabilia. I was struck by the camaraderie I feel with strangers when enjoying a game together, even if we're rooting for different teams. Once, after my divorce, I'd been traveling alone in Barcelona when Spain was competing in the World Cup against Italy, and watching a game in a beach-side pub with raucous fans cheering in Spanish had made my creeping loneliness wane.

Two days after the Giants won the World Series, Halloween arrived. We'd learned that West Hollywood is a mecca on October thirty-first. It was rumored many famous actors attended the festivities, hidden behind the anonymity of masks. My oldest friend Nancy, who has lived in L.A. her whole adult life and who loves Halloween (she's been known to throw her own elaborate costume parties) had never attended the West Hollywood revelry because it was notoriously difficult to deal with traffic and other logistics where 500,000 people gathered. But us? All we had to do was walk out the apartment's front door in costumes we'd improvised from the flotsam and jetsam in our suitcases. Our half-a-closetful of party costumes had disappeared with most of our belongings, but I had kept a boa and fishnet stockings for emergencies. Over the stockings, I pulled on shorts and boots, and I topped off my look with my cowgirl hat and glittery makeup. I applied glitter to Dave's face as well and draped my pink boa over his wildly patterned shirt.

At dusk, we moseyed two blocks into another planet. Spread out over acres of city streets, live bands blasted tunes on six different stages, from rock and roll to burlesque extravaganzas. Creatures undulated in elaborate costumes, from drag queens draping their arms around real cops, to ten-foot-tall aliens with articulating, illuminated appendages. Dave was engrossed with his camera, and I didn't un-drop my jaw for hours except to smile. I loved how traveling plonked us down into unexpected worlds.

The next day at Nancy and Andy's house, my longtime friend pulled a dozen garments from her closet and invited me to try them on. Shopping is one of her superpowers, and so is giving things away. I pulled on the slinky maxi dress she'd worn to our wedding. The pattern swirled with ginger and aqua, as though I was draped in an autumn day. As I played dress up, in each outfit I looked like a different woman. Maybe that defined nomadic living: trying on different lives. But no…we weren't *trying*. We were *doing*. As Yoda says, "Do or do not, there is no try."

Later we all piled into their Maserati. I'd never before been in such a fancy car, and I felt like a coddled celebrity being chauffeured to Santa Monica, palm trees and ocean-blue skies whizzing by. A few months before I'd been playing the role of a farmer's wife. And now I was a luminary. The cultural whiplash made me feel lighter, like life was a game to be played.

We ate breakfast at a local landmark, Patrick's Roadhouse, a funky forties-style diner at the beach. It's the kind of place where grease is king, and plates are piled high. I met Nancy at a party in high school when she was fourteen and I was sixteen. More than thirty years later, instead of sitting on her waterbed listening to Rod Stewart and bemoaning our boyfriend problems, we were hanging out with our husbands drinking mimosas. Like pentimento, that old world ghosted up and the two worlds melded. Simultaneously we were adults whose parents were gone, and teenagers whose parents were so alive we couldn't imagine otherwise.

Chapter Four

The Casita

Winter 2014

To drive the length of Baja, we traversed the peninsula six times, a snake undulating east, then west, then east again. On the tight and shoulderless two-lane road, we rolled through smoky desert forested with tree-sized Cardons and squat barrel cacti, bristly chollas, and chapparal yucca spiked with purple electrified spines. When a semi bolted past, our car convulsed.

At times, open spaces would unexpectedly close in, dwarfing us with toppling rock formations like a giant's Tinker Toys. We squeezed through a mountain pass. At its crest, a turquoise wash of sea colorized the sepia landscape.

Hurricane Odile, which had struck two months earlier, had spawned yawning potholes. Work crews directed us to veer off the asphalt to rutted dirt byways, the vehicles in front of us whipping up a rusty storm.

Every few hours we came to a checkpoint. Uniformed young men with submachine guns slung across their backs peered into our car, faces shiny with sweat. *De donde vienes y a donde vas?* I struggled to distinguish which question meant *where are you coming from?* and which meant *where are you going?* They waved us through—until once they didn't, signaling us to step out.

A kid—he looked younger than my university students—directed us to lift the hatchback. He zipped open our suitcases and yanked at the throats of our garbage bags stuffed with bedding and beach towels. Another guard bent into our back seat. Through the glass, I caught him reaching his hand into our bag of potato chips and crunching away. When the guys finished and declared *listo*, I held out the bag. He grinned, accepting my offer.

I later learned that seasoned Baja road-trippers stock extra bottles of water or Coke, bags of jellybeans or wrapped sandwiches, to relieve the young men's tedium of standing in the heat all day for little pay. One friend has been known to give out *Playboy* magazines, which may satisfy another basic need on Maslow's hierarchy.

If it had been Dave's and my decision, we would have made the trip in an unhurried four or five days, stopping in small towns to uncramp our legs and wander, eating fish tacos and fingering woven offerings from street vendors. When we sped past a pearly beach on the Gulf of California, also known as the Sea of Cortez, I ached to slip into the consoling waters. But there was no dawdling because my sister Ann, our caravan leader, was hellbent on her dream: freshly divorced and retired, she was starting a new life at Cerritos Beach.

Compared to Ann, we were driving in luxury. Chitty Chitty Bang Bang bulged with goods, obscuring the back window, but we had good air-conditioning, strong suspension, and all-wheel drive. Her beater Toyota Camry featured broken A/C and a stuck passenger door. Her black mutt Rama panted out an open window, dog hair and dust cycloning about.

Twelve hours in, when we finally stopped for the night, Dave could hardly unclench his hands from the steering wheel. The air smelled unknown—a complex wine with notes of raisin and diesel. I was too woozy to appreciate the hotel's arched entryway and Spanish tiles. I'd never before seen such a bright moon. Stumbling to our room, I shielded my eyes against its glare.

On the second day, after hours upon hours on the road, the highway opened up into four lanes when we reached the city of La Paz. Traffic slowed us down as we drove past boxy gray buildings and Spanish language billboards. Dave and I flashed our lights at Ann, signaling her to pull over in front of a hacienda-style hotel. We were so exhausted we didn't think we could make it the rest of the way. Besides, the sun was starting to set, and we'd been warned not to drive Baja in the dark—not because of banditos, but because cows and donkeys wander into the roads, and with lack of streetlights, you're in danger of totaling your vehicle.

Ann leapt from her car. She's one of those slender women infused with Energizer Bunny vigor. She takes after our mom, short and small-boned, whereas I'm tall and meaty like our dad.

"What's up?" she said.

We explained to her we were barely hanging on and hoped she'd be willing to spend the night at the hotel.

"But we have only another hour and we'll be there!" she enthused like she'd just spent a refreshing week at a spa. "Besides, look"—she pointed to a nearby bus stop where two women leaned against the wall. They were bulging out of tight clothes, their eyes thick with neon eyeshadow. "This hotel is a known hooker joint."

"Isn't there another hotel around here?" I asked.

"We'd have to drive back the way we came," she said. "Let's go. We're almost there! We can drive right into Todos Santos and have dinner."

Dave gave a weary shrug of resignation, and I nodded numbly.

As we followed her through city traffic that soon thinned out, we hoped her estimation of an hour was accurate. Was she so eager to get there it had skewed her sense of time? I ached all over flu-like, and Dave looked rigid as a plank. We were headed west, toward the Pacific Ocean with the Sea of Cortez at our backs. And then, as though Baja didn't want us to feel so bad, a sunset the color of a rainbow bloomed on the horizon, hues thickening by the minute.

By nightfall, we made it to Todos Santos, a town we'd heard was charming—but there was no way to tell in the absence of streetlights. In the warm evening, we sat at a table on the sidewalk to eat, while mosquitos feasted on our ankles. Finishing our meal, at last it was time to follow Ann the last ten minutes to our places.

After passing through the shadows of the tiny pueblo of El Pescadero, we took a right on an unmarked dirt road, bumping toward the ocean in the dark. Shadowy cacti held out their prickly arms. About a mile down, we turned right again and there it was: our small community of homes near Cerritos Beach dimly lit in the night.

When we unfolded our aching bodies from the car, a couple of dogs, tails wagging, emerged from the shadows to greet us and Ann's dog Rama. I struggled to wheel my suitcase across the dirt walkway.

"They keep promising to cement this," she said.

We pushed open our gate to a patio paved with uneven stones and a dead palm tree, a victim of the hurricane. A wrought-iron spiral staircase curled from the patio to the rooftop, reminiscent of the staircase in our Santa Cruz Love Nest. An ache creaked in my heart, and I shook away the nostalgia. Dave slid open the glass door to an empty box of a living room with a polished cement floor. Flipping on the overhead lights, the shade of yellow paint we'd chosen online shone brightly, but I was too stunned to be cheery. A shell of a kitchen stared out, blank spaces where cabinets and a fridge should be. And clearly our place was *not* "completely finished," as we'd been promised, because the kitchen bar-counter had yet to be installed. But, on the bright side, a four-burner gas stove with a diminutive oven had been installed, as had a multicolored Talavera bowl sink in the bathroom, although I noticed it wasn't the design we'd ordered.

In the bedroom, Dave dropped a bundle to the floor, the air mattress wrapped in plastic. We wrestled it out flat and plugged in the automatic pump, which roared like a demon in torture. Back at the car, we extricated sheets, pillows, and a blanket and, upon throwing them on the now-inflated pseudo-bed, collapsed like we'd scaled Annapurna.

As much as I hate sleeping on an air mattress, I was grateful for this one. When I closed my eyes I didn't think I'd wake up for twelve hours. But I was wrong. At some point in the murky night, I shifted to turn on my side, and my shoulder and hip slammed into the cement floor. In a mist of half-sleep, I realized the mattress had leaked out all its air. I reached over and pushed the button to re-start the deafening inflation process…and had to do so again and again, every few hours. Dave, being the skilled sleeper he is, barely stirred.

43

The next day, my sister said she'd thought we were blending smoothies in the middle of the night. But there was no way we could have done so because we had no blender. Or food, except granola bars. A desolate reality hit us when we awoke hungry and thirsty and wondering why we hadn't been better prepared. I peeled myself from the sticky sheets, the air conditioner having yet to be installed. The ceiling fan provided a modicum of air swirl. My mind was swirling as well. Not only did we need major appliances and furniture, we didn't own a broom, sponge, beach umbrella, or local cell phone. A year earlier, we'd been so eager to be free of material things…and now in order to live here we'd need to become consumers again. Our To-Do list was epic. I hated shopping and wanted to wave a wand to magically outfit our place. How were we going to handle all of this in my shaky, and Dave's non-existent, Spanish? Did we make a drastic mistake draining our savings to buy this dwelling that was supposed to be our house but instead felt like a husk of a dwelling in an alien land?

I straggled next door to my sister's casita and envy gripped me: she had a *couch*, and a *washing machine*, and *hot coffee*. She, bless her, poured me a cup, and we tromped up the stairs to her rooftop patio, where a slight breeze made the air feel…perfect. It was November, and I was wearing shorts and a tee-shirt like a kid on summer vacation. The desert's earthy smell and the sensation of warm, dry air on my skin unexpectedly softened my mood. The sky was such a deep blue it felt like I could dive into it. I slowly turned, looking in all directions. Our small resort had been built in stages, all the buildings constructed in sand- or brick-colored concrete, from the three-story condos near the pool, the bungalows beyond them, and our casita townhomes. I took it all in, the erect shaggy palm trees, the ones bent by the storm—and in the near distance, past a few rooftops, past khaki hills dotted with cacti, a slice of sea.

Soon Dave, Ann, and I were out for a walk, ambling along a dirt road populated with dozens of species of cacti of all sizes, the most impressive being the cardón, or elephant cactus, the largest species in the world which can reach up to sixty-five feet and weigh up to ten tons. Sadly, a few had been taken down by Odile's lashing winds, and others were missing limbs. We passed scattered small and boxy houses used by Mexican families on vacation, and sprawling ones owned by people who lived here year-round, with four or five dogs lounging around. Ann pointed out a few large, modern homes built by Canadians or Americans. Atop a cliff overlooking the crashing Pacific, the sun illuminated three white egg-shaped domes, a unique house built years before by Betty Marvin, the actor Lee Marvin's wife.

The beach swept at least two miles north, and we had it to ourselves. Rama pranced in the waves. I slipped off my flip-flops and curled my toes in the sand, waving at Dave who was taking pictures. No doubt about it, this place of desert and sea was beautiful in an unusual way. I reminded myself how fortunate we were to own a house, one that had made it through a terrible storm. We'd deal with what lay ahead *poco a poco*, as they say in Mexico, little by little. Perhaps I could embrace *poco a poco* as a life philosophy. Still, I wondered if this place would ever feel like home…whatever that meant.

The next morning I woke with anxiety pulsing through my body. We'd been able to go to a store the previous day to buy food and water, but those purchases had barely scratched the surface of what faced us. *Poco a poco* wasn't sitting well in the morning light. I felt empty, like something immense was missing from my body, like I was adrift in a black hole. Why hadn't we invested our money in the Love Nest? We were now probably priced out of California, unless we went back to full-time jobs…and maybe not even then. We had several small income streams—my pension, Dave's social security, my books/workshops/occasional online teaching…and we planned to rent out the casita when we weren't in it. Logically I knew if we'd chosen to keep working we would have missed out on all we'd seen of the world so far—and I would have had to delay my retirement. And chillingly, if I'd not retired when I did, I would have had to return to the classroom only weeks after brain surgery, or my medical insurance would have been deactivated. The timing of my retirement, which included medical coverage for life, had been divine. Yet my ego was on a rampage, grappling for security. But why now? Why didn't I go through this maelstrom of emotions when I found out I had a brain tumor? Or when we didn't own a house and were traveling in Sri Lanka and India? I tried to recall what Pema Chodron said about groundlessness, how we create our own suffering by grasping for security and satisfaction, as if those things can be nailed down. The reality of life, though, is change, motion.

The thought was making me seasick. It didn't feel possible to make a home on roiling waves.

I told Dave I needed to take a walk, alone. As I trudged on the dusty road toward the beach, my monkey mind jumped from branch to branch. I tried to step back from my thoughts, watching them to remind myself my feelings weren't *me*.

Near the surf school, a young man—maybe nineteen with a round, sunburned face—approached and asked in Spanish if I knew how far it was to the bus stop. When I told him about a thirty-minute walk, his face twisted and eyes grew wet. Switching to English, he gestured to two girls lingering behind him and said a friend had brought them to the beach last night then disappeared. His mom would be worried, and he couldn't call her because his phone had run out of juice.

I realized they'd spent the night on the beach wearing only bathing suits and shorts. They looked weary and in need of a mother. I felt a tenderness well up; they reminded me of my students, the ones who came to me with their problems, asking my advice.

I told them to wait, that I'd go get my car and drive them to the bus stop. A fresh energy came, and my lips softened into a half-smile as I thought about what my mom used to say: *When you're feeling sad or depressed or sorry for yourself, you'll feel better if you help other people.* I jogged to our casita and grabbed bottles of water and granola bars then hopped into Chitty Chitty Bang Bang, blasted the A/C, and sped over to pick them up. As we thudded down the rutted road, they gulped the water and tore into the food. They said they were on university break and had flown here from their hometown of Guadalajara for a beach trip. We chatted about what they were studying, and what I was doing in Baja.

The young man, Cesar, talked about how much he loved my blue car. He praised its creamy leather seats, moon roof, and CD player. He said he wanted to travel one day like I was doing.

"Can I be your dog?" he joked. While we all laughed, a shard of mortification sliced through me at how I hadn't been seeing all I have.

When I dropped them off at the bus stop, they thanked me. But I felt like I should be thanking them. My mood lifted, and I had a clearer vision about how to move forward.

Two weeks later, Dave and I had gathered for drinks on neighbors' roofs. We'd taken long beach walks and, sweaty, waded into the ocean. We'd shopped the Farmer's Market and swayed to live music on the playa. We'd given a ride to a hitchhiker, a young Polish woman who was traveling alone through Baja, and met a Swiss couple on bikes who'd ridden all the way down from Canada. We'd talked to people who'd retired here, others who came part of the year, and still others who lived in the nearby city of Cabo San Lucas and spent the weekends at Cerritos Beach. We met people who ventured here to escape the rat race—and others to escape the law. Some loved to surf or fish or just be near the sea. Others fancied four-wheeling or hiking through the desert hills. Some were born here. Others fell in love with the area and never wanted to leave. I was reminded daily there are so many ways to do this living thing.

Over the weeks, we'd procured some household items, living room furniture, and the all-important bed. A bilingual friend helped us, guiding us an hour south to Los Cabos to segundas (second-hand stores) and big-box retailers. A worker installed our air conditioner, and another had spent days constructing our kitchen island, a work of art he trawled by hand out of cement and then polished. Under the lip of the bar we slipped traditional rustic Equipale barstools made of tanned pigskin and cedar strips. I was nearly giddy the first time we sat there to eat a meal.

In downtown Todos Santos, Ann introduced us to Bahia, a sidewalk *mariscos* or seafood restaurant, where at plastic tables we ate fish tacos piled with coleslaw and salsa. The nearby tienda offered a bundle of warm handmade tortillas for pennies. Dave held them up to his nose and feigned happy tears. From the back of his truck, a guy in worn work jeans sold us a hefty bag of juicy oranges, and from a stand in Pescadero we bought potatoes, carrots, cilantro, and strawberries the size of baseballs. Pescadero, which means "fish monger," is known not only for its seafood but its agriculture. Cruising down the dirt byways, we were enveloped in the sweet scent of basil spread out in rows and mangoes drooping from the trees.

I tried to stay with the beauty but thoughts crept in about our to-do list that was longer than a politician's monotonous speech. I was glad the casita was small, because I didn't want owning a house to mean being anchored to never-ending home improvements. I didn't want my hobbies to be buying, fixing, cleaning…all the things *home* seemed to require. Things that affixed me when I craved flexibility, freedom, flight.

Chapter Five

Whale Sharks & Waterfalls

Spring 2015

We'd heard there were good stores in La Paz, an hour away—but we'd also been told the cops there pulled people over for a *mordita,* a word that literally means "little bite." We knew our blue Subaru with U.S. plates made us a juicy target for such bribery. We didn't want to get bitten, but we badly needed more furniture and sundries.

With no GPS on our phones, we had to rely on an old-fashioned map and advice from friends. We spent a sweaty day navigating unmarked streets and stopping at random segundas. We'd heard you could score good deals on charming pre-owned furniture in these thrift stores, but all we saw were couches with springs sticking out and dusty, wobbly ottomans. After crisscrossing dreary industrial byways, we located a big box store where we thought we could grab a cart and pile it high with household necessities, from a dish drying rack to laundry soap—and maybe we'd luck out and find a lamp.

I looked forward to relief from the humidity, but no whoosh of cool air greeted us. The A/C was down. We were surprised to see nearly empty shelves, items having been picked over, leaving dented and bruised detritus. Oddly, there were long lines at the checkout stands, and it dawned on me this post-apocalyptic scene was a remnant of post-hurricane upheaval. How could I have forgotten that some of these shoppers' roofs had been recently ripped off their homes? And that swaths of the community still had no electricity or running water? And here I was, bummed out because I couldn't locate a package of kitchen sponges. Having not crossed one item off our list, we limped out of La Paz hoping not to alert a cop hungry for a mordita. A disquieting sensation hovered at my breastbone—and I wondered if Baja could ever feel like home.

The next week, animated voices boomed through our screen doors. We opened our gate to our neighbors in the walkway. Their sun-caramelized skin glowed and their eyes sparkled. They told us they'd just spent a wonderful day in La Paz. As I wondered how the bleak city of La Paz could bring such joy, they said they'd gone swimming with whale sharks. Dave pressed for details. Being in the water with sea life is one of his passions. He'd been wanting to get into the Sea of Cortez but we'd been preoccupied with hunting down brackets to hang up our mop in the utility room.

"Um…swimming with a *shark?*" I whisper-hissed. I love the water, too, and as a former synchronized swimmer fancy myself a mermaid. There isn't a pool, lake, or calm sea I haven't enjoyed dipping into. But like everyone in my generation, I've been traumatized by *Jaws*, a movie I waited in line for two hours to be tortured by at age twelve.

Dave Cousteau explained whale sharks are not whales, and they are not flesh-eating sharks. They are the largest fish in the sea, non-mammalian vertebrates that can grow up to forty feet and almost 50,000 pounds. But they are gentle giants, filter feeders who eat plankton, not humans. He assured me the encounter would be safe—and mind-blowing. By this point in our three-year marriage, I knew to believe him when he said such things.

However, when we'd been in Hawai'i with our friend Christine the previous year, we'd had an ocean incident that made me question my seaworthiness. We'd taken the ferry to Lanai to swim with her and Kenny who both had about fifteen years on us, yet their bodies were firm from daily swimming, their skin crinkled and sun-goldened. With snorkels, masks, and fins, the four of us swam out to the open sea, seeking a reef Kenny had heard about. From the beach, the water had looked placid, but soon our bodies were being pushed and pulled by strong swell. We plowed through the chop, no land in sight. My stomach became unsettled from the constant motion and from involuntarily gulping salt water.

I wondered how Dave—an excellent swimmer and lifelong scuba diver—was feeling. I nearly panicked for a moment at the thought of being so far from shore, my body craving solid earth. I turned and floated on my back, my body bobbing as I gazed at the bottle blue sky. I tried to capture a feeling: the ocean as womb, the water amniotic fluid.

After nearly an hour of swimming, Kenny motioned us over. I paddled my fins—and through the looking glass of my mask, a magical world emerged: confetti of sea creatures in lavender, amethyst, malachite. Bulging fish, sleek fish, hundreds of silver fingerlings in a whirling cloud. Spindly corals with gangly arms, gem colors aglow. A turtle the size of a platter, drifting.

A few other snorkelers and divers appeared. I lifted my head and saw a boat and realized boat transportation was how normal people got out here. A crew member shouted out to us, "Are you okay? Do you need help?"

"We're fine!" Kenny shouted back.

I was tempted to hitch a ride. But, I reassured myself, Kenny and Christine knew what they were doing. I dipped my face back in the aquarium, watching the fish sway with the surge, reminding me to surrender, not fight. The saltwater cradled me, held me aloft. I thought about the book *Swimming to Antarctica*, Lynne Cox swimming for days in the world's coldest waters without a wetsuit. I thought of Diana Nyad, the first person to swim from

Cuba to Florida without a shark cage. Although she likely wasn't the first: people escaping Cuba have undoubtedly done so unreported. Humans are capable of extraordinary things—like performing and undergoing brain surgery. I reminded myself how fortunate I was to be living this life, to be alive—even to be in the water, because after the surgery I couldn't submerge my head for months. As though in response to my thoughts, my scalp scar audibly creaked, as it does from time to time.

Heading back, I followed Kenny and Christine, Dave the fish's tail protecting the rear. The waves had gotten choppier, and there was no bottom to see—just a gray infinitude. A curl of water splashed into my snorkel. I choked, wishing for gills. I could glimpse land in the distance and knew it was farther than it seemed. Nausea surged. The dive boat had melted into the horizon.

I focused on the line of land to level out my vision, in hopes of alleviating my seasickness. I'd never before felt this way in the water, ill and bone-deep exhausted. I'd taken the idea of an adventurous life too far. As we neared shore, breakers boomed like cannons. I could feel the power of immense waves forming as they passed below to lift and crash in an explosion of spray. I clenched at the thought that we'd need to swim through waves that would challenge professional surfers. But Kenny led us parallel to the shore to the next beach where the waves were smaller. I tried to body surf them, but they felt less like water, more like Jell-O.

Quaking, I glimpsed the bottom. Another numbing number of strokes and my tiptoes touched sand. A wave whipped me from behind, throwing me down. I choked as sand jammed into my bikini bottoms. As I struggled to surface, I knew I must use oceanic energy to take me the rest of the way. With a sloppy body surfing technique, at last I reached the beach, sputtering and bedraggled. I sprawled on the sand, my arms and legs quivering. Forcing myself to stand, I wobbled to the picnic bench in the shade where Kenny had already arrived and was munching on popcorn sprinkled with nutritional yeast, the feast of athletic hippies. He looked so at ease, and I felt lost. I was a little irritated at his blasé attitude toward such a treacherous experience, but I was also in awe of his strength and trust in the ocean. He was at home in Hawai'i in a way I'd never be.

My trembling fingers clenching a towel around my shoulders, I leaned into Dave, seeking grounding. He looked at me, eyebrows raised. I could read his mind, *What the fuck? Did we really do that?* I tried to smile to belie my bewildered state, but my face froze, encrusted in salt. The motion of the sea was still with me, a surging dizziness not unlike my post-brain-surgery vertigo.

Later, Dave told me the swim had been a stretch for him, but he knew I was struggling even more. Which is why, when he'd spotted a reef shark, he hadn't alerted me. He'd been excited but knew I might not be so thrilled.

Dave reassured me our Baja whale shark excursion would be nothing like the Lanai episode. We'd be in a calm bay, we wouldn't be swimming a long distance, and we could signal to the boat if we needed assistance.

On this, our second trek to La Paz, we followed our friends' directions to turn left at the McDonald's and head toward the malecon, an esplanade spanning the waterfront. It was lined with shops, restaurants, and small hotels on one side and the gulf's azure waters on the other, immediately reversing my earlier judgments of this city. We found easy parking in front of a defunct hotel with the faded words *Los Arcos* spelled out on crumbling adobe.

Across the street a guy leaning against his panga boat introduced himself as Omar. He charged us 1200 pesos (about eighty U.S. dollars) for a spontaneous, private charter. As we sped along the water, I struggled to ask Omar in Spanish about his life but was distracted by dolphins bounding by, silvered bodies glimmering as they arced over the sea. Moments later, Omar exclaimed, "*Mira! Mira!* Jump in!" My eyes followed his finger-point to a submerged shadow the size of a bus. As Dave giddily pulled on his mask, snorkel, and fins, I did the same, the *Jaws* soundtrack thumping in my mind. I soothed myself: *It has no teeth, it has no teeth.*

We dropped into the eighty-degree water in the pathway of the beast. He slithered toward us, revealing a face flat as a manhole cover, a speckled colossal body, and a pointy shark tail. As he drifted beneath me, he turned his head, and his primordial eye peered into mine. For a timeless moment, we were the same: two animals floating in this enigmatic universe. Every pore on my skin electrified and an ecstasy bloomed. All fear dissolved, as though my body would have been content to be gulped down whole.

After two hours on the water, we grew hungry. Thanking Omar, we tipped him, then walked through a skate park to an open-air restaurant covered in thatched palapa roof. Onto corn tortillas brimful with fish and shrimp, we piled goodies from the colossal salsa bar: pickled veggies, chopped cabbage, six different sauces. I drank my new favorite: *limonada con agua mineral*, fresh lime squeezed into sparkling water. Mexican limes are the best on the planet, as is Baja shrimp. In fact, I didn't like shrimp until tasting *camarón* in Mexico.

Next we drove south on a road that snaked through the desert hills, paralleling the Sea of Cortez. Suddenly, Dave braked the car and snapped a picture of an osprey atop a cactus, its head crowned by spiky feathers. The road ended at Playa El Tecolote, a dream-beach of calm aquamarine waters and sandy solitude sprinkled with shade palapas. I floated in the shallow sea that felt like being wrapped in another skin.

That outing emboldened us to venture through more of Baja Sur—and to realize we'd be fine if we went another week without a toilet scrubber and bedside stands. Dave researched and planned a four-day adventure to the East Cape, a forty-mile stretch of coastline along the Sea of Cortez.

As we maneuvered to our first destination, Cañon de la Zorra Falls, our car's shock absorbers were challenged on the pitted roads. At times it wasn't clear if we were going the right direction—and visions of us breaking down and scorching to death crossed my mind—but with the assistance of luck and a few scrawled signs, we made it to the entrance, a gravel parking lot aside a casita. The house's shady garden dripped greenery and overflowed with potted plants, driftwood, and tchotchkes. A brown dog lying in the shade didn't even lift her head at the crunch of our tires. A guy with the body of a featherweight boxer came out to greet us. We handed over a few pesos, and he pointed us to the trail.

The fifteen-minute hike was iffy in my flip-flops, and I rolled my eyes at myself for rarely having the appropriate footwear, a theme of my life. But every tentative step was worth it the minute we caught a glimpse of a pool of lime-green water gleaming amongst truck-sized boulders, a waterfall slivering down a crevasse. The cool water lulled my clammy body. Dave asked me to perform my signature synchronized swimmer's ballet leg, and he snapped a picture that to this day looks like a fantasy.

Next we drove to Santiago, a pueblo with a ghost town vibe. Seeking out food, we located the only grocery store, a tiny tienda smelling of mold. The cans and boxes on the shelves were dusty and out-of-date, and the one customer wandering the aisles had a scary zombie ambiance. I decided to view the whole thing as charming, but we didn't buy a thing.

When we arrived at the Palomar Hotel, an old hunting camp, I was enthralled by the terrace restaurant, fruit trees, and cooing doves. Our room, however, featured a mattress seemingly crafted from concrete and lifeless *cucurachas* that littered the windowsill. Too exhausted to care, we sprawled on the rock-solid bed for a nap.

When we woke famished at 5:20 p.m., we ambled to the restaurant—only to be told by Sergio, the owner, it was closed for the evening. I pointed to the posted hours of 9 a.m.-6 p.m. and he responded with a shrug. We scraped together lunch leftovers: half an avocado from our cooler, and a handful of cookies.

In the middle of the night, I was awakened by havoc: bawling doves, dogs yowling in the distance, and roosters crowing. The next morning the Palomar redeemed itself with tasty huevos rancheros and chilaquiles. When Dave asked Sergio how to get to Santa Rita Hot Springs, our host pulled out a pen and drew a map on a paper napkin. I had this unshakeable feeling we were characters in a book, like Paul and Jane Bowles exploring Tangier.

Sergio's directions led us to a short path we followed until we came upon a stream bounded by cacti and palms, an oasis steaming with thermal mineral-rich hot springs. We alternately soaked in the warm pools and in the cold water running down from the mountains, in awe we had this ecological wonder to ourselves.

Blissed-out, we drove to the pueblo of San Jorge, whose main features were a weedy basketball court and a doll house of a church with ten pews and arched stained glass windows. Later, we came across a monument at the Tropic of Cancer, which marks the northern boundary of the tropics. At the globe sculpture I placed my finger on the spot where we stood. The vastness of Earth made me feel insignificant in a spookily pleasant way. I like knowing I'm a speck in the universe, in this human form for a brief second in geological time. It helps me take everything less seriously—and to feel freer.

Soon we aimed the car south to Los Zacatitos. Our friend Roberta had invited us to come spend the night. I knew she was an artist, and I'd heard her house was special, but I was awestruck as we approached a purple dome standing out against the green-and-brown desert terrain like an Easter egg. Roberta was in her late seventies and had been driving alone from California to Baja every winter for years. In the 1960s and 70s, she was a Ford model and hung out with the likes of Sean Connery and the Rolling Stones. With her long silver hair and elegant, flowing clothes, she came out to greet us, her dog Angel at her heels. The house's dome ceiling was painted like the sky, constellations glittering. An ethereal bed floated on a pedestal in the middle of the room. Areas were organically sectioned off with bohemian furniture and antiques. That night we slept in her studio, surrounded by her photographs, paintings, and handmade jewelry.

In the morning we drove north to Cabo Pulmo for a final night. Even though the road was rough, I was glad we chose the ocean route rather than the smoother inland one, because we were treated to whale spouts and surfers. A stocky white bull and several cartoonish burros meandered by the roadside, and an upside-down RV next to the skeleton of a palapa brought a reminder of Hurricane Odile's force.

Cabo Pulmo was reputed to be one of the best places to snorkel in the region. We checked into one of the dive shop's cottages outfitted with red tile floors and an intricately woven palapa roof. The morning dawned with choppy waters, and we climbed aboard a boat appropriately named *Si no quieres no* ("If you don't want to, don't"). From the beach, three guys pushed the craft backward into the waves until the captain could drop the motor. It was a jerky ride to the only hard coral reef on the west coast of

53

North America. That Cabo Pulmo is a protected national park became evident as we swam with a dizzying array of fish so thickly packed together they brushed my skin.

The captain took us to observe sea lions splayed along jagged rocks. Some people swim with them, but I had no interest since my sister had been bitten by one the previous year, causing a bloody gash bigger than a *mordita* on her thigh. Give me a whale shark anytime.

Chapter Six

Some Dogs Bite

Summer 2015

The first night in Chicago, Bear kept me awake as he wandered around the bedroom scraping his nails on the hardwood floor. I'm not a fan of sleeping with dogs, especially ones that fart, snore, and clomp around. So the next night I dragged both dog beds outside the bedroom door to the hallway.

Bear was an intense young mutt who avoided eye contact and liked to run hard. Jake, on the other hand, was a gentle geriatric golden retriever with a lumbering walk. He followed me and plopped down on his pillow, but Bear had disappeared. I found him hunkered under the four-poster bed. I called his name and asked him to come, clicking my tongue, but he stayed put. I thought a treat might persuade him, so I ran downstairs for one, came back up and, on my knees, stretched my arm under the bed, calling his name.

When my fingers reached his lips, he chomped down.

I screamed and jumped away, my hand on fire. My finger was bleeding but fortunately still attached.

Dave came rushing into the room. I was wailing, freaked out by the pain but more so by the fact that he'd bit me, puncturing a hole in the delusion that the animals we cared for were temporarily mine.

Chicago was our third housesit in a few months, the other two in California, when we'd returned from Baja. Our time in California had been a cyclone of seeing friends and family, attending my niece's eighth grade graduation, rafting down the American River with our boat guide friend at the helm, and doing one of our favorite things: seeing lots of live music.

We'd left our car at Chambliss's and flown to New Orleans to attend Jazz Fest. Dave had been to this international music festival many times and regaled me with stories, so I had to see for myself. I gorged on the feast of music, from blues to Cajun to gospel, from soul to rock-n-roll and Brazilian jazz. In addition to spending days in the sun at the fairgrounds' stages, we flung ourselves into night shows, boogying with our friends until two in the morning.

When we returned to California, we continued fulfilling one of our retirement goals of seeing all the live music we could by attending an outdoor music festival in Santa Cruz featuring Bonnie Raitt. In July we drove into the Sierra Nevada foothills for the High Sierra Music Festival, a wild party of music and art and costumes and dancing with friends and strangers all day and into the night. The morning it was over, I woke up in our rented cottage knowing I'd pushed myself too far: cold sores that popped up from too little sleep and too much sun spread across my lips and I moaned to Dave we needed to stay there another night. But there was no more room at the inn, so I had to force myself up.

As we drove along a pine tree-lined road, I thought about how I wasn't twenty anymore and couldn't party with abandon and not pay for it. Why Dave was fine says a thing or two about our dispositions. He can be in the midst of a wild time and yet maintain his equilibrium. And he's an excellent sleeper, allowing his body to rebound. I tend toward episodes of insomnia and mania. Upon falling in love with Dave after a miserable divorce—and after having brain surgery—I wanted to LIVE! I rarely said no to an adventure as we stacked our calendar. But at that miserable moment in the car, I knew something would have to change. We'd need to transform from nomads into slow-mads.

Such a conversion, though, would take some time—and wouldn't happen in a straight line. In the three months since we'd left Mexico, before heading to Chicago, we'd slept in twenty different beds in California, between housesits, rentals, and friends' homes. While the pace threatened to deplete us, we giggled about having sex in so many different locations—and surmised that nomadic couples might have more stimulating sex lives!

On one sit, we'd again found ourselves in Santa Cruz, taking care of Marge the bulldog for Kamryn, my former student. I eyed the dog pillow in the bedroom and hoped all would be well. Yet, predictably, our first night with Marge, her snoring kept me awake. The next evening, as we came into the bedroom, she was already curled up on her pillow. As I dragged it across the hardwood floor, she stayed put. Lugging her into the hallway was a challenge because bulldogs are substantial creatures. To that point, her nickname was Large Marge.

She didn't complain about the new sleeping arrangement. No matter the time we arose, she'd be curled up, eyes open, waiting to follow us downstairs. She reminded me of an adorable toadstool, squat and white, splashed with black.

On my first walk with Marge, I leashed her and trudged up the steep sidewalk of the suburban neighborhood. Atop the hill, we climbed steps made from railroad ties—a portal leading from the sidewalk to a duff-soft trail through the trees. Kam had said Marge would stick with me, so I unclipped her leash.

When we entered a eucalyptus grove, my lungs filled with freshness, and I paused to watch the silver leaves tremble against ocean-blue sky. As I continued walking, I realized Marge was no longer beside me. I turned and saw she lagged far behind, trotting like a slow mini pig. I called out, encouraging her to come. She stopped, her sturdy legs planted.

"Come, Marge! Come!" I urged, slapping my thigh. She took a few steps and stopped again, staring at me like, *can we go home now?*

Kam had told me Marge loved walks. What was going on? Maybe she missed her owners.

I reattached her leash. She stayed by my side, panting. I'd once heard bulldogs can struggle to keep cool because of a clunky mechanism in their tongue or throat. It wasn't a hot day, but it was sunny. Was she sweltering?

When she lay down in a patch of shade, legs splayed and chest to the dirt, I panicked. Had I pushed her beyond her limits? We hadn't gone far, but I'd done a wretched job of honoring Marge's signals.

My heart thumped in my throat. I needed to get her to the kitchen's cool tile floor and her water bowl.

"You're okay, baby," I soothed. "You're okay."

Tucking my fingers beneath her meaty body, I fumbled her into my arms. It was like lifting a gym bag stuffed with dumbbells.

Her panting relaxed as I walked, but my knees threatened to buckle. When I reached the railroad tie stairs, I let her slither down. She walked like an arthritic to the house, plopping herself down next to the welcome mat. I brought out water, which she lapped up.

Dave appeared. "Is she alright?"

Had he said that accusingly? Years ago, when we'd been dating, I took him on my favorite hike one afternoon, straight up a hot mountain. He'd said, "This isn't a hike, it's a death march." Dave enjoyed hiking for being outdoors and taking pictures rather than for the extreme physical exertion I craved. I had learned from him there are pleasures in slowing down and looking around, but I didn't always lean that direction.

Marge was calming. I bent down and stroked her back. In a few minutes, she ambled into the house and curled onto her bed.

The next day, I let her lead the way on our walk. I told her we would go where she wanted, and only as far as she wanted. I was going to let her take the lead. Our walks weren't about my exercise, they were for her, so she could enjoy the smells of the day. Marge had become my guide in the pleasures of not rushing, and I loved her for it.

Bear in Chicago was the first dog in my care I didn't fall in love with. It was hard to adore an animal that bit me. But we reached a détente. I tried to be calm and assertive with him, and he responded in kind by relaxing around me. I came to understand he didn't randomly attack me; he'd been feeling cornered and self-protective beneath the bed. Besides, the wound was superficial. The bite had been a warning about his fear. With those teeth, if he were dangerous, he could have dismembered me. When I contacted the owner to tell him what happened, he said, "Oh yeah, he did that once to me, too." That would have been nice to know in advance. I added to our list of questions to ask homeowners: *Has your dog ever nipped or bitten anyone? What were the circumstances? How does the dog do with strangers? Kids? Other dogs?*

In our years of housesitting, I've discovered people prefer not to admit their animals' flaws, or they downplay them. I tell the hosts we can handle most anything, but we need to understand the dogs' dispositions. No animal is perfect. This usually helps them to reveal the warty truth.

The Chicago housesit was six weeks, a good way to slow down our pace. When we'd first arrived, we spent a day with the homeowners who toured us around their Hyde Park neighborhood of stately row homes constructed in red, white, and tan brick. Mature elms and maples shaded the sidewalks bordered with marigolds and geraniums. Concrete barriers blocked one street to through traffic, protecting a Georgian-style red brick house with white trim, the private residence of the Obamas. Down the street a plaque commemorated Barak and Michelle's first date at a Baskin Robbins.

We walked to the Lake Michigan waterfront and through the gothic architecture of the University of Chicago campus. The hosts kindly made us dinner that night and breakfast the next morning. Before they left, we attended a service at their Unitarian church in a grand ornate building. I'm not a church person, but in our mode of living many different lives, I wanted to experience everything. Without the Catholic rituals I grew up with— smoky chalices and silky holy water—it felt more like a business meeting than a religious event. I admired the inclusivity of all genders, sexualities, races, and cultures—and the Unitarians' commitment to social justice.

When the owners left, it didn't take long to get encamped in their row house appointed with Arts and Crafts furniture and leather sofas. Dave attacked their bookshelf teeming with presidential biographies. At first we were homebodies, reading for hours, walking the dogs, doing yoga, and taking care of business (me, writing and editing; Dave, researching the area and planning outings). One morning we observed a film crew through the window on the street below; they were shooting a made-for-TV movie about Michelle and Barak. We visited the farmer's market and walked across the street for free music in the park, a fun locals' scene. Living in this neighborhood for six weeks, we were transformed—at least temporarily— into locals.

I was pleased that the area was walkable, even in the heat and humidity. The air felt like a *thing*. Dusk was ethereal, with an opalescent sky, embryonic warm air, and fireflies floating around our faces like cinders.

The hosts had told us we were welcome to have guests, so we invited our friends Larry and Sofia who flew in from Mexico. At the time they arrived, our friend Kate was staying in the third bedroom, a stopover on her three-month road trip she dubbed her "Big Adventure." Together we launched into tourist mode, investigating the Art Institute, floating down the Chicago River on an architecture tour boat ride, and exploring Millennium Park where we took the obligatory picture of us reflected in the Bean, aka Cloud Gate, the famous curvy silver sculpture that hovers in the middle of the greenway.

At the park, we met up with Pam for a picnic and a free jazz concert. She and Dave had been friends since the days they hiked trails together in the Bay Area. Pam lived in Oak Park, a Chicago suburb famous as the home of Frank Lloyd Wright—and the place where Ernest Hemingway was born and grew up. She toured us around the neighborhood to see Wright's distinctive Prairie-style houses: low, open-plan horizontal structures that feel entrenched in the land.

That evening, we ate dinner at an open-air restaurant at Montrose beach serenaded by a Doors cover band. As people strolled on the sand in the dark, I was struck by how, if I didn't know better, I'd guess on this warm night I was at a beach in Mexico, not Midwest America.

As it turned out, our San Francisco Giants came to town for a baseball game at Wrigley Field. I'd been enamored of this old-fashioned stadium when I'd seen it on TV and was thrilled to be able to experience a park that had hosted Major League Baseball for more than 100 seasons. The visibility was perfect from our seats—of the players and the hands of the person behind the scoreboard manually updating the score, a vintage leftover.

When we'd booked the Chicago housesit, we'd had no idea we'd be seeing a Giants game, nor that we'd get to spend time with so many friends. There's something rich about leaping into the unknown, a feature of our wandering life. As I like to say, the void is fertile. When I mentioned on Facebook where we were, a distant cousin, whom I'd never met in person, asked if we wanted to get together for brunch. Anne-Marie brought her two sisters and her mom, Kathleen, my father's cousin. My parents had liked her name so much, they'd named me after her. I'd met her once as a girl, aged three or four, when my family had spent a summer in Illinois. Now she was in her eighties and on the fringes of dementia, her daughter had warned me. When I saw her, I fell into a time warp. She looked like my grandmother. It was dizzying hugging my namesake and, with my cheek next to hers, feeling my long-gone grandmother's soft skin.

I also met with a former student, De Ann, who now lived in Chicago. I'd run into her two years before when, newly retired and diagnosed with a brain tumor, I'd gone to campus to take care of final paperwork. When she'd asked me how I was and I told her I was having brain surgery the next week, she'd said, "Your surgery's on August eighth? Eight-eight? Eight is a lucky number for the Chinese." Speaking from the experience borne out of her Chinese background, she assured me I'd be fine. I'd been buoyed by her prediction, and she'd turned out to be right. And now it was another August, two years later almost to the day. We talked about the teaching she'd done in Africa, and the writing she was working on. Later she wrote to me, "I continue to tell people about my favorite professor in college"—melting my heart. Sometimes as a retired woman wandering around, the idea of my "life's purpose" would niggle at me. What was I giving to the world at this stage? De Ann reminded me of all the lives I'd touched as a teacher—and that had touched mine. And how that influence continued in ways impossible to map.

Dave pointed out, too, that housesitting was a kind of giving, an act of service. We allowed people to leave their homes and beloved pets worry-free, so they could go on badly-needed vacations, visit family and friends, or offer their own gifts to the world, such as working with the poor in India (as did the couple in Port Townsend) or volunteering their medical services in Africa (as did a doctor/nurse couple on another sit). I liked to think of it that way, even if unpleasant things happened—like getting my finger chomped by a dog or finding a bed uncomfortable.

I didn't miss the grind or politics of teaching, but at times I missed my relationships with students. I thought my days of teaching were over. Little did I know, soon I'd be teaching in three different places I never could have imagined.

Chapter Seven

Yes

Fall 2015

We'd been to L.A. a lot—but not *this* L.A. We were on a housesit in upscale Rancho Palos Verdes, a coastal Los Angeles-county region tucked in a peninsula. After Chicago, we'd flown back to San Jose and started the drive south to our casita, taking this sit as a stopover on our way. The house rested on bluffs overlooking the Pacific Ocean. The owners had installed a swing in the back yard, and swaying on it was like soaring over the sea.

The gig involved caring for two Siamese cats, Kozmo and Kalvin. During the day they'd wander onto the back patio and sprawl in the sun. In the evenings, if we were on the couch, they crawled onto our laps, purring and kneading as we petted them. They were quiet and easy, the only challenge being cleaning their cat box that was kept in one of the bathtubs. The boys didn't have the best aim, and so scraping up droppings became the price we paid for a free month in a split-level home with a ten-million-dollar view. The owners continued to pay for their housecleaners to come regularly, so I could hardly complain since cat-poop duty was my only cleaning responsibility.

I'm a dog lover but caring for cats makes it easier to get out and about. The seventy-ish degree sunny days invited exploring. We brought folding chairs to the beach and soaked in the salty air. We hiked down from steep cliffs to Abalone Cove, an ecological reserve. At low tide algae fluttered and anemones pulsed. We rode our bikes along the strand from Redondo Beach to El Segundo, a multiuse path lining the ocean for miles. I covetously eyed the sweet seaside communities of Hermosa Beach and Manhattan Beach, and launched into a fantasy about living there. But I reminded myself a) clinging causes suffering and b) our own casita was walking distance to a beautiful beach. I nudged myself to come back to the moment, not to get lost in some daydream of *should I or should I not try to live here*. I *was* here. We parked the bikes and stopped for lunch at a sidewalk café. While we ate, roller bladers and joggers whizzed by and, in the distance, gulls and surfers floated on the silvery horizon.

Some of our L.A.-area friends came to visit, including Jude, his wife Melissa, and his brother Brent. Jude and Melissa were new parents, and it was our first time meeting their baby boy, Miles. The brothers broke out their guitars—rarely do they go anywhere without them—and they played for hours as we sang along, the ocean unfurling below. As the horizon smoldered with sunset, Melissa swirled my multicolored hula hoop around her hips to the music. Miles nestled in my arms. Dave's face was aglow with the particular happiness he radiates when he's with these friends. It was one of those moments where you wouldn't change a thing, what Joseph Campbell calls "the rapture of being alive."

Of course no feeling lasts forever, and a few days later my body was jagged with tension. Perhaps having had three periods in one month had something to do with it. *I am peri-menopausal, hear me roar.* In an attempt to allay the worms crawling under my skin, I sat on the swing and did what Pema Chodron suggests: held my discomfort like a baby, cradling it as I had Miles a few days earlier. It helped me feel tender toward the unsettled part of me.

Later, on a walk, I saw a woman struggling to pull one of three refuse cans up her steep driveway. As often happens, my mom's words came to me, "If you want to feel better, help someone out."

I thought I'd frighten the woman if I grabbed one of her cans uninvited. She might think I was a murderer or a Jehovah's Witness.

So I said, "Hi! Would you like some help? It'll be my Random Act of Kindness."

She laughed and said, "Sure!"

I lugged her cans up to her garage, and she thanked me. I bounded down the road feeling the best I had all day. Perhaps this town wasn't my forever home, but wherever we were living, we had neighbors—and being a helpful neighbor felt good.

One of my goals in retiring early had been to focus more on my writing. Before we'd discovered housesitting, we'd rented a house in Tahoe to experience a season in the snow—and that winter I wrote most of my memoir, *Call It Wonder*, which explored our decision to live nomadically, our first year of travel, and my brain tumor incident. It had recently been released, and Nancy, my best friend since high school, threw me a book party at her art studio in L.A. Nancy is not only an artist but a staunch supporter of the arts, buying art and arranging openings for artists she loves. In high school, she could usually be found in the art room, painting. Sometimes I think we're happiest as adults when we're doing what we loved as kids.

For my event, Nancy organized her studio, set out food and drink, and invited a boatload of people. One of Dave's fraternity buddies came, as did one of my cousins and the daughter of Gabriele Rico, who features prominently in the book. Standing before the group reading from Chapter One, I projected photos on a screen behind me. One showed my scalp right after surgery, and then two weeks later with the staples pulled out and hair already sprouting like leaves of grass. The miracle of healing. There were pictures taken by Dave of our travels: kangaroos on a beach in Australia and a leopard we'd seen in the wild in Sri Lanka. As I thanked Nancy, I displayed a snapshot of us taken in 1980 at an outdoor concert, with our Farrah hair and New Wave cat's eye sunglasses. The event was wonderful…but also a bit nerve-wracking. The book's subtitle is "an odyssey of love, sex, spirit, and travel"—and the story exposes aspects of my past that are a smidgeon mortifying, such as my unconventional sex life and episodes of binge eating. But the book wouldn't have been true, or human, absent those events. It felt important to shine light in the dark shame-y places. A kind of healing for me, and perhaps for the reader. As writer and former bank robber Joe Loya says, you have to be willing to embarrass yourself to write memoir.

Soon after, my friend Patricia asked if I'd be interested in leading a writing workshop in Sonora at Tuolumne County Arts Alliance and giving two readings, one at Columbia College and the other at a bookshop and café downtown. Then Dave got notice his nephew was getting married in Northern California. As though the universe were conspiring for us to say *yes* to both, another friend asked if we wanted to housesit for her in Tahoe in December. Our plan had been to drive from Southern California to our casita, but visions of skiing danced in our heads. We decided Baja could wait and pointed Chitty Chitty Bang Bang north.

Pondering Patricia's invitation and Nancy's support of my work, I thought about how I didn't deep-down understand the importance of friends until I was going through my ghastly divorce. My friends showed up over and over, shoving my furniture into a moving van, listening to my pitying cries on the phone, inviting me to sleep in their spare rooms so I wouldn't have to be alone. My buddy Scott and I developed a ritual we called Beer and Buddha. Every week we'd go hear a dharma talk at a local temple, followed by happy hour. Those dates were like a life preserver. I promised myself I'd never again be a lazy friend, that I'd regularly reach out to my friends, that I'd tell them what they mean to me, that I'd champion their projects—and that I'd support *them* during the ups and downs of their own lives. I hope I've lived up to that wholehearted pledge. When Patricia signed her email, "Patricia, who so appreciates the day we met," I thought maybe I had, at least a little.

I thought again about how being nomadic could have led to my relationships growing thin. Perhaps in some ways they had, but in other ways they'd grown richer. We spent a lot of time with our friends when we were in their towns, and they knew wherever we were, they were invited to join us—and many had. It became like vacationing with our loved ones over and over again.

And when we're together, I feel *home*. So perhaps home is people, not a place. I had that feeling of warm belonging when, on our drive to Northern California, we stopped in the Sacramento area to visit my cousins and my 91-year-old Aunt Ruby. Ruby, who never took a music lesson, performed honky tonk piano for us. She told me playing music every day was her secret to longevity. My cousins are a playful family. They worship Disneyland and go there often with their kids (now adults) and grandkids; they enjoy all the Disney movies, can belt out any song from the soundtracks, and have Disney memorabilia stationed all over their bright house. The bedroom we stayed in had a different yet just as iconic theme: Coca Cola. The familiar swirling font spelled out *Coca Cola* in red and white on the bedspread, lamp, and vintage bottles and cans lining the dresser. One person's corny is another's fun—and while I'm not an avid Disney or Coke fan, I love how their home reveals their spirit. After all our time on the road, their house felt welcoming and cheerful. They are touchstone cousins, and they always share memories of my parents, as though they know such stories nourish me.

A week later, Dave's nephew got married in a Catholic church in Marin County. I grew up Catholic, and so the perfume of incense and the rituals of kneeling and standing aren't foreign to me. Neither is the fact that Catholics like to party. The reception flowed with wine, and we danced with everyone: the young people, Dave's sister Sue, and his brother, Milt. Looking around the room, it struck me that at some point we'd invisibly shifted from the age of those getting married to the age of the aunts and uncles.

I loved seeing Dave with his sister and brother. I knew he missed his hiking dates with Sue, and that he and Milt weren't in touch as much as he'd like. Knowing this made showing up for the wedding feel more important. I was glad we'd detoured, grateful for the flexibility of our lives. That was another reason I'd retired early. Yes, I'd sacrificed a larger pension—and sometimes I wondered what life would be like with more financial abundance. We lived on little money compared to many of our ilk. But mostly I was grateful for getting to choose how to spend my moments, my days. And for not having to devote every weekend to grading papers.

I titled the Sonora workshop "How to Believe in Your Writing." In my fifties, I was finally getting a handle on deeply appreciating that we are creative creatures who have every right to make what we want, no apologies or explanations. Who knew where this crazy desire to create came from? It was one of the mysteries I wanted to encourage the group to dig into.

After more than two years away from teaching, I had to shake off nerves as I faced a room full of women, and a few men, ranging from teenagers to those in their seventies. A longtime friend showed up with her mom. Their friendly faces helped the butterflies to settle, as did reminding myself people came because they *wanted* to write. I opened the day-long workshop with inspiring author quotes and led everyone through exercises, encouraging them to write freely, setting aside the critic in their mind. The energy in the room grew electric. People shared and laughed and cried. By the end I was buzzing and wrung-out—a reminder of how I used to feel after a day in the classroom.

Patricia and her partner Cindy hosted us. I had met Patricia at a writing workshop years before, when I was married to a woman. Patricia's book, *Between Two Women*, had recently been published, and we'd bonded over being writers and women who'd been surprised we fell for a woman later in life. When I married Dave, I wondered if she'd be uncomfortable, if she'd drop me as had a few of my lesbian friends. But Patricia remained my comrade, understanding we are more than the gender of the person we love.

Dave and I stayed in the guest room of their cozy mobile home. The front deck was covered in potted flowers and shaded by live oaks and bull pines. The interior had an office dominated by a writing desk, and a spacious kitchen opening out to a living room filled with mountain cabin décor, a homey place where I felt coddled and sheltered.

About ninety minutes from Sonora is Yosemite, a sapphire in the crown of America's National Parks. Dave and I headed there and hiked at Hetch Hetchy, a glacial valley with a reservoir drained by the Tuolumne River. After the intensity of interacting with so many people, it felt blissful to move my body under a peaceful gemstone sky. We traversed the dam and followed a trail for a few miles before settling on the edge of a granite cliff. We ate lunch to the grumbling and spray of Wapama Falls. That night we slept at Evergreen Lodge in a woodsy cabin. Whenever I was in Yosemite, I thought about my parents, who'd met there in the 1950s. Everywhere, California was filled with memories of what home used to be.

Afterwards, we drove back to the Bay Area, where my sister Crystal invited me to meet with a book group of her friends in an affluent East Bay community. The women expressed awe and envy that we'd downsized and were traveling freely. I find it's often people with the most resources—5,000 square-foot houses and seven-figure incomes—who say they desire what we're doing but can't imagine how to make it happen. Perhaps they're anchored by their choices. I don't judge people for having a lot of stuff (after all, it's the American way). Some people can manage life with a lot of possessions and not feel smothered. Me, sometimes I feel overwhelmed sorting through my belongings in one suitcase. Keeping my stuff simple and streamlined works best, although I don't always accomplish it, even though I own so little. When I had more possessions, the struggle to keep them manageable was worse: work clothes, twenty pairs of shoes and boots, overflowing bookshelves, drawers brimming with who-knew-what. It rattled me trying to sort through and reorganize jumbles of things I rarely used. I'd vacillate between feeling like my home was a nest and a prison.

At times I'm in awe of people's huge houses filled with beautiful things. I wonder how they rest amidst so much. I recall, though, at *two* different times, *two* wealthy friends of mine with multi-million-dollar chockful palatial dwellings told me they fantasized a fire would burn the whole thing down, freeing them.

I was touched when a few of the book group women said my memoir inspired them or prompted them to reflect on their own life paths. Some critics eye-roll memoir, saying it's navel-gazing or narcissistic. There tends to be an oblique misogyny in these dismissals of the genre—ignoring that renowned male writers like Phillip Roth and John Updike and Jack Kerouac wrote acclaimed thinly-veiled autobiographical fiction, and books like Frank McCourt's *Angela's Ashes* received high praise before the genre became "popular." To write, I have to ignore those opinions. I've always loved memoirs and novels in first-person that read like personal life stories—books by writers such as May Sarton, Maya Angelou, Erica Jong, Anais Nin. As much as I adore Virginia Woolf's novels, it's her collections of letters and diaries that grip me the most. As a girl I delved into *Harriet the Spy, Go Ask Alice, The Diary of Anne Frank*, searching in those girls' life stories for keys about how to live, how to think, how to create…how to *be*.

Our time in California was turning into a book tour. Next I gave a reading at my former place of employment, San Jose State University. The room was filled with my former colleagues and students, a few local friends, and current students who took notes, probably so they'd get class credit for attending. I talked a bit about the impact Professor Gabriele Rico, my mentor when I was a student there, had made on my life. After the reading, my former student Au-Co approached and said, "You are my Gabriele." It wasn't easy to speak with the lump in my throat, but I thanked her for her words and asked if she'd care to join the pack heading out to eat.

We gathered at Flames, a restaurant down the street where I'd spent many an hour imbibing, celebrating, and bitching with my professor friends. As we talked over plates of comfort food, Au-Co told me she returned to Vietnam every summer to visit family—and the last trip she'd fallen in love. She was returning next year to get married and wondered if Dave and I would come to the wedding.

I looked over at my husband, eyebrows raised. Our conversations about synchronicity and being open to opportunities came to mind. Something similar must have been coursing through Dave, because simultaneously we said yes.

Chapter Eight

Mandarin in Mexico

Winter-Spring 2016

We were living in my writer friend Suzanne's Tahoe house, with its open-beamed ceilings and fireplace, caring for big, white, bushy Ely, "the best bad dog in the world." A chow chow, he'd lived in four places before Suzanne adopted him, and one owner had been so abusive his jaw had been broken. It was amazing he trusted people at all—in fact, he was very loving—and while he coexisted with most pooches he sometimes erupted into dog fights. He'd been fitted with a shock collar which had been used on shock setting only a couple of times so he'd associate the noise with electricity; now it was just a "sound collar." Like all dogs, especially large ones, he needed a lot of exercise, and so he'd run as we snowshoed in the nearby isolated woods. We carried a remote to set off the collar in the unlikely event we encountered another dog. Eventually, we did see one walking with its owner. I tried to remain calm but on alert. I called Ely—he trotted right to me—and I attached his leash. I didn't have to use the buzzer because he merely whined as the other dog passed, and we continued on with no issues.

A few weeks later, though, a large brown dog charged us on the trail, and he and Ely barked and snarled at each other. I remembered Suzanne had said the neighbor had a brown dog who was an "asshole." Was this him? Soon the dogs were entangled and gnashing teeth. The buzzer was having no effect. A woman came running toward us, screaming and trying to pull the dogs apart. My heart pounding, I worried she'd get bitten, but the dogs separated, and as I leashed up Ely, she took off in a rush. There'd be no talking about what had happened. I examined Ely and found no wounds, although a few spots of blood were speckled on his white fur.

"What the hell, Ely?" I scolded him as we proceeded down the snowy trail. Clearly he'd already forgotten the whole thing as he calmly peed against a tree. My pulse was pounding, even though the event was over. We humans hold onto stuff. Nothing like a dog to teach you how to be in the present moment.

After a month, we moved to a nearby condo. This one was owned by one of Suzanne's friends, and we'd made a swap for a month at our casita. I missed Suzanne's hot tub with its view of pines and glimpse of lake, the access to snowshoeing right out the front door, and snuggling with Ely. But I didn't miss worrying about dog fights.

The roomy condo's main feature was a glass cabinet—a shrine of gaudy bottles of booze in all shapes and sizes. Although pretty to look at, it went to waste on us because we aren't cocktail people. We spent a good deal of our time researching Southeast Asia and talking about what we wanted to do after we went to the wedding in Vietnam. And then, one day a job announcement floated into my email inbox, a position teaching creative writing at a university in China. Most overseas teaching jobs required teaching English as a Foreign Language, with a focus on grammar and conversation. But creative writing? That was my one true love. I'd often fantasized about running creative writing workshops in dazzling locations. This job seemed like a way to fulfill that dream. And a year in one location would force us to do what we'd failed to do so far: become slow-mads.

Online, we located Nanning in Southwest China in Guangxi province, one hundred miles from the Vietnam border. We could go to the wedding, travel some, and then hop over to Nanning on a short flight. Synchronicity had struck again. We'd go to the wedding, I'd get to teach what I enjoyed, we'd have the opportunity to live in Asia, and we'd bulk up our coffers. After a Skype interview, I was offered the position and we now had two landing places—Da Lat, Vietnam and Nanning, China—around which to build an itinerary.

It was exciting and disorienting to imagine being in the tropics on the other side of the world while snow flurried out the window. My mind couldn't conjure up an image of where we might be living in China, but being in a tropical zone, surely it wouldn't have one particular problem we did here. For some reason, there wasn't enough de-icing salt sprinkled by the condo caretakers. To get to the car, we had to navigate stairs so icy I slipped and fell on my butt. From then on, I crept down like a toddler, clenching the frozen railing. I do love snowy nature, but by this point I was ready to head back to Mexico.

In March we drove to Baja, taking a luxurious four days from San Diego, instead of zipping down in forty-eight hours as we had with my sister. The roads were in better shape than the year before, most hurricane damage having been repaired. Each day in the car we practiced Mandarin by CD as the desert rolled by, the words tangling my tongue.

After nearly a year away, we arrived at the casita and plunged into the pool. This time, instead of an empty house, we were greeted by our red couch and loveseat strewn with bright Mexican pillows. The furniture was in a different configuration—the renters or the cleaners had shuffled things around—but in mere minutes we'd reordered it all. I was happy to have back my workspace, a rustic desk with blue chair, along with a bookcase that partitioned off an office area in the living room. Luckily, Dave's garden hadn't withered but instead had grown fuller and lusher. That night, instead of a leaky air mattress, we climbed onto our memory foam bed with a wooden headboard we'd found at a second-hand store. Shaped as a large half-circle, it was carved with a fanciful sun, face and rays beaming yellow and red.

I'd screwed up on the dates and accidentally accepted a four-day rental two weeks after our return. Shaking off irritation that my mistake meant we had to quickly give up our house, we decided to rent an Airbnb in La Paz, enjoying city beach life and warm evening walks along the malecon when all the families and vendors came out. Upon our return, I discovered a note. The renter had found my memoir on the bookshelf and wrote, "By the 10th page, I knew I was meant to find it. It feels like the book I've been searching for my whole adult life." She went on to say she felt connected to me, even though we'd never met, and she was now inspired to do what she'd forever dreamed of doing: write. She took a copy of the book (I had two on the shelf) and left money to pay for it, saying she'd mail the book back to me if taking it wasn't okay. Would any writer object? I doubt it. We write in solitude and then put our books out into the world, hoping they'll reach people but rarely knowing their impact. Publishing a book feels like laying your baby in a basket to float down the river.

A few days later, we joined my sister and some friends for a concert at Hacienda Cerritos, a palatial saffron-colored dwelling atop a cliff. The Hacienda was built as a private home by a rich tax-evader who landed in prison, and was now run as a hotel. It had arched entryways, red tile floors, elaborate colonial furnishings, and a bell tower. A patio overhanging the ocean spread out back featuring a swimming pool, a palapa-covered bar, and regal palms. Standing there looking over the Pacific, it's a 2,500 mile straight-shot to Hawai'i.

Several hundred people had gathered to enjoy the bluesy-rock band of David Raitt, Bonnie Raitt's brother, who had a house in the area. Last year we'd seen his sister at a Santa Cruz show, so this moment felt like cosmic dot-connecting. I danced barefoot until my feet bruised. Servers handed out tequila shots to the crowd for a toast at sunset. Ever since a haunting tequila incident in college, I haven't been a fan—but raising our thimble-sized plastic cups and cheering together in this sublime spot felt like communion.

A friend who was housesitting in Todos Santos, the town fifteen minutes north of us, needed a week off and asked us if we'd fill in. Todos Santos is a Pueblo Mágico, one of eighty-three small towns the Mexican government has designated as historic and deserving of attention (and tourist dollars). A few times a month, we drove down our bumpy dirt road and onto the four-lane highway—and in ten minutes, we'd be there to shop, eat street tacos, and wander around the shops and art galleries. We liked the idea of living in town for a week.

On our drive to the housesit, dozens of vaqueros wearing cowboy hats and boots paraded on horses along the side of the road. Later I learned they were community activists protesting the impact of Tres Santos, a planned hotel, restaurant, and Colorado State University campus. In addition to concerns about water rights—a troubling topic in the desert—a big issue was the high-end hotel being built on Playa Punta Lobos, where fishermen launched in the mornings and returned each afternoon with their catch to sell. It didn't go past me that the gringos spreading out all over Baja and building huge homes, many with water-demanding swimming pools, were also impacting the locals' way of life, as well as the natural environment. Of course, one could argue that bringing in money helped the economy. It was a tricky balance. Organizations of foreigners and Mexicans were working to address these issues, but I was aware my being in Mexico could have an impact for good and ill.

The housesitting gig was in a palapa-roofed house, sheltered by a stand of luscious palms in *el otro lado*—"the other side," the area north of downtown. Every morning we woke to doves cooing and a distant crash of waves. The steady breeze led me to pull on a sweater. The luxurious kitchen showcased a restaurant-style fridge (ours was half the size) and a chef-quality gas stove. We had two outdoor dogs to care for, Bonita and Negra, sweet lugs who required only a few pats and that their bowls be filled with dry food and water. We were asked not to take them off the property because their job was to guard.

People from the States often ask us if it's safe to live in Mexico. Statistically, Mexico has a lot less gun violence than the United States. Personally, I prefer attending gatherings without having it cross my mind that someone might mow me down like at the country music festival in Vegas, at Club Q in Colorado, at the Valley Transportation Authority in my former city of San Jose, and too many more to name...not to mention an unconscionable number of churches, synagogues, and schools. This kind of public mass shooting is a non-occurrence in Mexico. Stay out of the drug trade and you're likely to be fine. The prime concern for most in Mexico is theft. That's why people use housesitters and have dogs. Dogs may be pets, but their most important role is to scare away would-be thieves. I've known people who've had items stolen or their whole abode cleared out when no one was home. One reason our resort fit our come-and-go lifestyle: there was always staff present.

But of course theft happens everywhere. The only time in my life I've been robbed was in California when a burglar jimmied open the sliding glass door to my second-floor apartment. Fortunately, I slept during the invasion, and more fortunately the guy wanted only one thing: my money. He lifted my wallet out of my purse and slipped out the front door, getting away with eight dollars cash.

During our housesit, we hiked to La Poza beach, scrambling over rocks and past where the water flowed out of the *huerta*—the fields where peppers and basil grow. On our strolls down dirt roads lined with lush and dusty foliage, palm trees and cacti, Dave took pictures of spotted goats and grazing horses. Another day we ambled into town to do errands, including going to the optometrist to pick up my glasses. I liked the optometrist. He had a brilliant smile and knew little English, so interacting with him challenged me to communicate in Spanish. It was one thing to watch Spanish-language YouTube videos and practice on my Duolingo app, but another completely to chat with native speakers. I wished I could relax into speaking in another language, but the effort made my palms sweat.

While wandering through town, we peeked into art galleries, some of which doubled as studios. We could step in and, amidst paint fumes, observe the artist at work. The sounds of guitars and a drum seeped over from somewhere. Soon we discovered the main street was closed off and a makeshift stage had been erected. Crowds milled about in front of the iconic Hotel California. (Legend has it this hotel inspired the Eagles to write their 1976 hit. Although the rumor is wrong—and the band put the kibosh on the hotel constantly playing Eagles tunes over their sound system—the tale lives on.) Soon, dozens of cyclists rode in, wearing vibrant spandex, the end of a sixty-mile race that had begun in La Paz. Their outfits proclaimed they were from various Latin American nations: Costa Rica, Guatemala, Ecuador, and Peru.

One afternoon we went into a restaurant and sports bar with the sole purpose of watching a Golden State Warriors basketball game. On a barstool next to us sat an American guy, so of course we started talking. Rob told us he was ten months into a year-long around-the-world trip with his wife and two teen daughters. I picked his brain about where they'd been and what they'd experienced. He talked about having an adventurous mindset, one free of conventional limitations. He and his wife Nadia wanted to live *now*. They didn't buy a lot of consumer goods—they didn't even own a car—and they weren't afraid of spending their savings to travel. For many years, they lived and worked all over the world with international organizations, so this year of traveling with their daughters was a natural extension of their lifestyle.

When I asked him what they were doing once their year of travel was over, he said they were moving to Myanmar, where he'd gotten a job helping with the newly-elected government's transition. After we told him we were heading to China in August, he said we definitely had to stay in touch and try to meet in Asia.

We'd been planning to go back to our own casita that afternoon to water our yard, so we invited him and his family to our pool. Talking with the girls and Nadia, who was born in Abu Dhabi, it soon became clear the teens were Third Culture Kids, a term coined by sociologist Ruth Hill Unseem to describe young people who grow up in cultures different from their parents and essentially are citizens of everywhere and nowhere. They'd lived not only in the U.S. but in Jordan and several other countries before spending a year on the road. We also learned Rob had worked in Rwanda to help rebuild after the genocide, a task I couldn't begin to imagine. There was a calm nature to all four of them that felt borne from living an expanded, international life. When we said goodbye, I felt a deep knowing we would connect again—if not in Myanmar than somewhere else. And I was right.

Chapter Nine

People's Souls

Early Summer 2016

As our nomadic lives were about to pull us out of Mexico, I felt like I was suspended in mid-air. I knew what lay ahead: California, New York, Colorado, Vietnam, Cambodia, and China. Yet there was so much I didn't know. We'd be on the move, experiencing people and places and cultures new to us. How different than being rooted in our casita, living the rhythms of beach life.

For three months, I'd taken morning walks with my sister and her dogs. We'd celebrated Dave's fifty-eighth birthday around the community pool with a group of friends, dancing to tunes from the 1970s and eating handmade tortillas and tacos al pastor. Having the party catered by the owners of Dave's favorite restaurant in El Pescadero was his birthday present. We'd been able to enjoy our time here because instead of scrambling around to get the casita furnished and completed, we could hang out and *be home*. And now that we were leaving in a few days, I felt a tad wistful. When we'd left Santa Cruz three years earlier, I hadn't thought through how we'd be saying *goodbye* to one thing and *hello* to the next, again and again.

I had been regularly attending yoga class at Baja Zen. To get there, I walked behind our complex down a dirt road and then up a steep path rutted from rainstorms. The flat-roofed concrete building showcased a wall of sliding glass doors facing the ocean panorama. Sometimes during class we'd see whales spouting and breaching. I found myself involuntarily exhaling bone-deep when I walked in that room. Before class one morning Kylie, the teacher, and I talked about how we were both leaving Baja for a while. She, too, lived nomadically and was also pondering this lifestyle's uncertainties. She said, "You're going to like the poem I brought." At the session's end, as we lay flat on our mats in savasana, or corpse pose, she read a piece by C. JoyBell C. These words struck deep:

> *I have come to accept the feeling of not knowing*
> *where I am going. And I have*
> *trained myself to love it.*

I was reminded how living as a traveler was a metaphor for life. No one knows where they're going, not really. Life is more liquid than solid. I once again thought about how Pema Chodron's teachings encouraged us to embrace groundlessness, the shifting sand beneath our feet.

When Kylie finished reading, we rolled over and curled onto our sides: reborn from the corpse to the fetus. Death, birth. Goodbye, hello.

The previous year when we'd driven back to California, we'd crossed the border at Tijuana. The signage hadn't been clear and we'd discovered we were in a lane veering toward the city rather than the border. As we were snared in traffic, vendors descended on our car hawking plastic piggy banks, candy, straw sombreros. I clutched the wheel, and Dave kept craning his neck to see if we could merge into the correct lane, but cement dividers foiled us. A guy approached our car and told us in half-English that for forty U.S. dollars he could direct a group of guys to remove a divider so we could squeeze through. We appreciated his entrepreneurial ingenuity but declined, even after he dropped the price to twenty bucks.

Finally I was able to merge in, only to discover we were locked into the fast-track medical lane. When we inched to the guard booth, I explained our error, but the guard would have none of it. We couldn't pass through without papers from a doctor. He ordered us to drive around the city and to the back of the line. The words of one of my friends echoed in my head, "I would *never* drive in Tijuana." Inhaling deeply and forcing myself to unclench my teeth, I maneuvered down narrow pothole-ridden streets through chaotic traffic and an hour later, across the border. I wouldn't wish such mayhem on anyone, but powering successfully through did make me feel a bit like Superwoman.

Because of that incident, we decided this time to cross at Tecate, an hour east of Tijuana. The route added miles, but we'd heard it was a much better experience. Also, we now had an excuse to see the Valle de Guadalupe wine region. Baja peninsula's northern end is one of the oldest wine-growing areas. Jesuit priests cultivated vines there in the eighteenth century, and the first commercial winery opened in 1888. The roads were smooth, the traffic thin, and as the widespread vistas of green and gold vineyards floated by, I imagined Napa wine country must have been this uncrowded fifty years ago. We passed hacienda-style wineries, adobes with bell towers and arches draped in flamingo-colored bougainvillea. Having done his research, Dave targeted two of the area's 150 wineries. Sitting at an outdoor table with dogs curled near our feet, we sipped red blends and sampled cheese and bread, with specialty olive oils for dipping.

Crossing the border at Tecate could not have been more of a contrast from our Tijuana misadventure. We cruised right up to a line of two other cars. When the border officer started speaking English—and with a southern accent—it took my brain a moment to register that, of course, he

74

was an American. I'd been so used to inspection by Mexican guards who'd stopped us seven times on this 1,000-mile drive.

This guard asked us if "y'all have anything to declare." I knew we were supposed to disclose the wine we bought, and so I freely offered that we had two bottles each.

He dipped his head to catch my eye. "It's only one bottle per person."

"Oh, that's not what they said at the winery," I unhelpfully offered, while my mind played out images of having to pour out two bottles of excellent wine into the dirt like an underage drinker caught by the cops.

Apparently he pitied me, the naïve rube, and told us he'd let us through this time.

I supposed California winemakers had a strong hold on wine imports. Luckily, though, we had enough Mexican wine to share with our friends when we hit San Diego.

Before we'd left our casita, my cousin shared the sad news that her mother, my Aunt Ruby, had died at age 93. Then, tragically Ruby's son Bobby, my cousin, unexpectedly died soon thereafter at age 68 from a short illness. I was grateful we could make it to the joint life celebration in Northern California, at an Italian restaurant Ruby had loved. My sisters, nieces, nephews, and cousins filled the place, and we had one of those ritual gatherings filled with stories that brought out laughter and tears. I was glad I'd seen Aunt Ruby last year, viscerally remembering the way she'd held my face between her hands and said she loved me. Her death marked the end of a whole generation of that side of my extended family; now all aunts and uncles, along with my parents, were gone.

Also before we'd left, I'd received news that my memoir had been named a finalist for a Bisexual Book Award—and I was invited to the ceremony in New York City. At first I dismissed the idea of going since Dave and I had to prepare to leave for Asia—and we had tickets to fly to Colorado to meet up with a group of friends for a show at Red Rocks Amphitheater days before our departure. It seemed like a lot to take on. Besides, my book had been released by a micro-press, whereas most other books in contention were products of major New York publishers. There was no way I'd win. Still, I was honored—and I loved the idea of being in the presence of other writers and editors in a queer milieu. Dave encouraged me to go, saying I had worked so hard on my book and shouldn't miss out on the gathering.

I'd been to NYC only twice in my life and relished imagining exploring all over on foot, my favorite city activity. Besides, for some reason, I'd always wanted to walk across the Brooklyn Bridge. I'm not sure where I got the idea—perhaps from having thrilled as a teenager at the scene of daring in *Saturday Night Fever* on the Verrazano Narrows Bridge, an image that lingered. How our desires seep into our psyches can be a mystery. I whipped out my frequent flier miles to reserve a flight, and around the corner from the venue booked an affordable room at The Jane Hotel, a recommendation by the award event's organizer. I was stunned that there was a hotel with decent rates to be found in Manhattan—albeit the rooms were fifty square feet. The hotel had been built in 1908 as the American Seaman's Friend Society Sailors' Home and Institute, welcoming seamen who hopped off their ships when the Hudson River piers were bustling with longshoremen. In the West Village facing the Hudson, the vintage, nautically-inspired "Standard Cabin" rooms were described on The Jane's website as "old-fashioned, chic, and truly cozy." I also learned some rooms had housed traumatized Titanic survivors. I wondered if the place was haunted.

I was to be there three nights and took only a backpack carry-on. I planned to take a train from the airport into Brooklyn, and shouldering my pack, walk across the bridge followed by three-and-a-half miles north along Hudson River Park to the hotel.

The cross-country flight and transfer to the train went smoothly. But as I slid into a seat on the crowded train car, a gun dangled in my face. I was holster-level to a brawny cop standing over my seat, his hand gripping the loop above my head. Not my favorite scenario as I tend toward claustrophobia and gun-aversion. My stop was a half an hour away. I could feel my chest tightening, my heart thumping in my throat.

When at times I get uncomfortable on planes, I observe the flight attendants and think about how they fly all the time. The same idea came to me at this moment on the subway: I looked around at people whose shoulders jostled with strangers, at those staring at their phones or a newspaper, and thought about how being closed in could be thought of as comforting, or at the very least...normal. I thought about the cop, and how his gun probably had a safety on it, and how he might be glad to be heading home after a long night shift. That led me to remember Ram Dass instruct in a talk: "Practice seeing people's souls." He had specifically said to try this vague ritual in a crowded place like New York.

How did one see a soul? I wasn't sure. But I closed my eyes for a minute, took a deep breath, and opened them.

All the kids in the car lit up, emanating a warm shine. How interesting that it was easier to feel the souls of the babies and children, especially the little girl next to me—maybe seven years old—who was curled next to her mom.

The adults felt like they had shells—but I had time, and with patience I could sense warmth seep through their hairline cracks. I saw the individuality of each person, but also an electric pulse of connection among everyone.

As the train jerked to a stop, people squeezed out and others swarmed on. I wondered if I'd spaced out in my New Age musings and missed my stop. I asked the cop if my stop had passed, but he said he was sorry and didn't know. The mother of the seven-year-old girl told me it was only two away. She offered a smile and an explanation of the route. I wondered if my soul-peering was making people nicer.

I noticed her daughter—whose spirit felt like a golden, expanding bubble—was wearing a tee-shirt that proclaimed: "I ♡ being me." The heart was sparkly.

I said to her, "I love your shirt. I can't think of a better message to wear around all day."

We talked about how you can't help but be in a good mood when you're wearing such a shirt. When they disembarked, both mom and daughter waved goodbye to me. Maybe I'd discovered the key to dealing with crowds, of being a stranger in a big city. Ram Dass was onto something. This was some seriously magical shit.

My stop came. I had lucked into a mild sunny day with a flawless sky. I couldn't get that little girl out of my mind, with probably twenty braids on her adorable head and the proud way she wore that heart shirt. When I approached the bridge, it was swarming with pedestrians. Why had I thought the dream of traversing it on foot was singular to me? Later I'd read 10,000 people cross it every day. I couldn't help but notice, as though the love message were continuing to be relayed to me, a woman passing by wearing a tee-shirt with a heart emblazoned across the chest. A few minutes later, another woman jogged by with a pattern of hearts on her shirt. Next came a guy with a tee-shirt that announced, "Love Life," also adorned with a heart.

I glided across the bridge as Manhattan flaunted its iconic skyline, my spirit blasting like a skyrocket. It was a familiar elation, an exaltation I often felt while traveling in new territory, the world a feast.

The Jane Hotel transported me back in time. The lobby, illuminated by a vintage chandelier, featured emerald-green tiling, old-fashioned mauve wallpaper, and a majestic ceiling with elaborate moldings. Behind the ornately carved front desk stood staff members in bell caps and maroon uniforms. Keys were stored the old-fashioned way, in cubbyholes behind the counter.

But when I saw my closet-sized room, I couldn't imagine squeezing into that Thumbelina bed with only Titanic ghosts for company. I asked if there were other rooms available and was shown a "Captain's Cabin," featuring a queen bed with brass headboard, en-suite bathroom, and private terrace. I couldn't pull out my credit card fast enough. I rationalized the purchase as part of the special nature of this trip. I'd scrimp another way to make up for the splurge. Sitting on the balcony overlooking the bustling street, I transformed from a small-town California girl to an urbane city-dweller. But then I glanced down at my clothes—a blue dress from Ross Dress for Less and walking sneakers—and got a reality check. In truth, I didn't care. Having closetsful of Sex-and-the-City clothes and designer heels was never my thing.

For two days, I meandered around the West Village and Chelsea, taking in the city and consuming bagels slathered in velvety cream cheese. Bagels in other locales aren't true bagels, they are just sad, round bread. I window shopped, rambled through galleries, zigzagged along passageways viewing public art, and soaked in all the whirring human energy. I discovered a cozy bar and rooftop terrace at The Jane, an octagonal room where I drank a glass of wine and wrote in my journal.

By the time the book event began, I was so high on my escapade that merely being in the company of all those other writers was icing on the rainbow-flag cake. Nearly everyone in the community room at Westbeth Artists' Housing identified as bisexual. I had never been with so many people who, like me, had loved across genders. And these were people who had also written about that experience, one often ignored or belittled.

Married to a man, I'd felt my queer card had been revoked. I'd been with a woman for fifteen years. I'd forever been highly woman-centric and queer friendly. I'd marched for marriage equality and written about queer lives. Inequality incensed me, even as a kid. In 1979, as a straight-identified high school girl, I'd given a speech in my English class about why gays and lesbians should be able to adopt children. I don't recall where I got this idea because I didn't know any gay people personally until college. Did my divorce from my wife and my new life with a man erase all of this?

Some people dislike the word "bisexual" because in our either/or world that avows dualities, a third choice suggests you can't make up your mind, that you are indecisive or immature, that there's no way you could ever be monogamous. Of course now there's a proliferation of sexuality and gender terms (fluid, pansexual, nonbinary, etc.). Language is forever trying to keep up with the fullness of human experience.

I was conscious of how I was treated differently when presumed to be a straight woman, and how it was generally easier to move through the world with a husband. That reality was part of what motivated me to write my book.

When the time came for the memoir award to be presented, my book won. And at the evening's end, the final overall award of "Bi Writer of the Year" was also presented to me. Completely unprepared, I babbled thanks to the room of smiling faces, clutching two gold star-shaped trophies. I was stunned. Not only that people appreciated my book…but that I was acknowledged as an integral part of the bi community.

As though to stamp a seal of approval on my belonging to the queer tribe, when I returned to the Bay Area, my friend Laurie asked me if I wanted to go with her to the San Francisco Pride parade. I hadn't been in years. Everything felt sweetly familiar, from the Dykes on Bikes to the Mardi Gras atmosphere. I met a cornucopia of people who embraced me (many, literally). Laurie and I joined a group of women at a café and talked about travels and spirituality and books. We celebrated the flamboyance and cheered the camaraderie.

We didn't talk about the shooting at Pulse gay nightclub that had taken the lives of forty-nine souls two weeks before, but I felt its undercurrents. I sensed the bravery of every person present…and of all who have dared to thrive in the face of those who'd rather see you extinguished.

Chapter Ten

Spinning Planet

Mid-Summer 2016

Days before we were scheduled to leave, my visa had been approved but Dave's hadn't. Would I have to go to China without my husband? Or bow out of a job I'd already signed a contract for? Our intricately built, year-long Southeast Asia itinerary was at risk of toppling.

Four months, we'd gathered all the required materials to secure two visas: a working one for me and a spousal one for Dave. Our visa expert in the Bay Area had been wrestling with the bureaucracy for weeks. We'd been running around getting papers notarized, ordering documents (copies of my college transcripts and diplomas, our wedding license, and other papers we'd either gotten rid of or lost track of during our nomadic life). But the visa guy said there was one snag, related to the fact that Dave and I had different last names. I asked what our chances were it would be approved on time. He said it could go either way.

I jumped onto a housesitting website and applied for a gig in Thailand. I figured after traveling around Vietnam and Cambodia, if we wouldn't be making our way to China maybe we could spend a few more weeks in Southeast Asia. That's what I tend to do when chaos descends: try to lasso the turmoil, exerting control to fix the problem. In other words, I can forget to flow downstream, one of my favorite but ignorable mantras.

I was stressed and having a hard time sleeping. I knew it wouldn't be the end of the world if we didn't make it to China, but it would be an enormous disappointment. I'd been looking forward to the experience and had done a lot to prepare, including spending hours developing two courses. My suitcase heaved with books I'd be teaching, reams of articles, a clunky laptop, and a teaching wardrobe I'd constructed with hand-me-downs from my friend Laurie—badly needed after living mostly in yoga pants and flip-flops since retirement. We'd also handled other details such as registering our car, which would be sheltered in Chambliss's garage, as Non-Operational. That required a dreaded trip to the Department of Motor Vehicles, a place well known for its metal-chair, drip-torture, life-ticking-away ambiance. This time, miraculously, we were in and out quickly, even without an appointment.

"Have you ever before escaped the DMV in ten minutes?" I asked Dave in the parking lot.

"Only when repelled in horror," he deadpanned.

I laughed and suddenly felt lighter as I was reminded that humor is a good way to deal with life's frustrations and absurdities.

Tuesday afternoon my phone rang, and the visa handler's number appeared on the screen. In the thick second before I picked up, I knew whatever words I'd hear would pivot our lives.

"Both visas went through," he said. "Come to my office and pick them up."

And so that weekend we were able to relax and revel in the String Cheese Incident in Colorado before disappearing to the other side of the world. It was my first show at Red Rocks, an open-air amphitheater geologically formed by Mother Nature. Two 300-foot sandstone monoliths, Ship Rock and Creation Rock, have towered over that land for 250 million years—and they promote astounding acoustics. We danced to the trippy improvisational jams surrounded by dozens of friends in wild costumes, sparkly eye shadow, and boas, as balloons and bubbles floated past. While the band sang these words, I thought about how perhaps in a primeval age, our ancestors had performed their own rituals here:

> *Everywhere we're all colliding*
> *Come together, redefining*
> *Part of me part of you*
> *The sum of us comes shining through*

The horizon lit up with a marmalade sunset, and then as the sky darkened, the stage illuminated like a floating spaceship. Here Dave and I stood, specks on Earth, and in a few days we'd be 8,000 miles away. I felt like Alice in Wonderland—or *Wander*land—nibbling on the cake, shrinking and expanding in the vastness of time and space.

The sensation recalled Michael Singer's words in his remarkable book, *The Untethered Soul*: "You're sitting on a planet spinning around in the middle of absolutely nowhere… You're floating in empty space in a universe that goes on forever. If you have to be here, at least be happy and enjoy the experience. You're going to die anyway. Why shouldn't you be happy?"

Two days later, we were encamped at San Francisco International Airport waiting for our flight. Having checked in our suitcases, we carried only our backpacks, given to us by friends in Baja. We'd given away our packs when we were divesting ourselves of our possessions, and three years later our neighbors in Mexico offered us the ones they'd used on a trip to Ecuador. I liked to think that letting go of stuff seemed to magically boomerang other things in our direction when we needed them.

I prefer arriving at the airport early and lingering in the anticipation of taking off while I people watch or read, without stressing about missing the flight. Dave often says, "Do we have to leave *that* early?" This time, though, he was glad for our lingering when he noticed someone familiar. There in the same waiting area stood Jackie Green, the thirty-something musician with his signature Panama hat and dark beard. One of Dave's favorite artists. I'd never known Dave to approach a famous person, but he wanted to say hi to this man whose music he admired.

When we introduced ourselves, he shook our hands. Dave told him how he'd first seen him play when Jackie, a musical prodigy, was only nineteen. Smiling, Jackie took in Dave's appreciation and asked us where we were going. When we explained our Asia escapade, he expressed astonishment. He gracefully accepted our request for a picture, so our last photo on U.S. soil was a selfie of us smiling along with Jackie Greene.

Dave enjoys researching where we're going and making suggestions for things to do and see. He shares his thoughts with me, and I give my input. Together, we nail down an itinerary and spend time together at the computer booking flights and lodging. I'm the one who regularly scans the housesitting opportunities and applies. I also tend to take care of travel insurance. There were plenty of other details to hammer out for this trip; we kept lists, marking things off as either one of us took care of them. We enjoy preparing and envisioning, and rarely do we fall into disagreements about our plans. The only time I recall an argument around planning had been for our wedding: I thought the regular bar would be fine, but Dave insisted on springing for the supreme alcohol. He doesn't care for booze, but he wanted his friends to have the best. And so our guests imbibed single malt whiskeys and fine wines.

One sticking point for this trip had been that we wanted to travel light in Vietnam and Cambodia—but what to do with our mammoth suitcases crammed with stuff for a year in China? Dave worked it out that we'd fly into and out of Saigon (we soon learned most don't call it Ho Chi Minh City) and stay at the same hotel on both ends. While we set out to backpack for two weeks, the hotel held our suitcases.

As a teen, I dreamed of backpacking around the world. When I was in college in the early 1980s, before I'd heard the term "gap year", I'd wanted to take time off after my sophomore year. I sensed my white, middle-class, sheltered suburban upbringing had constrained me somehow. Living vicariously through books, which had sustained me for years, suddenly wasn't enough. My state university dorm life felt like an extension of high school keg parties, and my undergrad years were being gobbled up by a cloud of drugs and alcohol I felt helpless to resist. I couldn't put my finger on why I felt imprisoned. Working and traveling, I thought, would expand me beyond the tunnel-vision of my background. But my parents objected, asserting it was unlikely I'd return to finish my degree. They convinced me to stay. And stay I did, getting locked for years into high school teaching and a young, unhappy marriage. Divorced in my late twenties, I got a job teaching in Japan. And while living and traveling in that country for a year temporarily slaked my thirst for different worlds, I eschewed the chance to travel to other countries with a group of foreign teachers in order to return to the United States to be with my boyfriend.

And so now, at age 53, as I stepped from the Ton Son Naht International Airport into the steamy, bustling streets of Saigon, a backpack slung across my shoulders, the moment meant much more to me than taking a trip. I was stepping from the pages of books I had read into what was now my life.

My first reaction to Saigon was: where were all these people going? The tangle of roaring vehicles—mostly motorbikes—sautéed the humid air with smoky exhaust. Drivers wove around and between each other in impossible ways, their bikes stacked high with goods and passengers, defying gravity. However, no one was moving especially fast. The flow felt organic, like salmon during the height of spawning season. This place had been decimated by a horrifying, protracted war during my lifetime—and now it flourished. I wondered what remnants lived in Vietnamese psyches, especially the older people who'd experienced the unimaginable.

We'd planned a few days to unwind at a budget resort in Saigon. The room included my first experience with a wet bathroom, a cube with a shower that also sprayed on the toilet and sink. Mosquitoes zigzagged in the damp corners so again Dave came to the rescue as insect-killer. The bed was lumpy and the room stuffy, even with AC, and the broken overhead fan hung limply. Water was leaking from the ceiling at the doorway. Given my musings about the war, I was aware of my outrageous privilege when my stomach sank at the state of the room. The front desk attendant promised to send someone to install a new fan and fix the leak. Our saving grace was an Olympic-sized swimming pool with plentiful chairs and shade. We must have been the oldest ones there amongst the backpacker set. I reveled in lounging on the balmy afternoon—air that reminded me I was *somewhere else*—dipping into the pool then sliding back in the chair to read a few lines and doze.

We'd deliberately not made plans for our three days in Saigon, treating it as time to recover from jet lag and to rest up for what was ahead. We knew we'd need to recuperate from the crazy build-up to get there. Travel wasn't vacation for us, it was our life—so it wasn't about cramming in every excursion we could. We wandered out of the hotel onto the streets, cruising around the city to find food and to people watch. One afternoon the humidity abruptly swelled like a gathering wave, followed by a crashing downpour. We ducked under an awning while other pedestrians scurried for cover, like something from a movie set. Ten minutes later, the rain stopped, and we stepped back out onto the steaming streets.

The last morning we caught a cab to the airport for the 50-minute flight to Dalat. The air of this town in the Central Highlands was cool and crisp, a contrast to Saigon's mugginess. The shuttle dropped us off a few blocks from our hotel, making me grateful for traveling light. Everywhere was evidence this used to be a mountain resort town for the French colonialists, with the roasted essence of coffee and fresh-baked baguettes wafting from bakeries and the wrought-iron balconies and latticed gardens. Reputedly a replica of the Eiffel Tower exists somewhere in the city.

We woke the next morning, our fourth wedding anniversary, to get ready for the wedding of my former student Au-Co. In another layer of synchronicity, I pulled on the slinky ginger and aqua maxi dress that Nancy had worn at our wedding. A college friend of Nang, the groom, escorted us from our hotel through alleyways to Nang's family home. The house's entry, filled with shoes and a bicycle, led to a narrow staircase. When we walked up the stairs, Au-Co—whom I'd last seen in California at my book reading—came over and gave me a hug. She wore a sheer, informal white dress, her hair in a soft braid woven with delicate white daisies. About twenty people in the room chatted in Vietnamese. At five-foot-eight I felt like a Brobdingnagian, a familiar sensation from my time in Japan. People smiled at us, and a woman I took to be Nang's mother, clasped our hands in welcome. Au-Co introduced us to two of her friends from California, ushering us English speakers together.

Soon, everyone was invited to assemble in a room off the kitchen for the marriage ceremony, where an altar had been set up with flowers and burning incense. Au-Co explained that prayers were being said to the ancestors, a touching moment recalling the lineage that led to this couple being joined. Family members presented the bride and groom with gifts, and afterward we were led to the kitchen table for snacks. Next we were shuttled to a hotel for the reception, where more people joined in. Platters of steaming Vietnamese food—coconut salad, sweet and sour beef with mushroom, a chicken dish, seafood soup, bread, and fresh fruit—were served family style accompanied by Au-Co's mother on the violin. When she played Iz's Hawai'ian version of "Somewhere Over the Rainbow," I squeezed Dave's hand at the kismet; the song had also been played at our wedding.

The next day, Au-Co introduced us to James, an American who had lived in Vietnam for years and was married to a Vietnamese woman. Together they ran a brewery and pizza restaurant. He toured us around in his Russian jeep, taking us through the countryside where coffee is grown. We happened upon a farmer on the side of the road who was tending to silkworms. Thousands of white cocoons nested in the crevasses of what looked like a tall narrow bookcase. A guy crouched on the ground before white worms wriggling in bowls. He smiled up at me and gestured as though he were putting a worm in his mouth, and laughed. James said the guy was joking, that silkworms were never eaten raw, only fried.

We stopped at a coffee plantation with a deck overlooking a vista reminiscent of wine country. They served several different types of coffee for us to sample, including the infamous Kopi Luwak, which is created when a civet (a creature similar to a racoon) eats the coffee "cherries" and poops them out. The raw beans are gathered, washed, dried, and roasted. I wasn't thrilled at the prospect of putting in my mouth something that had passed through an animal's digestive tract but didn't want to decline an offering. It was delicious. Later, though, I did some research and decided I'd never again support an industry that snatches up creatures from the wild and imprisons them alone in tiny cages—just as I buy only free-range eggs in the States.

Back in Saigon, a taxi dropped us off at a dock to begin a four-day boat trip up the Mekong Delta through Vietnam and into Cambodia. When we'd made reservations, we'd been warned if the four cabins didn't fill, the trip would be canceled. Soon it appeared we were the only couple, and I wondered when they'd tell us to scram. However, they took us on board a boat that looked hand-crafted of gleaming wood. Our bear-den of a room had dark paneled walls, with blue towels molded into swans propped on the bed. The crew of five outnumbered us. Clearly, the advantage to traveling during low season—even though it was hotter and more rainy—was fewer tourists.

We sat on the deck as the rural world drifted by. People washing their clothes, soaking their cattle, or swimming waved as we passed. I thought about how all these people lived somewhere, had a place they called home. The first day, the boat docked and we disembarked with Thuy, our guide, a charismatic young guy. Together we rode bikes along dirt roads through the countryside, passing houses open in the front with men smoking and playing cards on slanted porches and women painting their toenails. In the vast fields, people were making hay and harvesting. Others sold fruits and vegetables at roadside businesses. There were restaurants with plastic tables and chairs, a beauty-shop hut adorned with faded before-and-after photos, and a closet-sized convenience store bulging with goods, its roof covered in rusty corrugated metal. The occasional truck rumbled by. When kids playing on a pile of dirt caught sight of us, they ran alongside our bikes shouting, "Hello! Hello!" When we yelled "hello" back, they doubled over in laughter. Thuy told us life was better in these rural areas than a few years earlier, now that residents had free time due to access to machinery and electricity. And, of course, cell phones.

At one point we stopped to observe a family in their yard pulling dragon fruit off a tree. An elderly woman walked over to us and, with a gap-toothed smile, offered with two hands a pink spiny fruit. I smiled back and accepted the gift, unexpectedly moved by her kindness. That evening on the boat, the cook sliced the dragon fruit and arranged it on a platter with sour-sweet mangosteen, juicy rambutan, and slick longan, which looks like a dragon's eye. The delicacies slid on my tongue and brought my tastebuds alive, so unlike the apples and bananas in U.S. supermarkets that are nearly tasteless by comparison.

One day, after seeing a floating market and houses on stilts, we stopped in the town of Sa Dec, a river port town burgeoning with colonial architecture along streets lined with shade trees and climbing roses. The writer Marguerite Duras, a French national born in Vietnam, lived in Sa Dec from 1928-1933. Her autobiographical novel *The Lover*, adapted into the Academy-award winning screenplay *Hiroshima, Mon Amour*, offers a fictionalized version of her love affair with a rich Chinese man that tore their families apart, a kind of 1930s Romeo and Juliet. Thuy took us to the lover's family home, an imposing Sino-Colonial house bedecked with French curlicues and Chinese-style peaks. We entered to a red and gold shrine, the Chinese ancestors' wooden altar, and a table inlaid with mother-of-pearl. The walls displayed old photographs of Duras, the lover, and his wife and children, as well as images of the movie production. The home had been closed to the public for years but with the Communist regime's loosening up, it was now a designated historical landmark.

As I tried to penetrate Duras' eyes for some writing wisdom, I thought about how she had penned a passionate, tragic story so powerfully that it hit a universal nerve. Nearly one hundred years later, her words were still alive.

Chapter Eleven

Like Drugs

Late Summer, 2016

After our jumping-around itinerary of the wedding, the boat trip down the Mekong, and touring several sites in Cambodia, I'd been anticipating relaxing on a secluded island. But now I wished I could bite a serpent's apple to escape this "paradise"—the Cambodian isle of Koh Rong. Indeed, it was all kinds of "wrong." I turned on the rigid mattress, my body slimy with sweat. The room had no A/C and no ceiling fan. I was suffocating beneath the mosquito net while rainforest creatures croaked, chirped, and hissed. But worst of all, the argument Dave and I had gotten into thundered through my head. Infuriatingly, he lay next to me snoring away, his tactic for making everything alright. I wished I had that talent.

I wanted to venture out into the night to find a café or take a walk to shake off the mental turmoil. But we were on a café-less tiny island amidst other backpacker cabins, and the lodge wouldn't be open for breakfast for hours. Besides, it would be dangerous to walk out there since it had been raining like someone overturned a sea in the sky, making the walkways slick and muddy. There was no Wi-Fi so using my phone was out. My Kindle had run out of juice, and this room had no outlets, much less electricity. That ruled out turning on a light to read. I took a deep breath, counted to ten, held it for four, exhaled for ten. Over and over. It was like trying to count sheep when your mind conjures wolves.

We'd been looking forward to Koh Rong as a quiet place to relax, especially after reading about its "paradise status" on TripAdvisor. I'd been excited about being unplugged far from civilization. I should have known better. "Paradise" is PR. Perhaps in the dry season the place had the makings of a utopia. Every online review depicted Instagram-worthy shots of aquamarine waters and clear skies reaching to infinity. No one had warned of stormy weather or the distressing three-hour boat ride.

At the dock, when we'd approached the transport vessel—an old fishing boat with bench seats—we'd nearly balked; instead, we'd boarded and prayed for calm seas. Our prayers were not answered. Minutes after launch, raindrops came bulleting down. Soon, waves rose, lurching us around and splashing over the sides while rain gushed down in sheets. Two of the eight passengers hung over the sides, heaving. I kept my eyes on the corkscrewing horizon, hoping I wouldn't be the next to barf. With rain now pelting us horizontally, I gazed up at the lifejackets shoved in the boat's rafters, while Dave calculated the best direction to swim if we capsized. The cherry on top was the stoic captain who chain-smoked while gasoline sloshed in plastic containers at his feet.

I did my best to reframe being on this bucking bronco as an adventure. I again thought of Pema Chodron's wise words about the "wisdom of no escape," how allowing rather than resisting what was happening could alleviate suffering. But my body would have none of my mind's calming shenanigans. In fight-or-flight mode, it gripped hard to survival.

When we'd arrived at Lonely Beach, an isolated strip on the island, the water wasn't dreamy turquoise but turd brown. My legs quivered as we made our way to the open-air lodge to check in. The hosts, a European hippie couple, cooked an aromatic dinner, but my throat resisted swallowing because a storm raged not only outside but between Dave and me. In our cabin, we tried to talk it through, but the issue felt intractable. When I went into the bathroom, I slipped and fell on the uneven river rocks embedded in the floor, the bruise rising on my leg mirroring the one on my heart. He'd said something that I'd found sexist and insensitive, and instead of talking about it, he'd shut down. Anger churned inside me, funneling me down a dark mental hole. I wanted to slam the patriarchy, the objectification of women, the world's insane beauty standards. I was sleeping with the snoring enemy.

I couldn't imagine spending a full week on this godforsaken Gilligan's Island. The next morning, Dave attempted to soothe our wounds by using the lodge's Wi-Fi to plan our escape. The hosts admitted an even larger tempest was headed our way and that it was possible the boat wouldn't be able to ford the passage. If we left on the day we'd planned, five days away, there was no guarantee we'd be able to get out in time to catch our plane. We requested to leave the next day, and again I had a sleepless night, imploring the gods for conditions decent enough to flee.

The boat ride back was just as jarring, and while my stomach roiled as a young woman spewed over the sides, relief spread to my bones with each nautical mile separating us from that sinister isle.

Back on the mainland, Dave had found us an air-conditioned room at a hotel with a pool at Otres Beach 2 in Sihanoukville for nineteen bucks a night. We were walking distance to a serene beach lined with feet-in-the-sand restaurants, a romantic place to lick our wounds. Tim Bluhm's song, "Hell is the Highway," played on repeat in my brain:

> The three worst days of my life
> Was quarrelin' with you.

If I didn't love you so bad
Would have only been two.

One afternoon at the pool, Dave started chatting with three Cambodian guys in their twenties who were taking a buddies' vacation. They lazed in the shallow side, cracking jokes and laughing. Dave, who doesn't like to drink booze, accepted a can of beer, and they all toasted. From my lounge chair, I watched my husband, admiring the way he enjoyed meeting people and blending in. I thought about how even though we'd been joined in matrimony, we were separate people, each with our own private worlds. In previous relationships, I'd insisted too much on "the merge," in Walt Whitman's words—which I'd thought of as the ultimate, divine connection between two souls. But after my last divorce, which had almost sent me over the edge of sanity, I'd healed by embracing *myself* as my own soulmate.

For all the spiritual talk of how we're connected, it's vital to acknowledge we're also separate. Each person is a world. It was okay I didn't have access to every crevice of Dave's being, that I couldn't understand what had angered me so. It was okay if we couldn't get to the bottom of the Koh Rong clash and instead floated for a while, not trying to fix things but allowing ourselves to soften and, hopefully, grow along the way. It was a delusion, anyway, to think you could completely understand another person. I understood my own soul, and when I touched the still, deep place inside, that was enough.

Before the Koh Rong debacle, we'd taken a boat from the Vietnam border to Cambodia and a bus to Phnom Penh, our stopover for a couple of nights before flying to Siem Reap. It was hard to wrap my mind around the fact that such a lively city—with its royal palace's golden spires, saffron-robed monks, high-rises, and humming streets—had not so long ago been the site of a four-year genocide.

As we walked around, tuk tuk drivers hounded us. Their scramble for money was understandable in such a poor country, but it became overwhelming to be harassed when we merely wanted to stroll. Eventually, Dave discovered that joking in a friendly way with the hawkers diffused them. He'd affect a facetious Australian accent and soon, they'd both be joshing around and cracking up.

In a short two months our bodies had been flung about on airplanes, boats, tuk tuks, ferries, taxis. I adored movement and watching the world go by. I once read that a dog in a car with the windows rolled down has an experience akin to an LSD trip because that rush of smells overwhelms the dog's brain. That's how I was feeling in Southeast Asia, especially at night. Darkness intensified the sensory effects as we moved through the maze of

89

streets, the hot, wet air clinging to my skin, the scent of grilling meat sizzling, lights dazzling me sideways from the markets, disembodied voices coming at us, *lady, sir, want to buy something?* I loved waking up the next morning with a light sheet over my body and eating luscious pineapple and watermelon on the lanai. In the afternoon, we'd swim at the beach or in the pool then escape the sun's intense heat in our room, propped in bed with pillows at our backs, hair damp, reading or dozing while a thunderstorm rumbled in the distance.

When Dave had told me his primary desire to travel to Cambodia was to see Angkor Wat, I'd said…what Wat? I'd been clueless about this World Heritage Site, a collection of seventy-two Hindu and Buddhist temples from the 10th to 12th centuries just outside the town of Siem Reap. Covering 400 acres, it's the world's largest religious structure. The main temple of Angkor Wat is the best preserved and most visited, a massive sandstone structure raised above the city with conical, elaborately decorated towers reflected in a still pond. Walking through the temple was dizzying. Everywhere I looked I could have stopped and gazed for hours at the intricate architectural features: pillars shaped like lotus buds; and galleries, passageways, and terraces decorated with statues, asparas (celestial nymphs), and extensive garlands. We lingered over bas-reliefs depicting the mythological, historical, and everyday world of this ancient civilization.

In his research, Dave had discovered it was popular to observe sunrise at the main temple, and sure enough I came across social media selfies of girls in glamorous dresses posing on the grounds at daybreak. So Dave's idea was to arrive at dawn, when most people had already left for breakfast. We had the place nearly to ourselves. His other inspired idea was to explore the less-visited temples in a succession of three mornings before the fur-coat heat wrapped around the city. By the afternoon, we'd be back at the hotel soaking in the pool. A swimming pool has become for us an important feature of traveling in steamy Southeast Asia.

We walked around Ta Prahm, the setting for the film *Tomb Raider*. This temple was overgrown by the forest; fig and banyan trees had spread their bulky roots across the stones, pushing walls and terraces apart, the branches and leaves intertwining to create a natural roof. A pleasingly eerie sensation crept through me as I imagined what the ruins of Silicon Valley might look like in a thousand years. We also explored the dreamlike terrain of Angkor Thom, a temple with faces the size of cars glaring down from every angle and phallus "lingams" adorning the temple. Some were as tall as trees, fronting warrior statues in elaborate stone headdresses.

Around the temples, children approached us for money. NGOs advised not handing out cash because the kids, who should be in school, were being used by adults who appropriated the funds. So I'd brought small toys and stickers to hand out. Of course they loved the playthings, but I couldn't help feel off-balance by the disparity between their lives and mine. As a kid I'd had everything: abundant toys and money and safety.

One day we took a boat trip down Tonle Sap Lake in the Mekong Delta River system and saw modern-day Cambodian village life. We glided past communities on stilts and floating villages of houses, shops, and schools bobbing on the water. Although the roofs and balconies were painted in bright reds, blues, and yellows, the residents seemed integrated into this wetland ecosystem. It struck me there were so many different ways we humans lived, and our environments shaped our lives. Traveling provided me with the opportunity to be sculpted by many different hands. As we floated by, people smiled and waved. I hoped our tourism wasn't an intrusion but helped in some ways. Probably, though, our presence was a complex combination of both good and harm.

We scheduled a driver to take us the two-and-a-half hours from Sihanoukville back to Phnom Penh. We had a plane to catch to take us to our home for the next year: China.

We'd been told to look for a new Lexus, but a twenty-year-old Camry showed up. A few minutes down the road, the driver stopped at a roadside stand and bought a bottle of water and two ears of corn. He offered us one, and we thanked him but declined. Soon he was munching on corn while weaving precariously in and out of traffic, speeding around trucks on the two-lane road, and averting his eyes to peel the silky hair off the cob. When he finished eating, he snapped his fingers every time we passed a vehicle. I wondered if the snap was a good luck charm of sorts. With the perilous way he attacked the road, I figured we could use all the luck we could get. Before we'd started traveling the world, his driving would have terrified me. But I'd soon learned that in few places do people stay in their lanes and follow the speed limit, if there is one, and I trained myself to relax about it.

The driver had a thin, long pinky nail. I wondered if that was a tradition. Or did it help administer powdery substances, or clean out one's nose? (Later I looked it up: While other uses might be side benefits, the main reason was a status symbol, proof he didn't have to make a living using his hands for hard labor.) He spoke no English, and of course my Khmer was non-existent. As much as I would have enjoyed chatting with him to learn about his life, it was liberating to be free of conversation. My mind could follow its own byways.

That was until he cranked up the music on the car's sound system. Leo Sayer crooned that he loved me more than he could say, and I was shot back to high school. Memories of my teen bedroom walls covered in band posters overlaid the rice fields buzzing by, stalls selling piles of unidentifiable objects and produce, and signs in English that made me scratch my head: *Hot*

Dip Galidini. Slow Down, Low Down. The surreal nature of the juxtaposition made me wonder if traveling was like drugs, just another opportunity to alter my consciousness, my face out the window like a dog on LSD.

Chapter Twelve

A Total Trip

Fall 2016

We lugged our suitcases from the air-conditioned airport onto the balmy sidewalk. We were finally in China, and I was woozy anticipating what it would be like to live and teach here for a year. It didn't take long to spy a young woman with glasses and shiny black bangs holding up our names on a card: *Dr. Kate Evans and David Rhine.*

A junior at the university, she introduced herself: "I'm Sue. But my friends call me Susan." I wondered how the fact that "Sue" is less formal than "Susan" was lost in translation. Of course her real name was Chinese, and I'd soon learn some Chinese people chose to take on English names for a variety of reasons—one being they didn't want their true name mispronounced by foreigners.

On the hour drive into Nanning, a "small city" of eight million, Sue asked if we'd ever been to Hollywood and seen movie stars. As the car maneuvered through traffic on an eight-lane freeway, we passed gray high rises and cranes like metal T-Rexes piercing the sky. She said she loved Hugh Grant and Julia Roberts—and began listing their movies she'd enjoyed. The closest I'd come to meeting a celebrity was Joan Baez, but I doubted mentioning this fact would have had the same cachet.

While we chatted, Sue every so often turned to the driver—a man whose intent face I briefly glimpsed in the rearview mirror—and they exchanged a few words in Mandarin. I told her I was envious she was fluently bilingual.

"I know another language, too," she said. "I'm not Han. I'm an ethnic minority." I caught a note of pride in her voice. Fifty-five ethnic minority groups make up almost half the population of China. Nanning is the capital of Guangxi, not a province but an Autonomous Region fostering the cultural sovereignty of the Zhuang, or Zhuangjia, people. I wanted to ask more about Sue's life, but I became distracted as the driver pulled up to the gate of the campus where I'd be teaching and we'd be living. As he turned left amidst a swath of flourishing subtropical foliage, I wondered what our housing would be like. It would be the longest we'd stayed in one place in three years.

Sue opened the apartment door, handed us the key, then skedaddled. High rises peppered the horizon, but our place—on the ground floor of a three-story building—was surrounded by lower structures. We'd been told our apartment would be cleaned before our arrival, but we were greeted by a dozen cockroaches crawling over the carcasses of their dead brethren, a rotting hole under the kitchen sink (clearly the cockroach freeway), black crud creeping on the bathroom floor, and stains streaking the walls of our now-home.

Vertigo overcame me, my internal elevator plummeting. Tears threatened but instead I grabbed a roll of paper towels and a bottle of cleaning solution that sat forlornly on the kitchen counter. Dave followed suit by locating a can of bug spray and murdering the pests then grabbing a broom propped in the corner of the room and sweeping them away.

After crazily cleaning on the heels of an international flight, we were shattered. But now that our new home was tidier and smelled more of cleaning products than mold, I could appreciate the living room window's view of a lotus pond. I also took in that this apartment was larger than our casita. Although the narrow kitchen had only one burner and a microwave, the sprawling living room was appointed in stylish lacquered furniture. There was a guest room/office with a bed and desk, and the main bedroom had an inviting bed the size of a California King. But when we fell into it that night, I had the sensation of being dropped onto a concrete sidewalk. No one had warned us hard beds are a thing in China. I fell asleep with images of a memory-foam mattress dancing in my head.

The next day we discovered the cushion-less wood couch and chairs in the living room were just as unyielding. I wondered if the Chinese thought comfort made you lazy. Were they trying to keep us vigorous? (Later I was told they believe soft beds and furniture to be bad for your spine and overall health.) No matter, we made it our mission to somehow procure a mattress pad and furniture cushions, which we thought might be possible before school started.

I'd received an official email saying: "classes should start on the week of the 4th of September"—two weeks away. *Should?* Even though I'd been warned by the Canadian administrator during my Skype interview that the Chinese dealt with time differently from Westerners—and we might not be apprised of the exact dates of important events until days prior—the *should* startled me. Unlike all the other places I'd taught, I'd been given no semester calendar outlining course schedules and breaks, no dates for faculty orientation or the first staff meeting. I kept a five-year planner, and so an extemporaneous agenda was going to be a stretch for me. I decided to lean into the fact that stretching meant staying flexible. As my former mentor Gabriele Rico used to say, "Flexibility is the essence of intelligence."

We set out to explore campus. The cooking-oil-scented air was so thick with humidity that sweat swamped my body the minute we stepped across the threshold. The sun shone hard through a hazy sky. We picked our way along uneven sidewalks, past serviceable buildings bordered by knotted banyan trees and bridges spanning fish-filled lakes grazed by the fingers of weeping willows. The conglomeration of high- and low-rises, one which housed a bank, reminded me we needed to open an account for me to get paid. I'd been told we'd be assigned an English-speaking student to assist us. The list of things we needed help with was the length of a Russian novel, with banking and setting up the internet at the top.

Although the new school year had not yet officially begun, the grounds teemed with people who lived there year-round. The university housed all employees and their families, from janitors to professors to retired personnel. It was a city within a city, with not only university buildings on the premises but a preschool, primary school, and middle school. Grandparents could be seen strolling with their grandkids while the parents were at work.

At an outdoor basketball center, young people shot hoops across the twenty courts, while others of all ages played badminton and tennis nearby. Exercisers stretched and sweated on park equipment. Kids scrambled around, shouting and kicking balls, while small groups of middle-aged and elderly people practiced martial arts. People peddled around on bicycles, and others zipped by on noiseless motorbikes, all electric as mandated by the city.

I couldn't help but contrast this peace and prosperity with the violent chaos that had descended upon this area during the 1966-76 Cultural Revolution, an era of vicious political upheaval targeting those accused of bourgeois and capitalist thoughts: professors, landlords, intellectuals. What many call the worst atrocity during that period occurred in Guangxi. Thousands were lynched, beheaded, and beaten to death—and some horrifyingly cannibalized by their political opponents. On this very campus professors were targeted, and at a nearby middle school students beat their teacher to death. As we walked past elderly women and men, I wondered what they'd seen, what they'd experienced, during that national nightmare. I also wondered how much the younger people knew about this part of their country's history. But I wouldn't be asking my students; my contract forbade me from discussing politics.

Circling back toward our apartment we discovered an open-air market. Tables were piled with produce, pyramids of eggs of whimsical colors and sizes, and overflowing bags of seeds, nuts, rice, and legumes. On one malodorous aisle slouched slabs of meat, chicken feet, and monstrous fish heads. Off to the side live chickens scratched in a crate next to a woman wielding a knife and wearing a blood-streaked apron. Another woman pulled a fish from a bucket for a customer and clubbed it to death before handing it over. There were no neat packages of cellophaned chicken breasts that allowed a denial of the cycle of life.

We bought a pomelo the size of a bowling ball, wrapped like a present in waxed paper. It quickly became my favorite fruit, pink and juicy with a satisfyingly resistant texture. We also picked up passion fruit, small creamy bananas, and a bag of oranges for only a few bucks. Under a shade tarp, stalls offered a dizzying display of random goods, and when I spied reading glasses, I bought a pair.

Later at the off-campus grocery store, we were able to avoid the bloody realities of butchery by buying already-cooked chicken and duck at the deli, as well as Dave's favorites: delectable fresh noodles and dumplings. Dave was in culinary heaven because like most Chinese he's lactose intolerant. He was thrilled that he didn't have to worry about dairy being slipped into unsuspecting dishes, as happens in a lot of the Western world. Soon we discovered Yann, a French student who lived above us. He cooked scrumptious soups, pastas, and desserts, selling them at a reasonable price and delivering them to our door. Figuring out how to feed ourselves was turning out to not be as complicated as I had thought it might be, since I'd been warned food in China would be different from the egg rolls and fried rice in America.

The next afternoon we had lunch at the home of a couple who worked on campus, an administrator named Li-Ji, his wife Sophie who ran a language school, and their four-year-old daughter. They also invited a French couple and their two little ones who were living on campus while he completed a post-doc. As we gathered around the outdoor table while Li-Ji played the guitar on a sunlit blanket spread on the lawn, my lightheadedness borne from so much change began to ease. The next day, Li-Ji and his wife showed us how to take the bus to Walmart. The bus was packed and hot; we learned later that for five cents more we could have boarded an air-conditioned one.

The only other Walmart I'd entered was in Mexico. This one was the same, except for a stench emanating from the produce area. There, mounds of spiny yellowish-green durian fruit, a popular delicacy in Southeast Asia, dispensed their infamous aroma some describe as a mix of turpentine, raw onions, and sewage. Later, in various spots throughout the region, we'd see people eating durian while wearing gloves to keep their hands scent-free. And we'd enter hotels with posted signs banning the toxic-smelling but apparently delicious fruit.

As we walked the aisles, we struggled to figure out what we were looking at: conditioner or shampoo or hand soap? Paper napkins or maxi-pads? We searched for tea, something we'd also looked for in smaller stores. That's right, we couldn't find *tea* in China.

Seizing a box of sugar with a picture on the front of a teacup, I brought it to one of the many women standing around in the aisle. China has excellent customer service…if you can speak. I kicked myself for not writing down the needed phrase in advance. I would have used my translator app, but our phones didn't work yet, and we'd neglected to pick up SIM cards at the airport.

Examining the box, several women surrounded me, chattering in Mandarin. In the midst of the commotion, I heard the word "cha." Oh, yes, in my brief, lazy study of the language, I'd remembered how much "cha" sounded like "chai." Tea.

"Cha! Yes, cha!"

One woman led me to an aisle of vaguely familiar packages. Closer, I saw box upon box of Lipton tea. I scanned for other types, but apparently Walmart sold only Lipton.

We'd hoped to buy cushions for the furniture, but no luck. Sophie told us she had a friend who owned an upholstery store and could make them for us, so we planned to do that later. We did, however, locate pads for the beds and some pillows—as well as mugs, plates, yoga mats, and a blender. Fortunately, the store offered a delivery service. At the counter, the non-English-speaking employees accommodated us through a combination of charades and smiles. Li-Ji had written out our address in Chinese on a card, which I presented at the counter and watched in awe as a young woman quickly copied the complicated script onto a delivery form. We had no idea when our packages would arrive, but they came an hour after we got home, right to our door.

Later that week, we met up with Kevin, a friendly redhead from Lincoln, Nebraska, who'd been teaching in Nanning for a couple of years. He invited us to join a group at the Queen's Head pub that night, a place owned by a Brit who'd lived in Nanning for many years. Dave decided to stay home, but I went along, crammed into a taxi with Kevin and Paul, a tall Liverpudlian in his thirties with a guitar case spread across his lap. Paul, formerly a professional musician in the UK, had been living and teaching in Nanning for three years. I was impressed by how he and Kevin were able to converse with the taxi driver. As we sped through the dark streets with thousands of other vehicles, the guys kept me laughing with stories of their faux pas when they first moved to China.

At the smoky, low-ceilinged pub, we joined a table of other foreigners, next to a group of locals with a young woman who coddled a feathery-eared dog on her lap. I was introduced to people whose names and affiliations I could barely catch above the music, two Serbian guys on keyboard singing Euro-pop. Soon, Paul joined them, and the music switched to rock hits from the seventies. I wondered how Paul, twenty years my junior, was so drawn to music of my era. Tattooed on his chest were the faces of Crosby, Stills, and Nash. Fueled by a few too many pints, I danced for hours, mostly with a hilarious gay Taiwanese guy.

The next morning, my head thudding, I moaned with a pillow over my face while Dave cheerfully jumped out of bed. Eventually I dragged myself up and decided it was time to deal with laundry. I stared at the washing machine. The buttons and dials might as well have been on the Star Trek Enterprise's console. I decided to walk over to the Administration Building, five minutes away, for help. A secretary said they'd send someone over. An hour later, I opened the door to a knock and was surprised to see the round-faced Dean, his belly straining against his buttoned suit jacket. I'd met him once before when I'd signed paperwork in the Admin Building.

He stood before the machine and pushed buttons at random. Nothing happened.

"I don't usually use a washing machine," he said.

"Do we need to get a woman over here?" I joked. We laughed.

After more fiddling, and translating the writing on the knobs for our sake, he figured it out. I took the opportunity to show him the hole that served as a cockroach interstate, and he promised he'd get someone over to fix it. I thanked him, and he seemed relieved to walk out the door. While Dave puttered in the kitchen, I slumped on our rigid couch, wondering why I remained in denial that drinking at night meant feeling the next day like I'd run a marathon with no training. I closed my eyes, thinking about how we'd been in China barely a week, and our travels through Vietnam and Cambodia already felt like a dream.

Days later, the Dean asked to meet with me. When I entered his office through the imposing door inset with beveled glass, he was leaning back in his chair, feet propped on the desk, smoking a cigarette like it was 1955. He asked me if I would serve as the faculty technology coordinator.

I thanked him for the offer and said I was sorry to disappoint him, but technology was not my strength. I suggested he could ask someone who was a techie.

"What about your husband?" he asked. "What is his educational background?"

I was surprised to hear him ask because being in China on a spousal visa, Dave had to sign a form at the police station swearing he would not work in the country—and an intimidating cop harshly commanded Dave to verbally reaffirm his status as non-working spouse. I was not allowed to do paid work other than teaching at the university—nor did I want to because one job was enough—but Paul and Kevin had told me almost everyone bent the rules, taking lucrative side jobs. Still, I was surprised that blatant rule-breaking extended to the Dean.

"Dave has a B.A. in Economics from U.C. Berkeley and does business development."

"Does he have any teaching experience?"

"No."

"Well, what's he going to do here?"

"This morning he went to the market. And now that you showed us how to use the washing machine, he's done a lot of laundry."

He humphed and stubbed out his cigarette. Nanning had a U.S.-in-the-1950s vibe, with capitalism now peering out through the communism, leading to more personal wealth and the burgeoning availability of consumer goods from sparkling kitchen appliances to fancy cars. On the streets women wearing knee-length, belted dresses pushed their babes in prams, working men wore conservative suits, and brides and grooms in wedding attire posed for photos in parks. Was the idea of the wife working while the husband tended to domestic details alien to the Dean? He lit up another cigarette and thanked me for coming by.

Except at the university, people in Nanning spoke less English than in other parts of Asia we'd visited. They tried to communicate through smiles and chatting with hand signals, and we did the same. There were lots of cute babies to dote over because the country had recently eased up on its one-child policy. Everywhere in the world, it was easy to express kindness and connection through the children.

While we both had struggled to learn Mandarin, Dave was a master at getting the gist of what someone was saying. He winged it and somehow communicated through body language and energy. He had no problem making up words and pantomiming. He even unintentionally threw in a Japanese or German word, the linguistic center of his brain igniting languages he knew. I wished I had such verbal ease in foreign languages, but my brain sputtered as it grasped at the meanings of individual words.

On a mission to paint our apartment, he found a paint store a few blocks away. One day, the paint guy delivered a batch for Dave's ongoing project. When the man came in, talking away in Chinese, Dave answered in English and showed him around, and this is what they sounded like:

Paint man: xxxx xxxxx xxxxx
Dave: Yes, see, we are using the dark blue as the accent wall in the bedroom.
Paint man: xxxx xxxxx xxxxxx xx xxxxx!
Dave: I know, right?

People enjoyed instigating interactions with us. They'd stop and ask uniform questions (*Where are you from? Do you like China?*) and take pictures. The attention could be unnerving. Strangers crowded us, wrapped their arms around our waists, and snapped a selfie…and another and another. And then they'd marshal Grandpa over for a picture with us, then a cousin, then a sister—and there would be the obligatory group shot. Eventually we'd smile and say *xie xie* (thank you) and sidle away.

Now and then I'd be standing on the street talking with a friend, and from the corner of my eye I'd see several people aiming their phone cameras in our direction. I thought this attention was all about my tall, blonde, whiteness…until I met an African American guy who had lived in China for five years and said it constantly happened to him, too. In a city of eight million people where most had straight black hair and were of smallish stature, a tall blonde or a taller Black guy with a shiny white smile was probably a *total trip*. His name was Willie, and he taught dance and used to perform with the San Jose Ballet company. Yes, we both had lived in San Jose, California and happened to meet in a café in China, a synchronicity that made me feel I was exactly where I was supposed to be.

Café Ukulele was co-founded and run by Paul, my musical colleague from England. With ukuleles for sale hanging on the walls, coffee and donuts at the counter, and tables and chairs facing a small stage, the café became a sanctuary of music and community. Dave and I missed live music. Walking around the parks, the tunes we heard mostly came from boom boxes—although in People's Park, we stumbled across a trio of elders making haunting music on traditional stringed instruments. Now we reveled in knowing on the weekends we could enjoy Paul perform, along with other expats and Chinese musicians. Paul was also a writer. We began to meet weekly at the local Starbucks—the only coffee shop within walking distance of campus—to give feedback on each other's pages. His friendship and creative connection became a kind of haven.

Soon, I started taking Mandarin classes, hoping to learn to speak well enough to at least be able to pronounce people's true names. In the class, the instructor helped translate my name, and I thought my new Chinese friends would use it: 凯特 (Kǎi tè). But whenever I tried to say my very own name, she'd correct my pronunciation. The subtleties were so profound I despaired of ever being able to communicate. Maybe when I met my students, they would help me. Classes were starting soon. Nervous excitement pulsed through me at the thought of returning to the classroom after three years.

Chapter Thirteen

People Are Not Their Governments

Fall/Winter 2016

It didn't take long to be reminded what a see-saw teaching can be. One day you're happy with the creative freedom, and the next you're plowed under with prep and grading. One day you're demoralized, wondering why the students are zoning out—and the next you're thrilled with their brilliance.

Then there was the fact that during the past three years, my work of writing and editing could be done in yoga pants, while teaching required real clothes—not to mention setting an alarm clock and brushing my hair. I had to go to campus only three times a week but still, for this retiree, it was an adjustment. I had forgotten how it felt to have to be *on*, meaning talking semi-coherently, at 7:50 a.m. Fortunately, my commute was five minutes on foot, across the street, past the lawn where early-risers played badminton or engaged in the watery movements of tai chi.

The damp-smelling cavernous classroom, with high ceilings and tall windows, was crammed with straight rows of blocky desks. The students had to strong-arm the desks into a circle or small groups because my pedagogy didn't allow for rows. Classes were forty to fifty students, and English language abilities were all over the map: some were fluent, others not so much. At faculty orientation, we'd been told the students were required to use an English name while at school. Most were common, like Amy, Robert, Gail. Others, though, were bizarrely humorous: Hamburger, Watermelon, and of all things, Xylitol. The English names requirement felt odd and colonial-y, and calling a student "Hamburger" seemed to erect a barrier between us (or at least make me hungry!). Perhaps some students felt the same and chose those names as an act of protest. In response, I decided to have one of our first activities be presentations on the significance of their Chinese names. The answers were pure poetry, revealing a lot of thought, intention, and meaning:

"My name means jade. My mom wants me to be like jade—beautiful—and to be a kind person."

"My name means a certain kind of tree. My parents want me to live as strong as that tree."

"It means to live a quiet, joyful life."

"Tolerant and praise-worthy."

"Elegant."

"A polite, educated person."

"Quiet but talented."

"Sunshine in the morning."

"My name means I will grow from a child to an artist of life."

Over the years, when I'd heard people in the U.S. claim that Chinese students aren't very imaginative, the arrow of my bullshit meter hit red. I believe imagination and innovation are part of human nature. Of course I knew rote learning, rather than critical and creative thinking, tended to be the primary educational practice in China, as in many countries. But that didn't mean inspiration disappeared. It might just need coaxing out.

Sure enough, in my courses, students wrote stirring poems and prose, made extraordinary video interpretations of poetry, and took inspired leaps. They showed interest in the readings, including Alice Walker, Sherman Alexie, Li Young Lee, Mark Doty, Shirley Geok-Lin Lim, lê thi diem thúy, Maya Angelou, Sandra Cisneros, and Jimmy Santiago Baca. In the memoir class, they enthusiastically acted out scenes from the stories—no surprise since performing was an important part of their worlds. Every weekend the immense campus theater was filled to capacity while students danced and sang onstage. On Halloween, a party filled the community space right out our front door. Sexily-clad students vogued like pros on the makeshift stage, and even some of the shyest sprang up to lip-synch. Everyone went wild when Dave (dressed as the Phantom of the Opera) and I (a zombie flapper) along with a group of other costumed teachers performed a choreographed dance to Michael Jackson's "Thriller."

Partway into the school term, the Dean asked me and two other teachers if we'd perform with him and several staff members in an upcoming talent show. At the conference table during the prep meeting, the Dean said Li-Ji would play the guitar while we sang an American song the Dean loved. He wanted us to listen first and then practice. He cued the lights and a screen dropped down projecting Peter, Paul, and Mary crooning "Blowin' in the Wind." My throat tightened with emotion at the thought I'd be singing an antiwar song with Chinese compatriots. As we practiced, I thought about how people are not their governments—and how divisiveness and racism lead us to otherize human beings, when most people want the same things: peace, prosperity, and love.

Dave was also lassoed into the talent show, and with a group of students performed a tai chi routine, wearing a white robe and face makeup that gave him odd caterpillar eyebrows. When my group sang "Blowin' in the Wind," footage of suffering soldiers from a war movie was projected on a massive screen behind us, and afterward the standing-room-only crowd roared.

City living was vibrant but also stressful, with its crowds, noise, and traffic. I missed wild nature. Perhaps the government understood the toll urban life can take because, in the absence of wildlife, a sound somewhere between the vocalizations of a frog and a dog chirped out of loudspeakers. When we'd first heard the noise, we had no idea what it was, but Dave learned its source from Lee, the eleven-year-old boy he was tutoring: the pseudo-nature sounds were intended to help ease the strife of urbanization. Dave got referred to the tutoring gig in his martial arts class. By that point, it became clear that no one followed the no-extra-work rules and that English speakers were in demand. Dave got paid to enjoy afternoons chatting with this smart boy, taking bike rides, and playing basketball.

Lee's family invited us to a mid-Autumn festival meal, where everyone participated in making pork dumplings. This holiday, also known as Full Moon Festival, falls on the fifteenth day of the eighth month of the Chinese lunar calendar, usually September or early October on the Gregorian calendar. Lee's mother's hands swiftly formed perfectly shaped and sealed dumplings, while Dave and I clumsily attempted facsimiles. Dumplings bubbled in boiling water near a round table where we and seven family members gathered around platters piled with greens, two kinds of chicken, and snake. I couldn't get past the scaly skin, more suitable for boots than appetizers in my opinion, but Dave braved a few bites. Later he told me it was so spicy he had to gulp down cold beer, which had been poured for the men.

After dinner, Lee's father made us tea at a special table, a carved desk housing numerous pigeonholes. A connoisseur of pu'er—a traditional fermented Chinese tea—he painstakingly unwrapped packets of leaves, some of which had been aged for years, and carefully poured hot water, steeping for a precise amount of time. As we sipped and compared flavors *ala* wine tasting, I felt honored to be part of this ritual—although when we stood up to leave, the caffeine coursing through my system made my head whirl.

We also were invited to a mooncake-making party at the home of Li-Ji and Sophie, where groups gathered around outdoor tables. A man weighed balls of dough and we rolled them out, added filling such as lotus paste and sweet potato, and pressed them into wooden molds to create elaborate designs before they were baked. I liked the belonging evoked when making food with other people, realizing the closest tradition in my family was dyeing Easter eggs.

As we made the cakes, the foreign teachers talked about how in past years the school had closed for a few days for the holiday. They were waiting to hear if that would be the case again. Soon I received a message saying we'd have five days off, starting next week. At the same time, I found out our friends Karen and Widi were on their own break from teaching at an international school in Chennai, India—and they happened to be in Vietnam. We made a plan to meet in Hoi An, and I felt a thrilling whiplash at the thought of returning to that country so soon.

Hoi An, a UNESCO World Heritage site, is a quaint village, one of the few places not bombed and destroyed during war, which left ancient temples and other antiquated buildings still standing. From the fifteenth to the nineteenth centuries, this port city located on the Thu Bon river was filled not only with Vietnamese but Chinese and Japanese families, which influenced the diverse architecture. We walked across a timeworn stone bridge built by Japanese merchants, the only known covered bridge with an attached Buddhist temple. We also visited a red-and-gold bedecked Chinese assembly hall with a grand gate, garden with ornamental plants, and an altar room. With other tourists, we crammed into a stuffy theater for an hour of traditional music, featuring women in colorful clothes with red fans dancing to drumbeats in a sly mix of noble and seductive.

Everywhere we went, people were fascinated with Widi because he spoke fluent Vietnamese, and I enviously watched his language abilities lead to instant connections. Widi is Indonesian, born in Java, but he learned Vietnamese when he taught in a Vietnamese refugee camp in Sumatra—the place he and Karen, who's from Massachusetts, met more than thirty years before. We'd befriended them on an Alaska cruise when we were living and working in California. Two years later, when we launched our nomadic lives, we visited them in India. I admired their status as citizens of the world, and befriending them undoubtedly inspired Dave and me to spread our travel wings.

The next day, we hopped on bikes and rode to Hidden Beach. It lived up to its name: underdeveloped and uncrowded. Dave and Widi did tai chi on the sand while Karen and I dipped in the water. There were lounge chairs, umbrellas, and food available—as well as massages. A beach massage has to be one of the most luxurious experiences ever. All four of us relaxed under healing hands while an ocean breeze blew over our bodies. After having spent the day before wandering ancient streets, and the day before that teaching in a classroom in China, I felt melty in time and space.

Dave and I took the trip back to Nanning in one day, which involved an exhausting mélange of taxis, flights, airport waiting, and a confusing transfer. When we hit the Nanning airport, we shared a taxi with a Vietnamese American woman who, as it turned out, used to live in San Jose. I thrilled at the synchronicity of now having met two people from the Bay

Area in China. When I told her I'd been a writing professor at San Jose State University, she said she wanted to write about her family's journey from Vietnam to America and needed a writing coach. Handing over my card, I was struck by how when the topic of writing came up, people all over the world expressed a desire to tell the stories of their lives.

In addition to our regular schedules, all professors were asked to teach two additional hours a week of anything we liked, a way to encourage the students to speak English in a relaxed setting of credit/no-credit courses. I chose yoga and soon faced twenty college students doing mountain, tree, and warrior poses. At the end we'd chant, "My body is a temple, my mind is a crystal, my heart is blissful" and sit for meditation, my voice guiding them to picture golden light pouring through their bodies. I hoped this practice would help those who were stressed about the myriad standardized tests they needed to pass. I knew some were the first in their families to attend university, and their relatives and sometimes whole town contributed to their tuition. A lot was riding on their success as they shouldered the burden of not losing face in their community.

Many students came from poor, rural areas. In the memoir class, a young woman gave a talk about the time she cut her little finger in half. At eight years old, she was working on the crops with her parents, when the scythe accident occurred. After getting her finger sewn back on, she had to stay in the hospital for five days for blood transfusions. Her parents would bring her food (hospitals in China don't serve meals) and then return to long days of field labor. She was scared, but she knew her parents needed to work, and she didn't want them to worry about her. "That was when I realized," she said, "I had a choice: to be scared or to be strong." She held up a two-foot sculpture she'd crafted of wood and red paper. On the overhead, she projected photos she'd taken of the sculpture in natural settings, some shot from below to make the sculpture look ten feet tall.

"This is my strength," she said, holding up her art with one hand and waving her bent pinky with the other.

I thought about how at age twelve I'd fallen from my bike and had been hospitalized for five days for a concussion and hairline skull fracture. My mom stayed by my side nearly the whole time, and I was four years older than this girl had been during her ordeal. I was enthralled with the way she'd used her creativity to bolster and express herself. Many of my students had that urge. Some admitted they wished they could major in the arts or English, but their families expected them to study math or science, a complaint I'd heard from students in the States as well. After presenting a professional-quality video he made for the poetry class, one student told me he wished he could major in film, but his parents said he must be an accountant. I thought about encouraging him to "follow his bliss," as I might have in the U.S., but that didn't feel right, given my outsider status in his culture. There was no way for me to truly understand the intricacies of his family life.

So instead I said, "Everyone has free time. Some choose to play video games, or do sports, or surf the internet. You could make movies if you wanted to."

In the next class, I talked about how the poet William Carlos Williams was a doctor, as was Khaled Hosseini, who practiced medicine while writing *The Kite Runner*. Wallace Stevens worked for an insurance company, Robert Frost was a teacher, and Haruki Murakami owned and ran a jazz bar. These writers, I said, show us it's possible to follow more than one path.

Later in the semester, as I was walking across campus, that same student pulled up beside me on his motorbike and gushed, "Dr. Kate, look at this!" He held up his phone and showed me a short film he'd made with his friends. He said he was now working on a full-length one. "I think after getting my undergraduate degree, I'm going to get a master's in teaching English." He smiled. "That way I can inspire my students to follow their dreams."

Teaching in China stretched me both as a professor and a person. In many ways it was similar to my experiences in the States, but there were differences. Unlike in my American classes, discussion was not freewheeling. The students wouldn't talk unless called upon, as much as I encouraged them to jump in. This likely had to do with the format of most of their education, but also that they had to express themselves in their non-dominant language. However, when I let them write or talk out ideas with a partner before speaking to the whole class, they got into it. They also enjoyed games and role playing and reading aloud. One day on my way to class, I saw one of my students standing in front of the lotus pond reciting a poem with our poetry book in his hand, gesticulating toward the trees. I had not assigned this; he was speaking the poem…just because, perhaps for his own pleasure or edification. In my twenty-five years of teaching, I'd never seen a student do such a thing, and I couldn't have loved it more. Another time, a student offered this reason for missing class, one I'd never heard before: "I am in my hometown until next Monday. My family is rebuilding the tombs of our ancestors."

As in the U.S., there were several students who came out as gay, either privately to me or in the pieces they wrote. There were popular students, shy ones, athletes, and class clowns. One day, a young man who usually had a joke at the ready seemed sick. I asked him if he was okay, and he said earnestly, "I'm sorry, I drank too much beer last night." I wondered if he was kidding, but the students burst out laughing and he gave me a hangdog look. I suggested he sleep it off. But he insisted on staying, his eyes half-mast the whole time.

Undeniably, I felt these students respected education and me as their teacher. One day, when I was feeling ill, I told the students I needed to dismiss class early. I expected them to cram their papers into their backpacks and eagerly take off, but they sat still, staring at me. "Really, I'm okay, I just need to rest," I said. They didn't budge until I walked toward the door, and they followed me out, grouping around me saying they hoped I'd feel better soon. Three boys accompanied me all the way to my apartment door, their regard for me as their professor clear in their actions.

The assistant provided for Dave and me—the godsend who helped us open a banking account and get Wi-Fi, who showed us parts of the city and campus we would never have discovered alone, the young woman who made shit happen and didn't take no for an answer from bureaucrats—was Tina. We spent hours together taking care of details and shopping and going out to eat, and once she took us to karaoke. At times I helped her with her homework. She was on the campus dance team, and we attended her performances.

One day I received a text from Tina asking if she could come over for a hug. I opened the door to a knock, and she was standing there in tears. I ushered her in thinking, *What happened? Oh my god, what if she's pregnant or ill?* She told me she was devastated because she'd not been chosen for an elite dance squad. I thought, *oh, thank god*, but my heart wrenched at her sorrow. I hugged her and handed her a tissue. She said she felt like a loser and was fooling herself that she could dance. Maybe her parents were right, she said, that dancing was a waste of time. She spiraled into more self-criticism, saying she *really* was a loser because she had failed the Gaokao, the National Higher Education Entrance Exam, a standardized test that determines one's college placement. She actually hadn't failed but had scored low, which was why she enrolled in the university's two-year program that helped students matriculate into the four-year curriculum.

"Then I'm so glad you failed because we met," I said.

Laughing through her tears she said, "Me too."

We talked about how good things can come from life's struggles and disappointments. I taught her the word "vulnerable" when I said it was beautiful she came to me with her feelings. I also mentioned some of my own failures, such as getting manuscripts rejected, but I kept writing anyway.

"I hope this won't ruin your love of dance," I said. "I know rejection hurts, but try not to take it personally. You do it for the joy, and because it's who you are."

107

She said it was hard for Chinese kids because of the pressure to be perfect and not lose face—and she knew most of her peers had similar feelings but hid them.

After an hour she said she didn't want to see her friends, so I asked her if she'd like to spend the day together. We did yoga in the living room, and then I showed her how I make smoothies, and she took selfies of us drinking them. Then she worked at our table on her laptop as I graded papers. In the silence, I'd sneak looks at her sweet, concentrating face, and I wondered if this was what it felt like to have a daughter. I knew my life would have been very different if I'd had kids, and I mostly didn't regret it since I loved my freedom. But sometimes the ghost of the child who could have been mine floated through my mind, and I briefly ached for her.

That evening Tina, Dave, and I went out to dinner and to the movies to see *Wonder Woman*. The next morning I saw she had posted a picture of us on WeChat (the Chinese Facebook) with these words, opening with a quote from the film:

"'The supreme happiness of life is the conviction that we are loved.' I think it was the reason why I thought about things positively soon after a huge blow. Just as Wonder Woman said in the movie last night, 'Love saves the world,' my little world was saved by you. Thank you for staying with me when I felt vulnerable."

For Tina's birthday, we took her to buy a new bike, her birthday gift. When her bike had disappeared the month before, we knew it was an opportunity to get a useful and meaningful present for this young woman who had done so much for us. At first she refused, saying it was too costly. But I told her the dollar was strong, it wasn't expensive for us, and we would be extremely sad if she said no. To get to what everyone called Stolen Bike Street—an avenue crowded with used (and perhaps actually purloined) bikes for sale— Tina perched sidesaddle on the back of Dave's bike. When I mentioned she seemed so at ease on the book rack as Dave swerved in the traffic madness and hopped over speed bumps, she said she was used to riding this way because when she was young, her family had no car. Her mother did not want to leave her and her infant brother at home so she put the baby in her bike basket, and Tina balanced on the back. Later, her parents left their town because her mother was pregnant with her third child, and they were ostracized by the community because of the "One Child" policy (which has since been abolished). I wasn't sure how they'd been able to have a second child without a problem, nor how entering a new community made having a third child possible, but for some reason it worked, and they started a profitable business—which allowed them to buy a car.

Next we took her to a restaurant of her choice. Because the menu had few pictures and no English, she ordered for us. A pot was set on the hot plate in the center of the table, and inside were...duck feet, Tina's favorite. Oh dear. With my chopsticks, I extracted one from the pot. It slumped there, a sad little extremity. I watched Tina happily chew away, spitting out tiny bones.

I took a few nibbles and was surprised to find it delicious, albeit not so satisfying because there wasn't much meat. The miniscule bones made eating complicated, equivalent to the labor of consuming a pomegranate. The pot was filled with other delectable things: potatoes, tofu skin, tofu cubes, quail eggs, taro root. Next came a plate heaping with seafood on ice to be cooked in the pot's savory broth: crab, shrimp, octopus, mussels, clams, and cockles. A side-dish was a Nanning specialty, noodles with miniature snails. I'd been avoiding that delicacy up to now—just as I stay away from escargot—but because of Tina I dug in and found I liked the salty dish.

After eating, Tina told us she had something she wanted to say, launching into a clearly memorized speech about how much we meant to her. She had barely begun when tears started streaming down my face. She thanked us for being so friendly and for never losing patience when she was trying to figure things out. She recalled when we went to the bank one day and it was so crowded we decided to leave and come back another time. "You said when things are *chaos*"—she remembered learning that word from Dave—"that it's better to go away and do something else." She also said she learned from us to appreciate the small things in life, and she was especially touched when one day she'd heard me tell someone she was like our Chinese daughter.

For my own birthday, Tina gave me a scrapbook that included pictures of our adventures. This took place at Café Ukulele, where we'd gone for live music, and soon the evening began to reveal itself as a surprise party for me. Paul sang my favorite song, Van Morrison's "Into the Mystic," which he had taught himself that afternoon. Two other teachers brought a cake, and everyone crooned Happy Birthday. I was in awe that in celebration of my fifty-fourth year I was surrounded by love from people I'd known for such a short time—and that "the other side of the world" was now my side of the world.

Earlier that day, the university had delivered a cake to our apartment, as they did for all university teachers. It was a sweet gesture and a magnificent cake, ringed on the top with tropical fruit...and tomatoes. The sodden texture and oddly savory taste led me to understand why one foreign teacher dubbed them "disappointment cakes." I brought it into class, where—after singing Happy Birthday in both English and Mandarin—my students devoured it. Knowing that some Chinese people who traveled to the U.S. didn't like the taste of our food, I marveled at how "differences" are just what we've grown up with.

Dave's birthday gift to me was an overnight at Jiuquwan Hot Springs. Leave it to my husband to locate a natural hot springs resort thirty minutes from our house. By now we could jump into a cab and get where we needed to go. We'd become proficient at using key phrases and translator apps, collecting business cards, taking pictures of signs and the fronts of buildings for later use, or having someone write down our destination in Chinese. The Hot Springs boasted one hundred pools, small and large, as well as saunas, mud baths, and fish-nibbling foot treatments. We soaked for hours then lay on warmed slabs of marble beneath an awning for a nap. That night I slept ten hours. My body needed rest after all the months of intensity—not only teaching but being immersed in an unfamiliar language and culture. The beastly heat also drained me. I'd thought siesta was only a Latin American thing, but in hot Nanning, every afternoon business closed down for a couple of hours. However, instead of napping I usually graded papers under the blasting air conditioner.

When I returned to campus, in the memoir class we watched the film *Wild* after having read a few chapters of the book by Cheryl Strayed. One challenge of teaching in China, I'd found, was trying to decide what to drill down on and what to gloss over. Vocabulary wasn't only about defining words but concepts, history, culture. In the course of teaching *Wild*, for instance, I'd introduced the students to Adrienne Rich, Jerry Garcia, "therapist," Pacific Crest Trail, Minnesota, the term "beacon" as a light and a metaphor for a guidepost, and a Simon and Garfunkel song. When we'd finished the unit and the students were filing out of the classroom, I'd felt good about my approach and the discussions we'd had. I'd liked what the students were writing about their own literal or metaphorical journeys. One student, however, lingered in the room.

"We cannot accept the sex of this movie," he said, surprising me with the force of his words. "Western and Eastern ideas about sex are very different. In the East, it is one man and one woman."

The film depicts Cheryl, played by Reese Witherspoon, doing heroin and having sex with strangers after her mother dies. Embroiled in grief and trying to change her life, she decides to hike the Pacific Crest Trail. Along the way, she has a tender one-night stand with a guy she meets in Portland. By the movie's end, we learn that four years after the hike, she married and now has two children. While I had been somewhat concerned if this material was appropriate, other teachers told me that as long as I was presenting the American experience, I could do anything. In the film and book, feminism is a central theme. Students, especially the girls, had been engaged as we talked and wrote about its tenets of freedom and equality. We had also discussed how destructive it can be to use sex and drugs to numb pain.

But now a young man stood before me apparently asserting I should not have taught this story. I knew students were appointed to regularly report to the administration about what happened in their classes. I'd submitted my syllabi in advance, as required, and had received only silence in return. Had anyone actually read it? I wondered if I was in deep doo-doo.

"I understand there are cultural differences when it comes to certain issues," I said.

"No one can accept this," he repeated.

"Well, these things happen. This is Cheryl's truth. I'm not asking that you agree with it. If your values are different, that's fine. It's good for you to know what you believe."

He began to tremble, and his eyes glassed with tears.

"College is so different. I thought I was conservative. But now I don't know."

I felt myself soften at this unexpected turn. I thought of all the students in the States who'd come to me with their personal problems. Was that what this was about?

"Yes, it's true," I said. "When you're away from home and treated like an adult, your ideas change and grow."

"And my girlfriend. She has been with other boys. I watch the movie and think about it. I cannot accept it. But I love her. She is my first love. She changed for me. One moment I want to stay with her, and another I think I cannot. How did Cheryl's husband marry her after all the men she was with? That would not happen in China. I was wondering...Dr. Kate...if you can give me some advice. How can I forget her past?"

Oh. My. God. I wanted to reach out and hug this sweet boy. I also realized he hadn't quite taken in our class discussions about slut-shaming and double standards. I took a breath and prayed I could guide him in some sort of helpful way, especially since ideas of shame in China were beyond my true understanding. I asked him how he knew about his girlfriend's past, and he said she told him. I pointed out how she must trust him to be so honest. His face went blank, as though he was trying to soak that in. I asked him what he was afraid of.

"I don't know." Students laughed and chattered as they passed by the window. "My friend told me he thinks she came into my life to teach me something."

His words touched me deeply, given my belief that every person who crosses my path is my teacher. "That's a wise friend. What do you think she might be teaching you?"

111

"I don't know. Maybe how to love?" I was so moved by this response that I blinked to hold back my own tears. "But it hurts in my stomach whenever I think about it. I just cannot accept her past."

He had said the word *accept* so much I eventually realized he was trying to deny what had happened. "Maybe you need to face this head on. Don't run away from it. It's not about accepting *her*. It's about accepting it happened."

He looked down.

"You can't decide what you want until you have put it there on the table. Fear is keeping you from seeing it. Do you understand what I'm saying?"

"Yes."

"And once you accept the truth, that is when you can decide if you want to be with her. People can love each other and choose to be together or be apart."

"Maybe you are right. I will think about this." He shifted his backpack on his shoulders. "Thank you, Dr. Kate. And please do not tell the others I talked to you."

"Of course. You do realize, though, there are other people in this class with your same problem."

He looked over his shoulder at the empty desks then back at me. "I don't know."

"There are. This is the human experience. You are not alone."

Before he left, I told him I was glad he spoke to me—and that we could talk again, any time. Alone in the room, I thought about how life, that trickster, had put this young man and me together in the same place, out of all the people and places in the world. His opening up to me had been a stark recognition that what young people grapple with has similarities across cultures.

Of course, I couldn't know how our conversation would affect him. The words of Cheryl Strayed voiced at the end of the film resonated: "There's no way to know what makes one thing happen and not another. What leads to what. What destroys what. What causes what to flourish or die or take another course."

And there were things I didn't say: that when I was his age I'd been sexually active for three years. That my undergrad college life was enveloped in a haze of drugs and booze. That I'd written about all of this in my memoir. I didn't think students could easily access my book in China, but if they had the will, there was a way.

I was aware being married to Dave draped me with a veil of straight-seeming privilege. In a way, I felt I was compromising my progressive pedagogy, but on the other hand I used course materials to explore such topics…and clearly students were thinking through powerful issues. That might have been why some students felt free to talk to me about their lives. And to come out. Perhaps they intuited more about me than I gave them credit for.

Still, I worried I had unintentionally developed a kind of Mary Poppins persona, floating down with my umbrella from California to Nanning before drifting away again. At least that was the plan: to leave after one academic year. Would resuming our nomadic ways mean missing an opportunity to go deeper? The administration had already sent me a new contract, and Dave and I had a couple of months to make a decision.

Chapter Fourteen

Heaven's VIP Room

Winter/Spring 2017

It was early December, and I had another school break, so Dave and I decided to take a trip to Hanoi, Vietnam's capital city. The land border between China and Vietnam was fortified by barbed wire, and armed soldiers signaled the Chinese bus to stop then climbed aboard to inspect identification papers before ushering us out. We were taken into a bland governmental building, down Orwellian hallways flush with cameras, and directed to stand in lines to repeat a showing of our passports. Eventually we were shepherded outside to stand on a curb for a Vietnamese bus to take us to Hanoi. At least we hoped so. We weren't clear on the procedure but were blindly following along.

A van pulled up, and people rushed to the rear seats, leaving only shotgun. The driver motioned for Dave and me to sit, but I pantomimed there was only one seat and two of us. His gestures made clear he wanted me to sit on the console between the two front seats. Dave and I concluded this must be a shuttle taking us to the bus for the next leg, a four-hour drive, so I climbed in and balanced on the rigid console, while Dave slid next to me. Minutes in, my butt was sore, and I was hoping we'd stop soon for the transfer. But after taking a few turns, the van merged and kept going…and going…and going. With no seatbelt and my face nearly mashed up against the windshield, the van whipped past slow-moving vehicles on blind curves.

"Holy shit, I think he's taking us the whole way like this," I said to Dave. My rear end had gone numb and my neck felt frozen at a permanent tilt when, two hours in, the driver pulled into a gas station. I stumbled out of the vehicle along with the other passengers who took a smoke or snack break. When it came time to pile back inside, Dave took the middle "seat" the second half of the way.

We made it to our destination intact, and the hazardous trip seemed worth it as I stood on an iron-balustraded hotel balcony taking in the fascinating, boisterous life of Hanoi's Old Quarter. Motorized and pedal-powered tuk-tuks navigated the narrow streets, women wearing conical hats hauled baskets brimming with flowers, and bicycles piled high with pineapples and melons lumbered along. It bent the mind to realize these streets were a thousand years old, and much of the architecture dated from the 15th century. Buildings with inclined tiled roofs and shops were wedged

114

together, burgeoning with merchandise nearly spilling onto the streets: bamboo stacked as thick and high as a transplanted forest, bundles of silk threads big as car wheels, and tumbles of plastic household goods in primary colors. Squeezed into the fray were five-story houses with narrow facades; these tube houses have a front room facing the street used for selling goods and a back for living, with a series of courtyards that go deep into each city block.

We spent our days walking, taking in people's daily lives, peeking into stores selling silk and embroidery, festival flags and religious articles, and miniature paper objects to burn for the dead. Pharmacies bulged with fragrant medicinal herbs, sacks and jars of leaves, roots, barks, and powders. We treated ourselves to luxurious yet inexpensive massages and pedicures, and I went to a hair salon—easy to access in Hanoi but difficult in China. The hairdresser spoke little English, and so I was able to express what I wanted with few words by showing her a picture of my haircut of choice on my phone. As for the spas, they had menus written in English, which required only pointing. The spa's solitude provided a refuge from the roaring motorbikes and cars careening down the narrow streets amidst gaggles of pedestrians and hawkers.

We walked to nearby Hoan Kiem Lake, thirty acres of fresh water surrounded by a park. The streets feeding into the area were closed off on the weekends, so we took a relaxing stroll amidst kids steering toy motorized cars and a band playing pop music to an appreciative crowd against a backdrop of the jade-green lake encircled by feathery foliage. We also hopped aboard a tuk-tuk to visit the Temple of Literature, an 11th-century shrine dedicated to Confucius. Amidst the picturesque pavilions with statues surrounded by ponds and gardens, young women draped like princesses in jewel-colored dresses were celebrating their college graduations. Featuring walls carved with the names of scholars, the temple was the site of the first national academy, which gave me a profound sense of being part of an ancient academic lineage.

Another afternoon we attended a water puppet show. The audience was filled with Western retirees, and I realized, alas, we were part of that target market. The stage was filled with water, the charming puppets manipulated by poles from behind a screen. Dancing wooden people, birds, fish, dragons, and water buffalo splashed out age-old stories, accompanied by musicians playing traditional tunes that resonated in my body, rousing an archaic pulse.

Hanoi is known for its street food for good reason. As we sat on low plastic chairs on the crowded sidewalk digging into bowls of noodles with savory sauces, I remembered having seen Anthony Bourdain in a Hanoi episode on a similar chair clinking beers with former President Obama. I'd been able to watch YouTube—and access Facebook, and many other websites blocked in China—only because my computer had a VPN, which worked intermittently.

Thinking of POTUS sparked a fresh memory: Three weeks earlier, I'd walked into class and my students asked, "What do you think of your new President?" Of course I'd been following the historic contest and had assumed the U.S. would be electing its first ever woman head of state. Voting for her via the FAX machine in the Dean's office, I'd wished my mom had been alive to see the election of a female President. I hadn't taken seriously that a man could win whose claim to fame was building hotels, starring in a TV show, and spreading lies about President Obama's birth certificate. Due to the time difference and the sporadic access to U.S. news, I'd not been aware the election had been called and was stunned when the students told me who had won. Realizing the nation would now be led by a misogynist authoritarian who spouted anti-immigration rhetoric had so distressed me I'd had a hard time focusing on teaching that day. So many countries had welcomed Dave and me: Mexico, China, India, Sri Lanka, Australia, Cambodia, Thailand, Vietnam. Most residents of those countries could not come to the States so freely. As a white American who could represent colonialism and warfare, I received almost nothing but kindness, and experienced basic ease of movement. No border guard or visa form had asked me about my religion, my political views, my financial status, or my feelings about their country. I knew many were denied what I had been gifted as an accident of birth—and I prayed hate wouldn't win the day in the land of the free that was founded on harboring immigrants.

A month after our Hanoi trip came a six-week holiday for Chinese New Year, also called Spring Festival. We wanted to explore more of China, but every time I had a break, so did millions of others, and navigating China's travel rules was complex. We'd bought train tickets to take us to Yalong Bay, reportedly the most beautiful beach in Guangxi. However, a few days later someone had outbid us and so our trip was canceled and our money refunded. We'd had no idea we'd secured only an *attempt* at tickets. We realized we'd fare better if we had Tina's assistance on a China excursion, and so at the start of Spring Festival, we asked her and her friend Rose to accompany us on a two-day outing. We'd be taking the bus, which had a more straight-forward ticketing system, but nevertheless Tina had to purchase our tickets on a Chinese website impossible for an English speaker to navigate. My colleague Michelle and her husband Joshua also came along. During the four-hour ride, a safety video played on repeat showing real bus crash footage. I tried to avert my eyes, but my gaze involuntarily wandered back to gruesome images of a bus rolling over and over, bodies flying across the seats like clothes in a dryer. The takeaway was unclear because there were no seatbelts on the bus.

Our first stop was Detian Waterfall, billed as the fourth largest transnational waterfall, half in Vietnam and half in China. A broad swath of cascades rushed down an oasis of lush tropical greenery, with jagged peaks in the background. The boat ride brought us close enough to feel the spray wet our faces and for the thundering power of nature to rumble in our bones. The next day we explored Tongling Grand Canyon, a karst cavern replete with an underground river and rich vegetation. Dwarfed by the scope of the place, we hiked on wooden walkways illuminated with multicolored lights for a Pirates of the Caribbean vibe—proof "cheesy" and "sublime" don't necessarily cancel each other out. When we emerged from the cave, we faced a stunning sight: one of the tallest waterfalls in Asia draping down like a goddess' boa.

As usual, everywhere we went, people wanted to take pictures with us. But Michelle's husband Joshua—a Ugandan reggae artist with dreadlocks, torn jeans, and swag—was the real star, especially with young guys who thought he was the coolest ever.

Next, Dave and I headed for a month in Thailand, by way of Malaysia, since flying through Kuala Lumpur turned out to be half the price of a direct flight to Bangkok. Kate Harris' words came to mind: "We're only here by fluke, and only for a little while, so why not run with life as far and wide as you can?" Our first stop was to be Koh Phangan, a Thai island that had piqued our interest since the foreign teachers at my university swooned as they talked about it. We were excited because Dave's dear friend and fraternity brother, Mark, would be meeting up with us.

A Burning Man aficionado, Mark rewired my stereotype of fraternity guys with his hippie van that reeked of pot smoke, his incisive intellect, his love of the natural world, and his knowledge of fringe media. Dave had told me that upon graduation, Mark had tried to fit into the corporate world. He became a top salesman of business forms but lasted only a few months. I had a hard time imagining him in a suit, especially since he hated wearing even a shirt. His whole life he'd been on the hunt for a place to live, somewhere he fit in, a spot he could call home. He had rented houses in Yellowstone and Zion, where we'd visited him among a cluster of family and friends. His explorations mirrored Dave's and mine. He'd recently driven a van across the U.S. and New Zealand—and before we headed to China, we'd spent time with him in his hometown of Alameda, California, an island tucked next to Oakland.

Dave and I had taken a housesit there for ten days, caring for a black cat with moss-green eyes named Uma in a downtown apartment on the main street above a taqueria. Within steps were innumerable restaurants and an old, restored movie theater. Mark lived a couple of miles away in the house he'd grown up in. His parents now deceased, the house was filled with a wacky juxtaposition of his mother's doily-draped flowery couches and collectable ceramic figurines mixed in with Mark's electric guitars, Beat Generation books, a laser light machine, and an assortment of bongs. He'd been adopted as a baby and, although he loved his parents, he rejected their conventional world. Throughout his twenties and thirties, he traveled around, couch surfing and at one point living in a converted tool shed. He was deeply involved in the underground raves in the San Francisco Bay Area until rejecting that world when trendy suburbanites soiled the scene, making it in his eyes too mainstream. Mark next conceived of and managed a workspace for nearly one hundred bands to practice and play concerts, including the then-unknown Green Day, in old warehouses in rundown Bay Area neighborhoods. However, bands regularly broke up and stiffed him, leaving him embittered. And so he brought raves to Maui and lived in a bachelor apartment with a group of other DJs. That world came crashing down when at a rave, a guy on a drug trip jumped off a cliff and died.

In Alameda, Mark led us on a bike tour. We rolled along the treelined streets and beside the silvery bay to the waterfront park where the ferry travels to San Francisco. I thought it was lovely, but Mark bad-mouthed Alameda—too humdrum, too bourgeois. His desire to find a place he belonged, his true home, fueled his wanderlust, as did his medical condition, a congenital heart problem that had recently required emergency surgery. It was easy to imagine him as fearless, but he had become nervous about traveling in non-English speaking countries where he wasn't confident about communicating during a medical emergency. Now, though, his recent heart surgery had prompted a renaissance. His signature sardonic wit had become infused with *joie de vivre*. When we told him we were headed to Southeast Asia, he announced he'd meet us there.

So now here we were, high on the island's turquoise waters and creamsicle sunsets and fresh snapper served whole. Koh Phangan seemed like a place I'd dreamed about. We didn't have much on our agenda other than a little exploring, beach massages, yoga, and swimming. That was until Mark roped us into checking out another part of the island for a dance party he'd gotten wind of—in a spot called Eden, no less. He'd heard about the island's secrets from Brian, a New Yorker and longtime island resident whom Mark called his Cosmic Concierge. A music connoisseur, Mark was always in search of an inspired scene, and he had the whole thing planned out so all Dave and I had to do was go along for the ride. With Mark in charge, there'd be no seatbelts to buckle.

118

That afternoon, a Thai guy named Squeekee Monkee pulled up in a black Toyota four-wheel-drive to take us to Haad Rin beach, home of the world-famous Full Moon Party that draws 20,000 revelers, jugglers, and fire-eaters once a month to dance all night to trance, reggae, and techno beats. Now, though, the beach was quiet since Mark had marshalled us here for another reason. The sun burned in the cloudless sky as we crunched through the sand past giant sound systems, strewn with cabaret furniture, and a roaming pack of dogs. Mark pointed to our destination high on a granite slope: concrete jammed into the hillside, the words "Mushroom Bar" scrawled in graffiti. He said it looked like a WWII bunker built by the shell-shocked, whereas the post-apocalyptic final scene of *The Planet of the Apes* flashed through my mind. Up several sets of stairs that appeared to go everywhere and nowhere, we found Mushroom Bar and a guy ready to serve.

"*Sah wah dee krop*, two happy drinks please." Mark grinned, his sunburned face crinkling around the eyes. He was shirtless as usual, his open-heart surgery scar snaking up his chest.

He was handed two smoothies created with yogurt, a variety of tropical fruits, honey, and most importantly, hallucinogenic fungi. "Elixir of the Gods," Mark sighed then amended, "Elixir of the Indians of the Americas to be exact," his nod to the earliest users of psychedelic mushrooms. He savored a few sips and offered us some. Dave and I declined, intuiting the day would be trippy enough without drugs.

Back on the beach, we approached a longtail boat, a wooden water taxi with an unhoused motor. It took eight people to inch the heavy craft into the water. We clambered aboard and the captain, standing at the stern, dipped his propeller-on-a-stick into the surf and off we chugged, around points, past hidden beaches. Mark noted that the bottom of the craft was littered with sawed-off gallon milk containers, obviously used for bailing. "I'm not sure if this makes me feel safer or scared-er," he cracked. Soon we were alone, other longtails in the gulf having dropped off one by one into the bays dotting the southern tip of Koh Phangan.

The boat whipped sideways as we neared land, then spun around to reach the shores of Sanctuary, where we disembarked at the pristine beach and hippie-chic spa resort sheltered in the rocky face of a cliff. A striking, organic structure tucked in the jungle caught my attention: an open bar and restaurant with bungalows in the back, crafted in polished, twisting wood. Hammocks, beach chairs, and a few thatched huts dotted the beach. We wandered past residents on the trail, some here for vacation, others for a health detox treatment.

Settling down on tables and ordering food, we watched the sun lower, smearing the horizon with flamboyant oranges and pinks. While Dave and I ate, Mark wandered off to a beach lounger for some "relaxed trippin'."

Later he told us he'd been joined by a woman from Manhattan who was there for a cleanse. He'd said, "That's cool. Would you like a sip of my happy drink?" She lunged at his offer and slammed a good third of the shroom shake, which set him belly-laughing.

When night fell, we made our pilgrimage to Eden, scrambling up rocks along a crumbling path, our only light source my phone. Now and then, shadowy people appeared from behind boulders only to disappear down jungle game trails. Our descent revealed the scene of Mark's dreams: an open-air nightclub at the end of the earth, electronica on a cliff, waves roiling below, the dance floor lit up with psychedelic lights and an array of dancers, eccentric in movement and dress. "Who knew heaven had a VIP room?" Mark exclaimed.

In the far corner, squid and snapper roasted on a grill. Incense wafted, and a German guy sitting against a railing casually smoked while shooting bottle-rockets over the bay. Two dogs playfully wrestled on the dance floor. People were seated at low tables on triangular pillows, and a smattering of hammocks held motionless lumps. Mark introduced himself to the DJ, a guy from a small town near Moscow, who to Mark's joy began playing "an expert mix of funky-soulful-house-tribal-with-a-touch-of-acid." We boogied for hours. As I waved my diaphanous scarf in the electric fan-breeze created to cool off the dancers, my ecstasy seemed Mark's doing.

Exhausted, we sat at a wobbly table in a separate lean-to with a view of the whole club. People of all nationalities came and went along a plank walkway that wound around a stack of rocks and into darkness. Our curiosity got the better of us and we decided to check out the mystery plankway that shook beneath our feet over a black chasm.

Rounding a boulder we beheld an illuminated, mysterious lean-to tucked in the hillside whose hand-painted sign claimed it to be a tattoo parlor and bar. The place was owned by Siam, a guy whose age could have been thirty or sixty, and was filled with unframed oil paintings, a matrix of his tattoo mandala designs. Two guitars lay at the ready, and his sound system spilled soulful house music to which a couple were swaying on a narrow dance platform. Another leaning structure stood to the right with "Stone Bar" sprayed graffiti-style.

Mark said, "Whatcha got?"

Siam replied, "Everything."

That meant kratom, molly, Jack Daniels, high-grade Colombo, ayahuasca, schnapps, the psychedelic salvia datura, limoncello, packs of cigs displaying bloody photographs of cancer surgery on the box, breadfruit tea, cocaine, psilocybin, Rolaids—and single-wrapped Mentos, complementary for his guests.

A few days later, the three of us headed by inter-island ferry to nearby Koh Tao. With lots of macho, tatted diver dudes strutting and a touristy atmosphere, Koh Tao had a rougher edge than Koh Phangan's hippie ambiance. While Dave went scuba diving and Mark explored, I found a yoga studio huddled in the rainforest and a place for breakfast afterward, my feet in the sand.

The sweet spot of Koh Tao was its world-class snorkeling. Mark treated us to a private boat for a full day, with two Thai guys skippering. After having seen so many sadly bleached reefs elsewhere, it was heartening to swim through magnificently healthy coral and swirling schools of vibrant fish. Back on the boat, his shirtless, tan torso displaying the lightning strike of his scar, Mark grinned and said he'd fallen in love with this part of the world. Perhaps the fact that we'd had to help hoist him up the boat ladder because he'd grown weak added an exclamation point to his desire. The next day, before we parted, he said he'd found home. He planned to return to Koh Phangan soon—and to stay forever.

Dave and I next flew to Chiang Mai, an ex-pat friendly, yoga-fied city filled with beautiful parks, temples, and street food galore. We met up with my former San Jose State University student, Sarah, who now taught in Chiang Mai, having landed there after a year of travel throughout India and Southeast Asia. Sharing the travel-the-world-and-write gene, we'd stayed connected on social media and the occasional email. She took us to a few temples and to the crowded Sunday Night Market, where you could buy anything edible on a stick, from insects to sweets. For Chinese New Year, red lanterns shone everywhere, accented with gold, making the night into a bejeweled shawl.

The next day, a van took us an hour north to Elephant Nature Park, a rescue and rehabilitation center where we observed the herd living in grassy hills surrounded by jungle, amidst rescue dogs, cats, horses, and goats. Elephants bathed in the river and played in mud pits. Some limped on feet mangled by landmines; others had been blinded by tourist flashbulbs in zoos and circuses. Many had endured further emotional and physical damage as a result of being broken in order to be ridden—a brutal practice which involves ripping the babies away from their mothers, beating them, and ruthlessly inducing pain. I learned no reputable elephant preserve allows visitors to ride elephants, which are among the most empathetic, intelligent creatures on the planet.

A long tradition of elephant trainers called mahouts, usually born into mahout families, learn to tame and control elephants through abuse. Elephant Nature Park re-trains the mahouts and gives them jobs working with elephants in peaceful ways, showing them how to use food, not pain, to coerce the animals to move to the watering hole or feeding platform. The men, along with legions of volunteers, worked hard on the premises and were able to build relationships with unruly bulls that tourists were not allowed to get near.

I swore the sweet beasts were thrilled to be living peaceful lives. They appeared to be smiling as they playfully threw dirt into the air, rolled in the mud, and frolicked in the river. No more cages, no more isolation, no more chains. When I was offered the chance to caress a hulking female's coarse hide, her eyes studied me, her lashes swept low, and she leaned into my hand. I inhaled the paradox of this gentle giant: rough skin, tender heart.

We spent the last few days of vacation in Kuala Lumpur, or KL as it's known in Malaysia. Our first stop was the Bird Park, the largest free-flight aviary in the world. I'm not a fan of caging birds, so it was a delight to walk the grounds seeing free-rangers of all shapes, colors, and sizes, from flamingoes, parrots, and peacocks to exotic breeds I hadn't known existed. Thousands of winged creatures roosted in the trees, toddled along the pathways, and floated in bodies of water. A few were housed in pens, notably the ostriches. When we fed them through a wedge in the fence, the fierce way they grabbed the greens, coupled with their I-could-slice-you-up clawed feet, made it clear why they couldn't be running around terrorizing tourists. Still, I wished they were in the wilds somewhere terrorizing lizards, but apparently all the ostriches in captivity had been rescued.

We enjoyed a day touring around KL on its hop-on, hop-off bus, lingering wherever we pleased. We checked out Chinatown (whose main feature was hawking fake brand-name watches), Little India, and the Petronas Towers—the tallest twin towers in the world. You can't gaze up at them without thinking of 9-11 and the human impulse to create and destroy.

Our hotel was near the massive night street food scene that we could hear and smell a block away. We waded through thousands of people, checking out stalls and open-air restaurants with gargantuan menus representing foods of many Southeast Asian nations. I happily munched on my favorite treat: deep fried banana.

We were also close to a pub street that, at night, transforms into a Vegas-esque pandemonium of crowds, music, and imbibing. At a corner café, we encountered a more mellow scene and enjoyed floating on a local trio's three-part harmonies. I marveled at all the city had to offer, and couldn't help but wish Nanning had such variety. Hunger sent us back out to the festive streets where we stumbled across a German restaurant with a warm ambiance. Weary of noodles and rice, I reveled in a luscious green salad and potato pancakes. Feeling like we could have been in Europe, I was enveloped by a surreal feeling of transcending time and space, no doubt aided by a German beer the size of a toddler.

122

This Southeast Asia exploration had reinforced for me what I loved best about travel: experiencing new things. That may sound self-evident, but it had taken me into my fifth decade to explore in the way I'd dreamed. As a kid, I'd fantasized about roaming around New York City with Harriet the Spy, climbing the Swiss Alps with Heidi, and playing along with Pippi Longstocking's shenanigans at Ville Villekull in Sweden. Ever since, I sought out other locales and other ways of living in every book I read.

I again thought about the fact that the university in Nanning had been urging me to sign on for another year. Dave and I would have to make a decision when we returned, but right now I wasn't sure I had it in me to stay anyplace longer than ten months. A zillion possibilities about what we could do next kaleidoscoped through my mind, shining like the universe's bling.

Chapter Fifteen

Don't Miss a Thing

Spring-Summer, 2017

I was now viewing China through a different set of eyes. I'd decided not to renew my contract and became hyper-aware about our limited time in Nanning. My gaze lingered on the lotus pond, on the grandma doing tai chi beneath a weeping willow. Even though it was a bustling city of millions, there was a laid-back quality to Nanning that I'd miss. I saw it in the traffic, which might look chaotic, but people at an even pace weaved around each other in a choreographed dance. An e-bike might cut off a car or pedestrian, but everyone swayed, seemingly unperturbed. One such move in California, and someone was likely to pull out a middle finger, if not a gun.

Having an exit date also made the things bothering me about our apartment easier to relax about: the mysterious stain spreading across the wall in the guest room and, in the bathroom (which Dave dubbed *Little Shop of Horrors*), unidentified goop seeping from the ceiling and the scratching of rats scurrying in the walls. I also felt less resistance to limited internet or the fact that a simple trip to the bank invariably took an hour or two. Soon: not my problem.

Was nomadic life escapism? Did I crave pressing the "Refresh" button more often than others? Or perhaps I felt most *me* on the move, a feral animal, gnawing at the rope if tied to one place. Was that home for me: being unfettered?

In the larger scheme, though, I knew none of the small irritants mattered. Most important were the people in our lives, epitomized by Dave's birthday party in May, held in our living room, a gathering of friends from China, Singapore, Russia, the U.S., and England. Paul played guitar, Mike bass, Daria keyboard, and Ricky flute. I debuted on the ukulele, which Paul had been teaching me. Together, we played one of Dave's favorite songs, Neil Young's "Heart of Gold," while Tina and her friend Jennifer performed a dance they'd created to the tune. Dave basked in the celebration of him, the friendship, the love.

Later, when I told Tina we were leaving, she erupted in tears, and we clung to each other, me whispering into her ear that when the school year was out, we wanted to gift her a trip to join us in Bali. I surprised myself by not crying as I dropped into the role of maternal consoling. But two months later, when Dave and I were all packed up and our suitcases had been stuffed into a taxi, she came to say goodbye, smiling and dry-eyed—and I was the one to weep. Her parents had nixed the idea of her meeting up with us on our travels. China wasn't easy to get to, nor simple to navigate, so it was painful to say, "see you later" when it felt like "goodbye forever."

Our first stop after lifting out of Nanning was to be the Indonesian archipelago of the Gili Islands: Trawangan, Meno, and Air. (In the Sasak language, "gili" means *island* and "air" means *water*, Gili Air being the only one of the trio with subterranean fresh water.) The area was reputedly a tropical nirvana. As we jolted along in a fast-boat, waves crashing over the bow, I prayed we weren't repeating the Koh Rong disaster with paradise dissolving into perdition. But when we neared the island, the sea calmed, sapphire waters lapped over snowy white sands, and I felt I couldn't have landed in a better spot to heal the wounds from leaving Tina—and to rejuvenate after the intense rush of finishing the semester and wrapping up our lives in China. That country had left its mark on me, an impact I needed to process.

Because there are no motor vehicles on the Gilis, people get around on foot, bike, and miniature horse-drawn carriages called cidomos. It was a magnificent sight to see the owners cool off their horses in the peacock-blue sea. The island of Gili Trawangan, known as Gili T, was small enough to circumnavigate on bike in half a day, even with stopping at will to eat and swim in the silky waters. We woke each morning to the haunting call to prayer blaring on a loudspeaker and fell asleep each night to the heartbeat of distant party music coming from the resorts at the water's edge. Instead of bothering me, these sounds heightened the tingling sensation of being *somewhere else, somewhere new*. The compelling juxtaposition of religious devotion and secular indulgence would become evident throughout Indonesia. Just as in Thailand, we found shroom shakes as available as roadside temples. Prayer and drugs, two routes for altering one's consciousness.

One morning at breakfast on the outdoor tables of the comfy family-owned B&B, we heard a young couple speaking English with American accents. Most travelers we'd encountered in Southeast Asia were Europeans, Indians, and Australians. I couldn't help myself; I had to ask them where they were from. Chicagoans, Danielle and Evan were on their honeymoon. We decided to share a boat for a day of snorkeling, since it was nearly the same price, and much more comfortable, to hire our own craft than to be stuffed into one with lots of other tourists.

We added each other as friends on Facebook—and since then we've watched them grow a family, welcoming two children. Our Facebook accounts are treasure chests of people worldwide we've met on our journeys. Social media often gets a bad rap, but to me it's a lush fabric woven with threads gathered on our travels. And because we keep track of friends old and new, we often reconnect all over the world. Obviously the internet has made travel much more convenient, from staying in touch with everyone, to planning and booking our itineraries. For those of us who have lived pre-internet, however, the convenience is offset in some ways by a (perhaps romanticized) remembrance of when traveling felt like getting lost, and time flowed like a lazy river.

When I lived in Japan in the early 1990s, teaching English, I wrote longhand letters, and after I mailed them, for days I'd imagine where my missive might be on its voyage to the other side of the world. My pulse quickened when an envelope or package was waiting for me at the post office. I spent hours in my studio apartment reading, days wandering the streets of Yokohama and Tokyo, reveling in the haunting yet delicious sense of being anonymous and adrift. There was no taking a picture or video and uploading it instantly for all to see. Video calling did not exist. A regular phone call was a rare and special event, involving buying a phone card and installing myself in a public booth, plugging one ear in hopes I could hear over a crackling line. In the internet age, there was no recapturing that feeling of vanishing into the world, although the far-flung islands of Southeast Asia came close.

The reefs we floated over from the boat with Danielle and Evan were divine, but the snorkeling turned out to be just as great right off the beach. One day Dave and I walked into the crystalline water and were instantly surrounded by five or six sea turtles munching on algae in the shallows like antediluvian mythological creatures.

Paradise was interrupted when we realized we needed to deal with a rookie mistake we'd made. We had crafted an itinerary of two months in Indonesia but when we entered the country, we were granted only thirty days, the limit for U.S. citizens. However, we'd learned it could be possible to extend our visas, so we asked around and were told to see the "guy with the mustache" at a travel booth on the main dusty road. Dealing with bureaucracy everywhere is a challenge—more so in a place where the rules seem, well...flexible, and you don't know the language or the culture. Handing over cash and our passports to "the guy with the mustache" was a pure act of faith.

Days later, our passports were returned, but to finalize the extensions, we had to board a crammed ferry—really a fishing boat, overflowing with passengers sprawled on the floor—to get to the passport and immigration office on nearby Lombok. We'd been told the ferry would depart "about" 9 a.m. It took off at 10:30, but hanging out on a beach sipping a coconut wasn't the worst way to wait for a ride. We had vague instructions about how to meet up with a guy who would drive us from the pier to the inland city, and he materialized as though we dreamed him up. We thought we'd already paid for the transport, but he insisted we hadn't...so maybe we got bilked. Dave was irked, while I felt a few dollars was not a big deal for us but may have been for him. After we procured our visas in a government building, the driver took us to see an elegant mosque with a green and gold minaret. It would collapse the next year in a devastating 7.5 earthquake centered two miles away, tragically killing nearly a thousand people and injuring many more.

From the Gilis, we took a speedboat to Amed, a village on the easternmost point of Bali. Disembarking meant stepping from the wobbly craft onto an even wobblier floating dock with no handrails that was being buffeted by waves and undulating like a Slinky. I was thankful for the balance yoga gave me. Such physical challenges reminded me to be glad for traveling before it was too late. We hadn't nailed down what we'd do when we could no longer travel; we figured the answer would unfold over time.

We stayed a week at the Blue Star Bungalows on Jemeluk Beach. From Blue Star's rocky black-sand shore, Dave and I were able to walk right out into the water for world-class snorkeling. Emperor angelfish, lined surgeonfish, and sixbar wrasse flurried about. Blueberry-colored seastars and midnight-velvet giant clams draped over elaborate coral formations. Our skin softened from the water, we ambled into town for dinner. There we shared a meal with a German couple, him a filmmaker, and her the head of an NGO that promotes equality for women in developing nations. They told us about their work and lives, more of the world's cornucopia, and I was reminded how much I treasured such encounters made possible by wandering.

The tropics may be heavenly, but paradise has bugs. When we were checking into the cottage, Dave spotted a cockroach clinging to the inside of the mosquito net. We were worried about trying to catch it because we didn't want it to disappear into the sheets. We alerted the front desk and soon two guys showed up. One, wearing a glove, grabbed it, and it hissed like a cat! I jumped and let out a screaming laugh. Not as funny was a bug bite Dave got on his calf that itched mightily. It became infected, pus-filled, and streaked with red. At a clinic, the physician indicated necrosis, dead tissue that must be scraped and cut away without anesthesia. Dave had to return several times to endure the painful procedure, but we were grateful inexpensive and immediate care was available. Many U.S. citizens move abroad because they can no longer afford health care. Even with insurance, my thyroid medicine in Mexico costs less than my co-pay for the same pharmaceutical in the States. Too many Americans stay in jobs they hate, or delay their retirement, because they rely on the accompanying medical coverage—and of course the numbers who've gone bankrupt when they've fallen ill are staggering. Most people I meet agree the U.S. for-profit medical system is broken.

Iluh, the charismatic owner of Blue Star, told me I could remember her name with the acronym, "I Love You, Honey." And I did—love her, her small hotel, and Amed. Iluh told us tourism hadn't come to Amed until relatively recently. When her husband was growing up there, everyone was poor; no one had electricity and most kids didn't go to school. Things were changing but still, children wandered the beaches when they should be in class, hawking handmade bracelets and other items to tourists. Iluh suggested we buy only from adults and give kids school supplies instead, so at a local store we purchased multicolored pens we handed out.

One girl, around seven years old, approached me as I read on the beach. I'd given her a pen the day before, but she started with her usual pre-sales pitch: "Hi! Where are you from?"

I exaggerated a pout. "Don't you remember?"

She grinned. "Germany?"

"No."

"France?"

"Nope."

"Italy?"

"I'm from a big country that has many states."

She nudged herself onto my chair, her little thigh sticking to mine, and pulled from her bag a small notebook with a rough sketch of the United States. "Here?"

"Yes." I grabbed a pen from my bag and wrote "California" with an arrow to the West Coast. I wrote in other states, and she repeated all I said. Next I drew a kitty and she exclaimed, "Cat!" I taught her how to spell it. We did dog, fish, chicken. I drew a tree. I pointed to each animal and said, "animal, animal, animal" and when I got to the tree, I asked, "Is this an animal?"

When she said yes, I pointed at each animal again and when I got to *tree* I asked, "Animal?"

She fell quiet and then, catching my eye, said, "Flower." Pressing hard on the paper, she drew a flower next to the tree. She pointed at the animals, saying "animal" each time, only to pause when she got to the flower and tree.

"Plants," I said.

I could tell the moment she got it. Gleefully, she went back through: "Animal, animal, animal...plant, plant."

We spent more time together in an impromptu English lesson, writing words accompanied by pictures, her tiny hand on my forearm—one of my favorite moments in thirty years of teaching.

When we decided to travel to Indonesia, Dave said we must see orangutans. One of the last places in the wild that orangutans live is Borneo, the third largest island in the world. Borneo is divided into four regions: Kalimantan (part of Indonesia), Sabah and Sarawak (Malaysia), and Brunei (an independent sultanate).

We flew from Bali to Kalimantan by way of Jakarta, where we met up with Paul and Fran, who'd taught with me in China and were on summer break. Paul, the tall musician from Liverpool, brought along his ukulele. Only in his thirties, he'd lived many lives, having been a professional cricket player in Australia and half a popular musical duo in the UK before deciding to teach in Asia. Fran, who hailed from Nashville, was an animated sprite in her fifties always up for an adventure.

We were taken to a dock to board a klotok, a traditional river boat that would be our home for the next three days. For hours we drifted down the Sekonyer River, the steamy jungle floating by, our faces fanned by the motion-produced breeze. At times the captain slowed for us to observe the proboscis monkeys in the trees with their Jimmy Durante noses. There wasn't much human population, but we saw a few homes on stilts whose inhabitants fished for a living. It amazed me that the cook whipped up meals of rice and noodle dishes, shredded salads, fruit, and a carnival of lime and chili sauces while crouched in the cramped, low-ceilinged kitchen below deck.

The first night, we slept on the boat shrouded in mosquito nets. What I'd imagined would be a romantic night cocooned in jungle sounds turned out to be virtually sleepless. The bedding was scrawny, and the clammy air stifling. And in spite of the net, I found myself scratching at bug bites. I was thrilled to learn the next night we'd be sleeping in a hotel with the promise of A/C and warm showers. Turned out there was no hot water and the air conditioner didn't work, but a fan kept the air tolerably circulating, and the comfortable bed dropped me into dreamland.

When we reached a forest trail the next day, we trudged past a sign that proclaimed:

Please DO NOT:
- Feed the orangutans
- Eat in front of the orangutans
- Touch the orangutans
- Warning: Do Not Swim in the River There Are Lots of Crocodiles

In spite of this caution, I'd seen the young male Indonesian guides bathing that morning in the river.

Soon, we came across a furry red orangutan gripping a tree trunk above our heads. According to our guide, she was a seven-year-old female, recently independent from her mother. She eyed us soulfully, and I wished I could scoop her up and give her some motherly love.

The trek next took us to orangutan feeding stations, where the wild creatures were fed twice daily due to their dwindling habitat, and to bolster the tourist economy. At the stations, the workers dumped out passels of small bananas. Soon, orangutans came swinging from the trees and dropped down to the platforms. The big ones ate what must have been close to a hundred bananas in steady succession. The mothers smashed fruit in their mouths and then pulled out wads to feed the babies. Afterward, a worker swept the peels off the platform for a patiently waiting warthog to dine on.

Our last day, we waited and waited after the banana distribution, wondering if the orangutans would ever show up. Eventually, high in the trees: movement. Dozens of red-furred humanesque creatures scurried across the treetops, squeaking, hooting, and barking, more than we'd seen in one place. Four bulky females dropped to the platforms, plunging in death-defying drops from limb to limb while tangles of children played high in the trees. It was a play-date for the kids while the moms went "shopping"—a community of creatures who compellingly seemed like ancient ancestors.

When the boat dropped us off, we waited for a vehicle to take us to the airport for transfer to Flores. A compact car pulled up, too small for more than two passengers. Our guide said another would come soon, but I felt my blood heat up as I transformed into the She-Hulk Ugly American, demanding to know why the proper vehicle hadn't been sent and what would happen if we missed our flight? As Fran and Paul ducked into the car, no doubt relieved to escape my rant, I flushed with shame. The next transport came within minutes, and as Dave and I were taken to the airport, I bemoaned my behavior, wondering why I had lost my shit after having such an amazing experience on the boat. "Don't be hard on yourself, it happens to everyone one time or another," Dave graciously said. But I continued to cringe at what the Indonesian guide must have seen, a spoiled Western woman upset at not getting her way. I wanted to go back and apologize profusely, to fix everything, but that was impossible.

Dave had turned me on to the allure of the wild animal encounter. In our travels we'd come across not only orangutans but sea turtles, kangaroos, platypuses, an echidna, mongooses, water buffalo, jackals, baby skunks, monkeys, wild horses, elephants, peacocks, monitor lizards, macaques, crocodiles—and, in Sri Lanka, a leopard. Now, our next wild animal experience took us to southern Indonesia at Komodo National Park on Rinca (pronounced Rin-cha) island. The little I learned about Komodo dragons in advance included that they can grow up to nine feet long, they appear sluggish but can move quickly, and their prey don't die from their vicious bites but from the Komodo gift of deadly bacteria. On our way there, Paul had asked the driver if he'd heard of Komodos attacking people, and he regaled us with a terrifying story about a ranger who'd neglected to shut the office door and was killed by a Komodo that had slunk in. Nerves trembled in my gut at the sight of our guide carrying not a gun or a machete...but a pronged stick. I was skeptical that a nudge could keep such monsters at bay.

Our first glimpse of these dragony reptiles occurred at the ranger station, where they casually hung out on the grounds, with baggy, scaly chain-mail skin, dagger claws, yellow eyes, and darting, forked tongues. When we passed the station and walked along a forested path, I recalled the taxi driver's story, and my skin slithered. I don't appreciate horror movies, but at that moment I understood terror laced with thrill has its pleasures.

Our guide pointed out a mound of dirt, a Komodo egg nest. As he spoke, specks of dirt flew from the nest and a female lifted her dinosaur head over the edge. My heart skidded when she opened her mouth to reveal a cavernous pink hole and hissed...a moment Dave caught on camera. He also snapped a shot of a swarm of thousands of bees writhing on a tree limb we'd walked right past. Komodo National Park ain't no Disneyland.

We spent another few days with Paul and Fran in nearby Flores, and then together headed to Bali where we were joined by Daria, a Russian foreign student we'd befriended in Nanning. With her angelic singing voice, Daria harmonized with Paul as he played the ukulele in the communal outdoor area of our guest house and on an open-mic stage in Kuta where they were the show-stopping performance. As we had at the Ukulele Café in Nanning, Fran and I jumped up to dance.

In the beach area of Uluwatu and the fishing village of Jimabarin, we experienced local music and bodies telling stories in dance performances, the dancers clothed in elaborate traditional garments and swaying like waves, moving their arms and eyes and heads in ways I didn't know the human body was capable of. Dave and I said goodbye to our friends, promising we'd meet some other time in some other place in the world—and when we landed in Ubud, we happened upon an outdoor Jazz Festival, a wonderful welcome for us music lovers.

Ubud was made popular—some say ruined—by Elizabeth Gilbert's *Eat, Pray, Love*. Yes, this town of 30,000 residents features touristy restaurants and shops, and traffic clogs the main thoroughfares, but it's colorful and lively and imbued with Balinese culture. Besides, I had nothing to compare it to since this was my first time there. Although I'm not immune to nostalgia,

I tend to feel it's wasted energy to exalt an idealized past rather than living what's right in front of me.

As I walked the streets, incense and flowers perfuming the air, I passed ancient temples wedged between stores. Dogs sniffed at offerings placed three times a day on the dirt roads—bits of food to please the gods and to provide good karma. Kites and birds bedecked the sky, and ribbons of rice fields glowed green and gold. Daily I passed statues of gods and goddesses swathed in moss that was somehow incandescent. I hiked up the steep stone stairs to a yoga studio overlooking the humid rainforest canopy, sweat drenching my shirt. After class, Dave would come pick me up on a motorbike and we'd cruise the streets, eyeing all the color and clamor, then stop for lunch before going back to the small family-run hotel for a dip in the pool and an afternoon nap.

Although shopping isn't my jam, some days I enjoyed browsing through the goods sold in booths and boutiques. One way to keep our costs low was by not buying stuff we didn't need. Our living space—be it the casita, the car, or suitcases—couldn't hold much. Currently we were living out of backpacks, so if I did buy a new piece of clothing, it was only to replace something stained or torn. My main struggle was shoes: I liked cute flip-flops with sparkly doodads, and even though my chunky, pragmatic Keens sandals could suit all purposes, I jammed a pair of superfluous footwear into my luggage. Although I never cared much for shopping and collecting things, at times I wished we could accumulate more art. Overall, though, Dave and I lived light, spending most of our money on experiences, not things. My mindset about accumulation is reflected in Dan Brook's words: "The more things we have, the more things we have to organize, guard, and defend. Physically, cognitively, emotionally. In this sense, property becomes a sort of prison, as what we own, also owns us."

In Ubud, I encountered interesting women everywhere: in yoga classes, in a goddess workshop, in cafes. We talked: Not *what do you do?* But *who are you, what matters to you, what is your life?* I met Marilyn, a woman in her seventies who came from the States many years ago and started a business with a Balinese family, and they now lived all together. I befriended Deanne from Australia, a musician who traveled alone for a personal retreat. Her stories reflected a happy albeit unconventional marriage to another musician. She and her husband performed together but lived in separate houses in Sydney, and she regularly traveled alone to Bali, her favorite place. Each day I greeted Coco Wayan, an ancient yet youthful Balinese woman selling goods from a cart. I bought coconuts from her, and she'd tease me about heading to yoga again, her grin stretching across her whole face. I asked myself how we happened to collide here on the planet at this exact place and time. Every moment in Ubud felt slightly enchanted. And then, surreally, I stumbled across a square of cement in the road, artfully embedded with these words: "Be where you are, don't miss a thing, Kate."

After two months in Indonesia we headed to Koh Phangan, the island Mark had claimed as his home earlier in the year. We were rendezvousing with Mark again because he'd enrolled in a writing workshop I'd be teaching at the Sanctuary, the upscale, bohemian resort we'd trudged through on our way to Eden, the open-air club where we'd danced all night.

I'd always dreamed of teaching at an exotic writing retreat, but for some reason my wish wasn't coming true by sitting around waiting for someone to offer me free round-trip tickets to lead a workshop in Bora Bora. Then I'd met Brian, Mark's "Cosmic Concierge." A writer, Renaissance man, and New Yorker, Brian had been living on the island for several years. He was the kind of guy who did crazy shit like travelling to Afghanistan, Iraq, and Nicaragua without a predetermined itinerary or lodging, serendipitously finding places to stay and people to interview regarding how they felt about the U.S.'s military interventions in their countries. Such brazen acts led to his book, *WAR: The Afterparty*. Turned out he, too, had thoughts of running writing retreats—and after a few chats over meals, we'd set the wheels in motion, planning via Skype between China and Thailand.

We wanted the experience to be empowering, even transformational. Toni Morrison's words were our guide: "If there's a book that you want to read but it hasn't been written yet, then you must write it." We also wanted novice and experienced writers to be welcome. Fortunately, working with diverse groups was my wheelhouse. I feared dealing with the logistics and minutiae to get such an event off the ground. But Brian and Dave (our helpful consultant) took care of most of that, leaving me to my strength: developing curriculum.

After months of planning and prepping, there we were, writers together, having journeyed on airplanes, trains, taxis, and boats to converge in this rarefied corner of the world. My longtime friend and super-supporter Nancy came in from L.A. with a couple of her friends. Others arrived from the States and Australia, and a few from the island. It was a different season than the last time we'd been there: hotter, muggier, more mosquitoes. I worried the magical bubble had been burst when everyone who'd reserved the unique treehouse-style rooms switched to the less elegant ones for the A/C. To get to our gathering place, we had to traipse up a steep terraced hillside laced with stairs in the clammy air, and people arrived wild-eyed, wet clothes clinging to their bodies. But soon we fell under the spell of writing and sharing our stories—and as happens at the best retreats, summer camps, and sometimes sitting next to a stranger on a five-hour flight, we quickly bonded as intimates, gut-laughing and spilling tears. Afternoons we swam in the warm bay, ate from the Sanctuary's bounteous menu, had spa treatments, napped in hammocks. The last evening one participant, Romi—an Australian writer and therapist who lived on the island—led us through a labyrinth constructed with stones, a meditative experience and a chance to reflect on what the week had meant to us.

Again I was reminded how teaching—even in such privileged and exquisite circumstances—consumes me in both senses of the term: it's fascinating, and it eats me up. Dave and I knew I'd be exhausted when the workshop was over, and so we'd planned to spend our final two weeks in Asia alone in Phuket, the country's largest island in the Andaman Sea. When we weren't sweating in the sauna followed by the cold plunge, or playing ping-pong in the hotel's basement, we devoted our days to exploring the island by motorbike.

I'd spent my adult life echoing my mother's sentiments about motorcycles: so dangerous you need a suit of armor to ride one. Her first job as a nurse had been in the ER, and she pointedly told stories about the meat-grinding horror of motorcycle accident victims. Dave, on the other hand, grew up flying around on motorcycles and dirt bikes like many boys in rural Northern California. Ever since we met, I told him I'd never get on one and I preferred he not, either. What changed my mind? Thailand and Indonesia. I went from, *no fucking way* to *alright, I'll try it*. Soon I was finding excuses for us to hop on and drive around, my arms encircling Dave's body as he steered us here and there. My job was to settle into the sweet spot between alert and relaxed—a baby monkey, clinging yet surrendering.

One night after dinner of a whole fresh fish and cashew rice, Dave mounted the motorbike and I slipped on behind him. My head encased in a pink helmet, I thought *astronaut*. Instead of steering us to our hotel, Dave spontaneously turned up a hill for a night jaunt, going nowhere for no reason. He sped in the dark, climbing up and up, the ocean an indigo satin sheet rippling below, lights from the city dotting the skyline like stars. I held on, my heart pressed into his back. My skin was sun-tight from a day at the beach. The night air was thick with humidity, deepening the sensation of being in another atmosphere, encased in an intimate pod.

The day arrived that it was time to leave Thailand; we'd spent nearly a year and a half in Asia, and this departure felt seminal. I left a splinter from my heart there, assuring myself I'd return some day.

Twenty-four hours of traveling and we touched down in the States in Hawai'i, soon arriving at the Lanakai waterfront home of our friend Candis. I dropped my bag and hugged her petite frame, my fatigue so profound I felt I could melt into the floor. Instead, she drew us out to her backyard facing an expanse of aquamarine bay.

"Let's get in!" She enthusiastically lifted her shirt over her head.

I looked over to Dave. Smiling we began to disrobe and all three of us plunged into the Pacific's warm waters in our most natural state.

Chapter Sixteen

Litmus Test

Fall-Winter 2017

As Tom Petty sings, everything changed then changed again. Upon returning to California we were planning to head back to Mexico but then a message popped into my email from Suzanne, who invited us once again to housesit in Tahoe during ski season to take care of Ely, the Best Bad Dog in the World. Although I'd not imagined we'd replicate a gig—I craved novelty—after so long in tropical climates, I thought longingly of inhaling fresh cool air, snowshoeing along trails, and whizzing down mountains. As improvisational travelers, jumping on opportunities when they crossed our path had become our forte. We said yes.

We had a month to fill beforehand, though, so we retrieved our car from Chambliss's house and drove to the Pacific Northwest for two housesitting gigs. Our first stop was Seaview, a seaside town in Southwest Washington on the Long Beach Peninsula, embraced by the Pacific Ocean on the west and Willapa Bay to the east. I had been to Long Beach with my family once before, in 1972 when I was ten years old, where we dug for clams. I remembered the icy sand's gritty feeling and the wildness of the vast beach.

The housesit took place in a Victorian gray-and-white jewel box with gables, peaked roof, and white picket fence. It was stuffed with antiques, and the upstairs bedrooms had the cozy, low sloping roofs of a refurbished attic. The owners, Bill and Sherrie, were a doctor and nurse probably a decade older than us; they were headed to Nigeria on a medical mission. I was astonished to learn they'd traveled to more than 90 countries.

Our animal roommates for two weeks were Freckles, a curly black-and-white cocker spaniel rescued from a puppy mill, and an orange Scottish Fold cat named Robbie, who resembled a loaf of bread with ears bent like envelope flaps. Most days we bundled up and walked Freckles through the neighborhood of eclectic beach homes and paths lined with fragrant pines, cottonwood, and ash. In ten minutes of ambling we reached the Pacific Ocean crashing on a beach so wide and long, its blue-gray melted into the horizon.

We brought Freckles on our hikes through old-growth forest dripping with ferns at Cape Disappointment State Park, so named by Spanish explorers who failed to get to the Columbia River, foiled by a massive sandbar at one of the most treacherous channels in the world. Dave's research also led us to Willapa National Wildlife Refuge, a conglomeration of salt marsh, mud flats, grasslands, and coastal dunes home to more than 200 bird species. As we traversed the wetlands, the bay spread before us and thousands of birds confettied the sky.

The contrast between this place and urban, humid Nanning couldn't have been more pronounced. Difference itself fueled my desire to wander; I liked seeing life through fresh eyes. Change made me feel alive and more in tune with the moment, with whatever was in front of me. Perhaps if I were a real Buddhist, not a wannabe who dabbled in New Age thought, I could realize heightened consciousness through meditation alone. But apparently I pursued spiritual insight through travel since immobility wasn't my way.

In Seaview, we were thrilled with the food. A few blocks from the house we came across a small cannery where we bought a case of smoked tuna, infused with pepper and lemon. Nearby we discovered a luscious bakery that served non-disappointment cakes—and further down the road a restaurant with mouth-watering fish and chips, tuna melts, and craft beer on tap, delicacies I'd been dreaming of. I didn't need to eat another rice or noodle dish anytime soon.

We huddled in the house with the fire roaring in the wood-burning stove, playing cards or reading, the cat curled at my feet. I needed to regroup after the wild time we'd had in Hawai'i at Candis's. Petite and in her fifties, she had more energy than most people I knew and had thrown an all-night rager our first night there. Dave and I had fallen into bed in the wee hours, only to wake up to the group twirling on the lawn welcoming the sunrise. The next night we'd jammed with other friends who brought over mandolins, ukuleles, and guitars. Earlier that day Candis had taken us to her friend's uke shop, and I'd bought a caramel-hued beauty made of cedar and mahogany. Later she showed us her newly developing farm in a valley surrounded by chartreuse mountains, where she was growing fruits and vegetables and turmeric for making tinctures, and also raising chickens for eggs.

In the past, I'd seen her smiling and chatting and dancing for days on end at music festivals, appearing every few hours in a different glittery getup, and her vitality awed me. The first time I'd met her she was wearing a sparkly outfit over a back brace with a halo since she'd broken her back skiing—but nevertheless she'd shown up to the concert. I loved our time together, but on the heels of an international flight, part of me had wanted to rest in bed. Why hadn't I? An age-inappropriate mix of FOMO and not wanting to be rude to the hostess, who probably wouldn't have cared if I'd napped. Predictably I'd worn down my immune system and gotten sick. A few days of rest at Chambliss's back on the mainland had helped, and then snuggling under a quilt in the warm Victorian and spending tranquil hours in nature soothed me to the bone.

By the time a visitor descended on us in Seaview, I was ready: My friend Anne came to visit. I hadn't seen her in nine years, but when she walked through the door, the gap in time melted away. We'd met in our MFA program in Creative Writing; she was not only an accomplished poet but a visual artist who painted, drew, and sculpted. We enjoyed our time together in a low-key way, taking beach strolls, talking about life and writing, and wandering through nearby Sou'wester Historic Lodge & Vintage Travel Trailer Resort, a pine-fringed hodgepodge of classic RVs, suites, rustic cabins, and camping spots where, coincidentally, Anne had once been artist-in-residence. When I'd asked Bill and Sherrie if it would be okay to invite a friend to come stay for a few days—making sure they knew we completely understood if they said no—they'd responded enthusiastically. We've learned most hosts are open to guests because they want people to enjoy the place they call home. And besides, if they trust us with their house and pets, they trust us not to throw wild parties.

One afternoon, after Anne had left, a neighbor alerted us to white smoke gushing out of the chimney. A volunteer firefighter, he recognized a chimney fire when he saw one. Sure enough, the wall that funneled the smoke from the living room up to the roof was scorching to the touch. The neighbor recommended we monitor it for a few hours to see if the blaze would self-extinguish, which we did anxiously, the fire department on speed dial. Fortunately, the fire died out, and we didn't burn down a house we'd been entrusted to care for. I worried that we'd done something wrong, but by email Bill had been apologetic, saying that particular chimney design was susceptible to such problems, and he should have warned us. Now we had another item to add to the list of questions for homeowners.

Our last morning there, gusts shrieked at the windows as a storm with a severe wind advisory descended on Washington. Counter to our desire to burrow under the covers, Dave and I tumbled from bed to feed the dog, pack up, and clean the house before Bill and Sherry returned. Our next gig, in Seattle, wouldn't start for a few days. We had planned to drive up the Olympic Peninsula, exploring beaches, trails, towns—but no way, not with this storm. We decided to hunker down for a few days, probably at a hotel or BnB in nearby Astoria.

I stuffed the sheets in the washing machine and scoured the kitchen while Dave vacuumed. I knew from our email exchanges Bill and Sherry had worked long days in Africa in 100-plus degree heat and would appreciate a comfortable return. While Dave packed the car, I took Freckles for a last walk to the beach, savoring each moment with this sweet little being. Although wind whipped my hair into my face, the sky was a sheet of blue. Rain wouldn't roll in for an hour or two, but the storm made itself known with mountainous waves smashing onto the sand. I thought about how we hadn't yet figured out where we'd be spending the night, and our Subaru had developed a leak in the back—not a major problem unless you're driving through a downpour with your trunk packed.

When Bill and Sherry walked through the door, Freckles wiggled her whole body with joy, which relieved me of the shred of remorse I felt when saying goodbye to a dog I adored. They asked where we were headed next, and we explained how the storm had put a kink in our plans.

"Why don't you stay here a few more days?" they said.

As it turned out, they had come only to pick up the animals and head back to their main residence, a few hours north. It took a moment for reality to sink in that this was their *beach house*. Even though I preferred light consumption, I marveled at how having more than one residence proffered power and flexibility. And in their case, generosity. Dave and I shared a glance. He held the car key in his hand, a reminder that our packed Subaru sat snug in the dry garage.

"Really?"

"Sure. We won't be back here for a while."

We pulled our stuff out of the car then took a run to the grocery store. That was a first, a reversal of our leave-taking. In those few days, I kept expecting to see Robbie curled on the couch or Freckles nosing her leash hanging near the door, ready for a walk. The storm lashed the house and after it eventually blew through, we hit the road beneath a crystalline sky. On our three-hour drive to Seattle, we stopped at a mechanic shop. In the time it took us to go to lunch, he fixed the leak.

Matt and Trevor, our Seattle hosts, were heading off for a safari in Tanzania. Their home in an upscale Seattle neighborhood had an *Architectural Digest* air, with its sleek high-end furniture, distant mountain views out colossal windows, and a walk-in shower for a party of ten. The guys' packed luggage stood at the ready in the entryway. They took half an hour to show us around, meet the two golden retrievers named Dakota and Charlie, and Kitty the cat—and then took off. Waiting for us in the kitchen were two bottles of Washington state wine, a box of locally made chocolates, and a gift certificate for their favorite restaurant, which we decided to use on my birthday the following week. Their gifts reminded me how much homeowners appreciated us, how housesitting wasn't a one-way street.

Charlie was the younger dog, and when we tried to walk him, he pulled like a reindeer on a sled. I soon learned throwing the ball for him in the back yard for an hour before the walk made him more manageable on leash. Climbing the Seattle hills tightened up our glutes; this was not dog care for the lazy. But in spite of the dogs' size and energy, Kitty was the queen of the domain. I had to laugh when I saw her taking her time at the water bowl, both dogs panting behind her waiting their turn.

During this time, I was working on revising and re-releasing my second novel, *Complementary Colors*—based on the story of how I'd met my ex-wife, the first woman I ever loved. When the novel had been released, she and I were going through a divorce after fifteen years together. I sat like an earthquake survivor in the ruins, the book in my grip fictionally portraying my now destroyed relationship as an exquisite encounter between soulmates.

Back then I could not imagine promoting a book of lies. Even though it was fiction, it was so close to the bone my skeleton ached when I glanced at the cover. How could I stand in front of people—quivering, manic mess that I was—and read a love scene based on the woman who broke my heart? When my first novel had been released, I had done radio programs, print interviews, readings—resulting in sales, reviews, and best of all, emails from readers who connected with the story. I didn't have the heart to do publicity for *Complementary Colors*, and while it found its way into a few readers' hands, it mostly limped off into oblivion. A few years later, the press that had published it folded, and the book went out of print. When I was teaching in China, my colleague Paul ordered my books and read them all. He loved *Complementary Colors* and encouraged me to re-release it.

At first I balked. But ruminating on Paul's words, I became curious. I borrowed his copy and devoured it in a day, rediscovering that it was the kind of book I like: a story of a transformative time in a woman's life, featuring art and poetry and sex and love. I didn't feel anymore that the book was a lie. It was *emotionally true*—and emotional truth is timeless, not dependent on "the way things turned out."

Jan of Coyote Creek Books, who'd put out two of my other books, took on the project and developed a new cover featuring art by my friend Nancy. I wanted to check in with Dave, to ask how he felt about my spending time and effort bringing this book about my relationship with someone else back into the world. He never said I should put the story behind me. Instead, he said that without my life experiences, I would not be who I am now—the woman journeying through life and the world with him.

We were lucky to have found each other in the second chapter of our lives. When we'd first met, we were working grueling hours—him in an office, me on campus—and had no idea three years later we'd transform into a nomadic couple. I hoped Julia Child's words about her husband Paul in her wonderful memoir, *My Life in France*, applied to us: "Travel, we agreed, was a litmus test: if we could make the best of the chaos and serendipity that we'd inevitably meet in transit, then we'd surely be able to sail through the rest of life together just fine."

Chapter Seventeen

"End of Paved Road"

Winter-Spring 2018

After Seattle then Tahoe, we exchanged snowy mountains for the desert. In Palm Springs we cared for two cute poodle mixes named Gracie and Oliver, as well as a school of koi in the backyard pond next to the swimming pool. Tending to the fish required more than sprinkling food on the water's surface. One morning the dogs were yapping at the sliding glass door, and Dave ran outside just in time to shoo away a great blue heron at the pond's edge who'd been angling for a snack. We also had to keep our eyes peeled for prowling coyotes as we walked the dogs, even on the suburban streets. Because neighbors had lost their dogs to coyote attacks, Gracie and Oliver were not allowed in the yard unsupervised.

Another task involved placing poems in a glass-doored box on the sidewalk: a fresh poem a day, written by Joe, one of the hosts. I'd loved this idea when I'd read about it in the listing—and perhaps we got the gig because in my application I'd pointed out I was a poet, too. I'd also mentioned the Bisexual Book Award since they highlighted they were a gay couple, and I'd wanted to signal not only were we LGBTQ+ friendly but part of the community. I'd made personal connections in other applications; for instance, when in one I read the dog needed thyroid medication daily, I wrote, "I need mine every morning too, so we will be thyroid buddies." A different gig mentioned Mazy, their dog, and I commented that I'd once had a pooch with the same name. I enjoyed featuring these connections to make our applications stand out.

The Palm Springs house included a casita out back, so happily we were able to host our friend Cathy, my former colleague who is also a writer and an intrepid traveler. To research her most recent book, *Champion of Choice: The Life and Legacy of Women's Advocate Nafis Sadik*, Cathy had traveled alone around the world to developing countries. She gathered stories of struggle and survival to help readers understand the impact Nafis Sadik made in her U.N. role to improve women's lives—and to illustrate why such efforts must continue. I deeply admired Cathy's work, both as a writer and a professor who contributed more than her fair share to bolster the students and the department of English. Also, Cathy knew how to have fun! She was a great hostess, be the party at her home or following a campus literary event.

On Christmas Eve, the three of us went out to dinner at Bernie's Lounge and Supper Club. With its deep red walls and black-and-white booths, it had the feel of a place the Rat Pack would hang out. And indeed, Frank Sinatra and his entourage had made Palm Springs their playground for decades. It was like being transported back to the 1950s when the next day we entered the Casablanca Lounge, adjacent to Melvyn's Restaurant which was owned by Mel Haber until his death in 2016. Photos adorned the walls of Mel standing next to Bob Hope, Marlon Brando, Lucille Ball, Jerry Lewis, and Liza Minnelli, as well as presidents and sports figures. While we sipped our drinks, the player at the grand piano belted out "Fly Me to the Moon."

During the days, we shared from our writing, made meals, and explored the downtown boutiques, the streets lined by towering palms, and the glamorous Walk of Stars, honoring hundreds of celebrities such as Liberace, Dinah Shore, and Elizabeth Taylor. I'd thought of Palm Springs in these terms, a place to shop, dip into a pool, and rub elbows with the memories of Ava Gardner and Sammie Davis, Jr. However, once again my husband did his research and discovered numerous places to spend time in nature—winter being the best time of year to avoid baking in the desert heat.

One early morning Dave and I hiked Tahquitz Canyon Trail on a section of the Agua Caliente Indian Reservation's nature preserve. As sun seeped from the edges of the San Jacinto Mountains, the buttery light illuminated a herd of big horn sheep defying gravity as they clung to the slopes, their antlers curling like fat horns-of-plenty. On New Year's Day, we ascended 8,000 feet in an aerial tram, being lifted from the warm desert floor up through four different temperate zones equivalent to traveling from Africa to Alaska. At the cold summit we pulled on our jackets and took a loop hike and then paused to rest on boulders, gazing out at the view of Chino Canyon while sipping hot tea from our thermoses. I'd read on a clear day you could see all the way to Mexico from this spot. I didn't know what country I was looking at. Besides, borders didn't mean anything here, where beyond the granite cliffs blue-tinged mountains tiered the horizon. I leaned my head on Dave's shoulder, feeling his warmth against my cheek, and thought about how the new year promises a clean slate. I had no resolution in mind, except to bring myself back to the present moment again and again.

Upon leaving Palm Springs, we drove to L.A. and left our car at Nancy's to fly to New Orleans for the 40th anniversary performances of The Radiators, Dave's favorite band. After a whirlwind trip that involved dancing until two a.m. three nights in a row, followed by raucous brunches and dinners with friends, we returned to L.A., ragged around the edges yet set to drive to our casita. Again, though, our plans took a U-turn when Nancy connected us with her friends Janice and Jim who needed caretakers for their forty-one acres in Northern California for two-and-a-half months. In the six months since we'd left China, we'd not stayed in one place longer than three weeks, so an extended period in a quiet place surrounded by nature sounded luxurious. We imagined settling into a different rhythm, one that didn't involve so much packing and moving about. Of course we could have done the same thing in Mexico, but we wanted to help out Nancy's friends; and since it was high season at Cerritos Beach, we'd bolster our income renting out the casita. I thought the secluded Northern California house would be a good place to write; I wanted to start a book about our wayfaring life, about living in other people's houses, about what home means. So instead of driving toward the border, we headed north.

Around then, I received a message from Daisy, whom I'd met in the MFA program. I had officiated her wedding to Tung a few years before, a ceremony she'd designed in spite of the demands of their embattled families, his Catholic and hers Buddhist. She'd asked me—someone not affiliated with religion or either family—to preside, and she'd centered the service around poetry rather than religious texts, her way of rebuffing family pressure and creating a meaningful event. Since then they'd had a darling boy, Luc. Although she'd struggled with fertility, eventually she was able to announce she was pregnant again, this time with a girl. Tragically, though, during a routine ultrasound, they discovered that the baby had died in utero. Daisy had to be induced to give birth to the daughter they'd named Thi Aracelli—Vietnamese for "Poem of the Altar of the Sky." I couldn't begin to imagine the sorrow they'd suffered. Daisy told me a story that tore me up: while in labor, she had felt her daughter's presence as a toddler. She saw them in a golden field together, dandelion fluff floating around, and Thi had picked a fistful of wildflowers and given them to Daisy, calling her "Mama."

Although some were telling Daisy to forget the tragedy and try as soon as possible to get pregnant again, she wanted to have a funeral—and she was asking if I'd officiate. Our decision to return to Northern California had been divine timing, in that we'd be able to offer them our support. At the memorial service, Daisy read a wrenching letter she'd written to her daughter. Thi Aracelli came alive in the room through her mother's words— and then Daisy, and we, had to let her go. When she said, "My baby girl has gone where I can't follow," every heart in the room must have cracked. As painful as it was, I was grateful to be there, witnessing Daisy's vulnerability and strength.

Janice and Jim's house felt like an elegant cabin with its hardwood floors, polished stone fireplace, Japanese paper lamps, and Craftsman-style furniture. It sat on forty-one acres in Northern California, east of the college town of Chico, amidst manzanita, pines, and oaks. The air smelled of dirt and pine needles, the nostalgic scents of my childhood. At dusk, frogs in the pond bellowed in chorus with the crickets. Behind the pond sat an old silver Airstream, and next to that a "She Shed" cottage with sliding pine doors, bookshelves stuffed with fashion magazines, and a stained-glass window that filtered in pink and green light. The house had only one bedroom, so we'd sleep in the cottage for two nights until they left. I already knew I'd make it my writing studio.

As serene as this place was, though, when we'd first arrived I felt my gut clench. We had driven down a long road that eventually passed through the town of Forest Ranch (one restaurant, one store, and a post office) and turned off onto another road which narrowed, then narrowed some more, as it curved around the mountains, a canyon drop-off disconcertingly close. We had to stop to let another car edge past. At the "End of Paved Road" sign, gravel spurted beneath our tires. Another mile or two and a few turns later, we reached the house, and I wondered how we'd ever find it again. How hard would it be to get to the store, a restaurant, a doctor? A feeling of being trapped tensed my body, but at least we weren't there during fire season.

When we arrived, Janice and Jim were in the throes of preparing to leave in two days, the house piled with belongings, and the kitchen counters sprinkled with coffee grounds from the espressos they made every few hours in a fancy silver contraption. I wondered if it was caffeine that kept them both so svelte. Ironically, they were headed down to Baja, to their house in Loreto, about six hours north of our casita. They planned to take two of their three dogs; the older laid-back golden retriever, Gracie (same name as the tiny dog in Palm Springs!), didn't travel well and would stay with us. The hilariously-named Poopy, a Chihuahua, slept on the bed with them, and Spirit a one-year-old, long-legged Belgium Shepard puppy was so strong of mind and body, he insinuated himself into all situations, pushing himself in front of us, stepping on our feet, and chewing whatever he could get his mouth on. Jim and Janice joked they could leave him with us since Dave was Dr. Doolittle, and we joshed back that we hadn't agreed on puppy duty. They loved Spirit, but they probably would have appreciated a two-month break from him, only to return with him well-trained. I didn't blame them, but we weren't signing on. It would have been like caring for a toddler.

The plan was to spend two days together so they could show us the property's ins and outs. People often don't realize how much is involved in maintaining their lives until we ask questions: gardening schedules, vet and neighbor phone numbers, plumbing and appliance quirks, how to handle the five remote controls needed to watch TV or listen to music. Even a small home has many moving parts, especially if animals are involved. Some homeowners are so organized that the minute we arrive they do a quick orientation, hand us a list of numbers, and take off. Others prefer a more organic style; we hang out and chat, and as they do tasks we shadow them and talk them through, Jim and Janice's approach. There was a lot to learn about their property: what to water and when, where the rakes and shovels were kept, where to dump the food remains in the compost, how to take out the garbage at the end of the road, which trails went where.

While we unpacked our groceries, Dave and I decided we'd cook dinner for everyone. We sat on couches with trays on our laps to baked chicken, salad, and polenta, pushing the puppy back with our knees and telling him unsuccessfully to sit and stay. Jim, a retired criminal defense attorney, told us most of the adjacent properties had pot farms—and that many growers were his former clients. Marijuana had recently been legalized in California, yet appallingly many people remained behind bars for weed busts. The conversation evolved into a laughing discussion of the drugs we'd tried in our lives. After dinner, Jim and I jammed a bit, him on his guitar and me on my uke.

The second night they took us to dinner at an outdoor restaurant in Chico. There was an ease being with them, and they felt like new friends. Yet with all our moving around, and on the heels of the emotions tumbling through me after the funeral, I was tired and felt pushed to the edge, the way I used to feel the last few weeks of a teaching semester, as though I was holding my breath until I could rest and rejuvenate.

After dinner we drove down winding, dark roads, past shadowy, towering trees, to a place inaptly called Helltown, juxtaposed against the neighboring town of Paradise. In these communities, musicians who were passing through played in people's homes, and Jim had scored tickets for the four of us. The house was filled with well-off former hippies, children of the sixties and seventies that welcomed us to the fold.

The music featured a young man and woman who filled the room with rich harmonies. He played some kind of fancy acoustic guitar, and she stomped her foot to the beat, her tympani created on a wooden stage the homeowners had permanently outfitted in their living room. Guitars and mandolins and odd stringed instruments I couldn't identify hung on the walls. The music was spirited and soulful, and in the middle of the first song, I caught Jim's eye, then Janice's, and Dave squeezed my hand. The fatigue I'd been feeling earlier lifted, in the magic of musical intimacy. Dave—who has been to hundreds, if not thousands, of music events in his life—said this occasion would stand out for him as extra special.

The next morning, we hugged goodbye and after they piled into the truck and lumbered off down the dirt road, we entered the now-quiet house. Although part of us wanted to collapse on the couch, we craved diving into the well-tuned ritual of settling into our housesit: finding the best spots for our clothes and toiletries, our computer and phone plug-ins, our books and food. That night, Dave built a fire in the wood-burning stove. With its high beam ceiling and leather sofas and woven rugs, the place resembled a cozy mountain cottage. We snuggled under a blanket, dog at our feet, reading our books (he: Isabel Allende, me: Haruki Murakami), later turning on the TV for *Jeopardy* followed by a basketball game. In less than a day, we'd settled into our temporary home.

Our first morning alone, we walked with the dog down to "Gracie's Pond Trail," designated with a rustic hand-made sign, and she jumped into the water, joyfully dog-paddling. The pond was fed from a nearby spring. What a pleasure to walk a dog unleashed, along quiet trails, without another person in sight. On the way back to the house we inspected the wood-burning sauna Jim had built hidden in the forest, including a cold plunge and a deck with lounge chairs. The temperatures weren't cool enough for a sauna to sound appealing—in fact, the grounds and trees were tinder dry—and, besides, starting it up looked like a lot of work. Dave thought he might get inspired to do it when the temperatures dropped.

Back at the house, I walked to the She Shed, noting lizards rustling in the bushes, gnats swarming my face, and goldfish gleaming in the pond. Far-off birdsong echoed through the still air. As I unrolled my yoga mat on the narrow deck beneath the trees, the fast train we'd been on for months, maybe years, had ground to a halt.

After yoga, I sat on the cottage's couch and propped my laptop on my legs. A lack of internet connection made me feel even more blessedly isolated, and I quickly dropped into the dream of creating, time losing its linearity in a flow of words. My fingers glided across the keyboard, and occasionally flipped through old journals, thoughts drifting by like leaves on a stream. A voice in my head barged in: *How is this ever going to be a book? It's a chaotic jumble.* I bristled then breathed deeply, telling the mean librarian in my mind that I didn't need her right now, that I'd invite my critic in to edit when I was ready. I thought about the books I loved, about the time I'd discovered May Sarton's journals, and all those subsequent memoirs I'd read, stories of dramatic lives and simple lives made rich through the alchemy of language. I settled into the reminder that I was writing what I liked to read—and that I was drawn to books that showed me what people do with their living time, with their cornucopia of moments, days, years.

After a couple of weeks alone—including a sudden temperature drop and a peaceful snowfall we viewed through the house's plate glass windows—we headed into Chico to meet up with Barbara, a longtime friend of my parents. I hadn't seen her in many years, and she looked the same as I remembered, with her bright eyes and white-toothed smile. The loss of my parents swept freshly through me for a brief moment, soon replaced by the comfort of being in the presence of someone who'd known and loved them. There were fewer left every year.

Barbara played the ukulele in a music group and had invited us to join in. The room was filled with people in their fifties through nineties, a group called Tuesday Tunes that led sing-alongs in retirement homes and homeless shelters. Most were playing ukes and guitars, but there were also banjos, a violin, a guy with a harmonica, and a few with bongos. Incredibly, a woman plucked on a harp towering in the corner. Some participants simply sang along. As I played, I felt the power of union through music, akin to a holy experience: church without dogma.

With Jim and Janice's blessing, I informed friends they were welcome—and over the next two months we had five waves of visitors. With our friends, we walked the trails, played music, cooked food, got silly with Cards Against Humanity, and conversed into the night serenaded by frogs and crickets. First came Stacey with Junebug, her energetic brown lab. Jumping from the car, June charged into the pond and mouthed a goldfish, the tail slurping through her lips like a string of spaghetti. We cracked up but after that kept her away from the pond, veering her to the streams and swimming holes on our hikes. Next came Roger and Marilen, followed by Debbie and Tony. And for Easter my former colleagues Kelly and Cathy bounded in with bags of groceries and cooked enough food to feed a small village. The perfume of Kelly's homemade blueberry scones lingered in the house after they'd left—as did the echoes of all we'd shared about our lives.

Our last guest was Mark, who'd come to California from Thailand for medical checkups. He rolled onto the property in his van and hauled out his guitar and amp in preparation for an evening jam. First, though, he told us about his plans to throw a three-day combination 60th-birthday-party-and-Burning-Man event on Koh Phangan, featuring music, art, and performances by Thais and expats. Would we come? We'd been planning in the fall to get housesits in Europe and visit friends in Italy and Switzerland—but how could we pass up celebrating Mark's birthday at what was bound to be one of the coolest events the island had ever seen? Besides, given his heart problems, it was a miracle, as Mark himself said, that he'd made it to sixty. The party would be epic. So, yes, we would come.

When it came time to leave, Dave started up the car while I stroked Gracie's head, thanking her for the companionship and telling her that her owners would be here in a few hours. As we drove down the narrow dirt road for the last time, winding our way past isolated houses shaded by sugar pines and black oaks, I was grateful for our time there and glad to be headed out before fire season. In seven months I'd be hauntingly reminded of those thoughts when seeing reports of the catastrophic Camp Fire. The inferno came within two miles of Jim and Janice's property, destroying the neighboring town of Paradise, killing 85 people, burning 400,000 acres, and incinerating nearly 14,000 homes.

Chapter Eighteen

Into the Mysteries

Spring-Summer 2018

We were hanging out in Chambliss's back yard in San Jose, having arrived the previous day from Forest Ranch. It was a bright spring afternoon, hummingbirds darting at the feeder and the persimmon tree puffed up with waxy leaves. As we chatted about our plans to leave for Mexico in a few days, his neighbor, Jackie, came through the gate. Her golden retriever Sammy bounded in and wiggled up to each of us for a greeting. I rubbed Sammy then threw a tennis ball out to the lawn for him to chase. Over the years, we'd befriended Jackie and her husband Todd, as they stopped by on their dog walks. This time, though, Jackie had come solo, worry etched on her face. She explained they were supposed to leave for a two-week cruise to Greece day after tomorrow, and their dog sitter had fallen ill. She didn't know what to do and was thinking she'd have to cancel their trip.

Dave and I shared a look, and I voiced the understanding that had passed between us.

"Jackie, we can do it."

"What! Really?"

"Yes! We love Sammy, and we can postpone our drive down to Baja."

Jackie came over and hugged us—and I wanted to thank *her* because spending two weeks with Sammy would take the sting off having said goodbye to Gracie. I missed our Forest Ranch golden shadow, the way she sprang along the trails and plopped herself by our feet. The same breed, Gracie and Sammy looked like siblings, so it felt meant to be.

When my last dog, a Pomeranian named Max, had died I considered adopting another. Dave and I were both working long hours and the idea of nomadic life hadn't yet seeped into our consciousness. However, we did want to travel, and he reminded me we'd have more freedom to do so without worrying about pets. He loved animals and at one point had volunteered at the Humane Society to walk dogs awaiting adoption. His experience of spending time with animals without possessing them inspired his advice to me: "You can think about every dog you meet as your dog, as part of the great big pack." His notion was prophetic because now, all these years later, we lived that way, dipping into others' lives, caring for their animals—and then releasing them back to their beloved owners as we moved on.

These animals, this sleeping in others' beds, this cliff-dwelling and cliff-diving, wove the fabric of the anomalous life we were living, one I never could have imagined...except vaguely. I hadn't dreamt about this exact life but had wanted the *feeling* of it: the freedom to improvise, to lift the curtain of convention, to embrace the words of Walt Whitman: "From this hour I ordain myself loosed of all limits and imaginary lines." Our way of living wasn't perfect, but I was beginning to feel it fit me better than anything else I'd tried.

Our change of plans opened up another door: my sister Crystal asked if I'd go with her to Yosemite National Park to spread our parents' ashes—or actually the last third of their remains. Our parents had met in Yosemite in the 1950s when Mom was a nurse in Curry Village and Dad was driving a tour bus during his college summer break—although my sisters and I have different memories on this point, and it's possible he was working as a garbageman. It would have been like him, though, to have several jobs, so perhaps he was doing both. Upon our parents' request, a third of their combined ashes had been buried in their small-town cemetery, and a third dispersed into the San Francisco Bay. The last portion had been stored at Crystal's house for six years.

Crystal, her nineteen-year-old son Evan, and I took the four-hour drive in the early morning. I wondered aloud if we'd have to sprinkle the ashes surreptitiously because I wasn't sure distributing cremated remains in a National Park was legal, but Crystal assured me she had applied for the permit and carried it in her purse. That was very much like her, a woman who took care of things. Approaching the gate, we discovered it was National Parks Day, which meant free entry. We laughed at how our frugal father would have delighted in this.

Soon we were hiking across the valley floor with the crowds who apparently had gotten the memo about the day's complimentary admission. Granite cliffs dwarfed us humans. Seeing my parents' grandson carrying their ashes on his back in a pack sent me into tender and raw ruminations about the cycle of life.

We climbed up a steep trail, leaving behind the masses, until we found a mineral-scented clear tributary of the Merced River. At the edge of the rushing water, we stopped, took in the scope of it all, then released the last of our parents' bodies into the mysteries.

When Jackie and Todd returned, Todd—who is a professional chef—prepared a batch of paella on his barbecue. With several neighbors, we feasted in celebration of Todd's and Dave's birthdays, which were a day apart, and we toasted to Dave's entering a new decade at age sixty. The next day, we loaded up our Subaru, which would carry us the length of California and beyond.

The minute we hit Baja Sur, I rolled down the window and breathed in the familiar mix of salt air and dust that whispered, *welcome home*. What this meant for me as a nomad, I wasn't sure, but I tried to grasp the sensation, only to come up with an oxymoron: a sense of foreign familiarity. Perhaps choosing to reside in a country you didn't grow up in means that place will always be home/not-home.

At Casita Once, Dave launched into house and garden projects, while I wrote, edited books, and taught yoga by the pool twice a week. We reveled in the fresh produce available: small creamy bananas, sweet onions, avocadoes, limes, and strawberries. We picked papayas from the orchard behind our house. We played backgammon and cards with friends and ate communal meals. On Mondays I jammed with the Todos Santos Ukulele Club.

From a neighbor, we bought a yellow Can Am four-wheel-drive quad we named Mantequilla (Spanish for butter), Manny for short. Dave steered over the bumpy dirt roads with me perched on the rear passenger seat. The sounds of nails pounding and saws buzzing came from all directions with home construction sites popping up where there had once been only cacti strewn across barren land. New restaurants and stores were appearing as well, and our resort was expanding, a new phase of units being built. But mostly El Pescadero remained rustic and rural, with its rattlesnakes and roadrunners and unpaved roads winding through the gold-brown hills.

A short quad ride down the beach, past the popular surfing and swimming area, we could access unpopulated ribbons of coastline and isolated sunset spots. Once, as we bounded across the sand astride Manny, dozens of diamond-shaped black-and-white mobula rays popped up from the water, briefly gliding through the air on their winged fins before splashing back into the sea. Later, we stopped riding on the beach when we learned of the damage vehicles can do to nesting sea turtles. But we still enjoyed trundling along the dirt roads to get to friends' houses, to pick up treats from an out-of-the-way market, or to ride to the spot where we observed caracaras, iconic birds of Mexico. Falcon-like, caracaras have orange and white beaks and sturdy bodies. We'd noticed a nest atop a tree-sized Cardon cactus and made it a point to ride by every so often in hopes of seeing the parents feeding the chicks.

One day we joined a group for a day-long ride into the Sierra de Laguna mountains. It was gritty, exhilarating, and exhausting to be on the quad for so many hours, bumping through arid sub-tropical forest and across valleys, the granite mountain range rising purple in the distance. When we reached a sandy oasis, we all dismounted and waded in a cool stream and ate lunch in the shade. In one crazy moment, a vehicle got stuck in the mud and Dave used Manny's winch to help pull it out, struggling to not flip over.

Soon after, I got a message from Lee-Ann, an Australian who'd attended the writing retreat in Thailand. She happened to be in San Jose del Cabo at the home of Jeff, her partner she'd met on Koh Phangan. We drove an hour down the freeway to spend a night with them at Jeff's adobe house adorned in colorful Mexican tiles and outfitted with a pool and lounge chairs. We went downtown for dinner, walking along the cobbled brick streets, fairy lights swinging overhead. It was surreal and wonderful to be laughing and eating in Mexico across from the woman I'd last seen on an island on the other side of the world.

The next Sunday I attended a service at the local Catholic Church in El Pescadero with two friends. As the congregation sang in Spanish, I thought about how much my mother would have enjoyed the experience. Even though she gave up on religion later in life, she was drawn to the church's rituals and admired the nuns and priests who worked for social justice. At the end of mass, two children about eight-years-old and dressed in white were baptized. They then were lifted up by their father on one side and the priest on the other, to the congregation's applause. Witnessing this communal and familial love, I couldn't help but think of all the countries that had welcomed us contrasted against the horror of children being separated from their parents at the border who were trying to escape poverty, violence, and persecution. I thought it would be impossible for anyone who sat in the pews with me that day to support such an appalling policy by the U.S. government to discourage immigrants from transiting.

For Dave's and my sixth wedding anniversary, we drove five hours to Loreto, on the Sea of Cortez. Jim and Janice, whom we housesat for in Forest Ranch, had offered us their Mexico home for a few nights. We arranged to have a panga boat pick us up from the beach. I took in a deep lungful of the Sea of Cortez's salt air as the captain steered us over the turquoise waters and by two small islands, Carmen and Danzante. He anchored at a spot where we snorkeled. On the ride back a super-pod of *dolfinas* surrounded the boat, squealing and jumping. I asked the captain how many there were and thought he said, *cincuenta* (fifty).

"De verdad?" I said. "¿No mas?" *Really? No more?* I'd thought there had been hundreds.

He explained he'd said not *cincuenta* but *sin cuenta*...literally, "without counting." Too many to count. My Spanish lesson for the day.

My sister Ann had moved into town and rented out her casita. That's how we met Susanna and Doug. They also housesat on occasion, and we discovered even more in common, including our ages, love of live music, and Santa Cruz, where Susanna had lived for years. Susanna and Doug had met when they crewed in the Baja Ha-Ha, a sailboat race from San Diego to Cabo San Lucas. I was excited to learn they now split their time between Bali and the Thai island of Ko Lanta. When we told them how much we loved Southeast Asia and that we were headed back soon, we devised a plan to meet up in Indonesia in the fall.

Susanna regularly sat on the beach to paint *plein air* watercolors. When she mentioned she needed her website edited, I did so in exchange for one of her expressive paintings of Cerritos Beach we framed in cactus wood. Susanna and I spent a day together at a nearby restaurant where, if you bought food or drink, you could soak in their saltwater pool. In this serene setting with an ocean view, I learned we had something else in common: dramatic health events. I told her about my brain tumor, and she shared she'd recently had surgery for stage-four colon cancer. I admired her empowered approach to treatment, a well-informed combination of conventional and alternative methods. Bright-eyed and full of life, she'd gone vegan and quit drinking booze (and Doug had done the same), after reading studies linking colon cancer with ingesting animal products and alcohol. Her doctors were amazed at how well she was healing.

I was glad to have new friends who didn't drink. In Baja, it was easy to get caught up in the It's-Another-Tequila-Sunrise lifestyle, day drinking by the pool, cocktails at sunset, wine at communal dinners. I'd enjoyed a lot of drinking in my life, but in my fifties, booze had stopped being my friend, often leading to insomnia, migraines, malaise.

I had decided to stop drinking for a while, curious if living without alcohol would improve my life. I was surprised by how many limiting thoughts popped up: *Won't I be a buzzkill, a party pooper? Only boring people don't drink. It's the lifeblood of fun. Also, it's sophisticated! Look at those Europeans imbibing at their elegant sidewalk cafes!* I realized I hadn't spent more than a few months without drinking since I was a teenager. Perhaps giving up booze was the next level of shedding, after having discarded my job, town, possessions, and a brain tumor the size of a walnut. When I decided to lean into my curiosity about my patterns, I noticed a desire for a drink often popped up around four p.m. Happy Hour was in my blood. I also began to see how deeply I associated pleasure and relaxation with drinking. Surely there were other ways to chill out that didn't have such consequences.

One day I endured an hour-long super-craving for a glass of wine. The desire was so strong, it surprised me. I didn't pretend it wasn't happening, and I didn't impulsively act out (unless you count eating jellybeans). I observed my mind buck like a wild horse and actually laughed as a voice in my head developed all kinds of rationalizations about why I should imbibe. I told myself to go buy a bottle if that's what I really wanted. Instead I drank a glass of sparkling water with a dash of grapefruit juice and went for a swim, and the desire waned. As Joe Dispenza says, "A habit is when the body becomes the mind." The mind knows what it wants and doesn't want. But the body has become so habituated it overrides the mind. The question is: Who's in control? The bucking bronco, or me?

Now I rarely drink, but when I do I try to mindfully enjoy it. I prefer not having hard and fast rules about being sober or drinking at every social occasion. When I do drink I accept I'll feel less sparkly for a few days, like I'm wearing a long dress and someone is stepping on the train. By now I've been to lots of parties and other events and had a great time without drinking alcohol—reminding me what's most important is human connection, not what's in my glass. Sure, it's fun to get high from a little wine now and then, but now I know I'm also capable of what Pema Chodron calls "the joy of happiness without a hangover."

Chapter Nineteen

Burning Man, Buddha & Bugs

Fall 2018

We figured after flying out of Mexico, packing up in California, and taking an international plane trip it would be a good move to rest up before Mark's party. So Dave and I first spent a week on Koh Samui, a short ferry ride from Koh Phangan. We stayed on south Lamai Beach at a budget resort far enough from the throngs for privacy but close enough for easy access to things we wanted to do. Dave was working on his advanced diving certification, so when I was alone I walked down the beach then up hilly streets, past a golden temple where people prayed next to a *muay thai* boxing martial arts studio where people beat the shit out of each other. In an open-air room, I took yoga classes then dipped in the nearby pool and, at the adjoining restaurant, ate a smoothie bowl and wrote in my journal—luxuriating in my favorite things. Time slowed and expanded as I walked back, wading in the ocean along the way, a beach dog or two joining me in the warm, lapping waters.

I was in my element, happy to be back in Southeast Asia, as I clung to Dave while he spirited us around on a motorbike, up the hills for sprawling views of neighborhoods shrouded in greenery. Pink, yellow, and red blossoms cascaded down the slopes, the sea stretching below. Once, riding the back roads, we came across an incredible sight, thousands of coconuts piled beneath trees, gathered by humans who were nowhere in sight. Coconut was abundant: we slaked our thirst with fresh coconut water and filled our bellies with green coconut curry. Almost daily, we indulged in Thai massage on the beach overlooking Grandmother and Grandfather rocks—so named because one resembles a tree-sized phallus, the other a vulva cave. I loved the ritual of washing my feet in a bowl filled with floating flowers before submitting myself to the masseuse's touch. Too bad affordable massage isn't as ubiquitous everywhere in the world, it's so beneficial to one's health. Of course, "affordable" can point to underpaid labor, and I internally struggled with that reality while also knowing paying for a massage and tipping well helped the individual practitioners. While it doesn't take scientific research to see that massage does wonders for the body, mind, and spirit, the Mayo Clinic points out it increases circulation and reduces stress, lowers blood pressure, and improves immune function.

And god knows we needed our immunity boosted in the face of Mark's week-long extravaganza of art, workshops, dance, and music. People from all over the world descended on Sea Garden 2, a funky resort clinging to a cliff overlooking the Gulf of Thailand. Mark never had much money— in fact, at one point he lived in a shed in a friend's back yard—but he was an only child who cared for his elderly ill parents and they left him everything when they died. So now he was able to commission over fifty artists and musicians to create a captivating array of Burning Man-style art pieces and performances. Like many regional burns, it was much smaller but in the spirit of the original Burning Man, where once a year 80,000 people gather in Nevada's Black Rock Desert to create a temporary metropolis dedicated to community, art, and self-expression. Each day brimmed with events, starting with morning yoga and "Ecstatic Disco Dance" by the pool, culminating with a DJ mixing tunes until the wee hours.

Entering the grounds was like walking into Mark's brain. One area was set up as Jam Camp, with drum kit, guitars, bass, amps, and mic, a mannequin stationed out front. In another room you could trip out to a 3-D mapping projection as geometrical shapes emerged from the walls. On the grounds people lay beneath trees on meditation mats, while others played ping pong under refrigerator-sized woven dream catchers. One wall featured a participatory art installation, brushes and paints at the ready for anyone who wanted to add to the mural. On the lawn, fire dancers with dreadlocks threw around blazing hoops while snaking their bodies into the splits. Translucent jellyfish the size of mattresses draped from tree limbs, lighting up at night like hybrid creatures of land and sea.

Down the steep, uneven steps along the cliff to the rainforest garden below, lighted paths led to teepees erected on the sand for workshops and gatherings. A wooden temple towered over the beach, a carving of the sun radiating from its center. Next to it loomed the effigy of "the man" to be burned the last night, a wooden triangle for a head, and arms and body made of driftwood. I recalled how Mark had shown Dave and me the 1970s cult horror film *The Wicker Man* about an earnest Methodist burned alive inside a human effigy woven from wicker. Clearly Mark was drawn to the idea of "burning down" mainstream society's structures and strictures—a gift of liberation he offered to everyone there.

Mark's DJing from the poolside booth started around sunset, while the masses wearing everything from bathing suits and fringy hats to capes and sparkly makeup danced to the electronic rhythms. At one point each night a group of drummers emerged and pounded out tribal beats to the throbbing electronica, braiding together ancient and futuristic strains in a way that brought out my goosebumps. Presiding over the festivities was a silver robot the height of three men, with a boxy head and aluminum body, a red

156

heart centered on its chest—which made me think of Mark's heart, how it beat with a unique percussion. Maybe his heart "problem" was also the source of his power, the dynamism that made it possible for him to create such an experience.

I led yoga in the mornings near the pool, amazed that people who partied all night showed up. Usually around midnight I'd collapse in bed, but it wasn't easy to sleep with the music thumping through the walls like the telltale heart. The whole experience was undeniably epic and exhausting in equal measure. Due to all the energy I expended, combined with so much swimming and loud music, I ended up with an ear infection I treated with over-the-counter antibiotics. When we left, I was simultaneously relieved and sad it was over. The explosion of human ingenuity, infused with love, reverberated in my core. We were amazed by what Mark had manifested, but not surprised.

Dave and I boarded a plane with his longtime friend Craig, who'd been at the Burning Man event. On Phuket, a Thai island on the Andaman Sea, we spent a week together motorbiking around. We went to beaches, watched monkeys scramble in the trees, and visited temples with pointed roofs, white pillars, and red and gold embellishments. We rode to the peak of Mount Nagakerd to view the area called Big Buddha, which displayed multiple buddhas. Most striking were the white one the size of an apartment building and the gold one on a snaky coiled platform, a white cat burrowed in its folds. On an expansive banyan tree, people had fastened thousands of fluttering gold hearts inscribed with words in many languages: *peace and love to all*; *here's to a happy life*; *pray for each other*. We stayed at Pacific Club Resort at Karon Beach for its herbal steam room, rooftop pool, and breakfast layout the size of a wedding banquet—and still spent less money than we would have living in California for the same amount of time.

Saying goodbye to Craig, we took a cab to northern Phuket to visit Nadia. We'd met her and her family in Baja, on the last leg of their trip around the world, and now they were living in Phuket. Rob, who did international peace-relations work, was on assignment in Kenya, but Nadia (who trained humanitarian workers) welcomed us with open arms, even though we'd met her only briefly once before. We also got to spend time with their daughters: a fourteen-year-old who'd just returned from Africa where she taught art therapy to women with HIV in prison, and a seventeen-year-old who recently developed and implemented a school project to build roads for a poor community in northern Thailand. I was in awe of these young women's awareness of humanity's needs and admired how their parents had raised them as world citizens.

157

Nadia took us shopping at the local market, and as usual in Southeast Asia I was enthralled at the colorful abundance, with people and dogs wandering about, such a different feeling from a cold supermarket. Whole fish overflowed on platters, bowls brimmed with mollusks and nuts and seeds, and dozens of kinds of greens and root vegetables were on display. There were many varieties of bananas, small and large—all of which made the one type of banana available in the U.S. seem ridiculously boring.

Nadia also brought us to a gibbon rehabilitation center. Ear-splitting shrieks emanated from these adorable creatures, with their fuzzy heads and shiny marble eyes. From there we hiked through the rainforest to Bang Pae Waterfall and slid down mossy rocks to swim in a natural pool, washing off our sweat in the cool water. Nadia took us to restaurants where we feasted on whole snapper, sea grapes, glass noodles with prawns, and crab curry. But the best part was talking with Nadia, conversing intimately about our pasts, our travels, our inner explorations, as though we'd known each other for years, not days.

Leaving Thailand, we flew to Malaysia for our first international housesit. Ralph and Junnie—a British and Malaysian couple—picked us up at the airport in Penang, an island connected to the mainland by two bridges. Their penthouse, hovering on the twenty-eighth floor overlooking the pure blue Strait of Malacca, was filled with antiques. Eyeing their state-of-the-art kitchen, I was glad I'd be able to cook after weeks of eating at restaurants. The living room's sliding glass wall opened up to the sky and ocean, seabirds hovering. It was like living in a dazzling, high-end treehouse. My housesitting bubble burst, however, when Ralph warned us to avoid getting attacked by an acid-spewing insect called a rove beetle that scorches human skin.

"I got burned on my testicles," he casually mentioned. "And my armpit. The burn transferred to my inner arm. Lasted for weeks and was so painful. If one lands on you, don't swat it. Blow on it so it will float away."

Well *that* wasn't on the website's description of this gig. Junnie taught Dave how to spray the balcony plants to discourage the pests, and we were instructed to keep the windows closed at night with the A/C on, since the menaces were drawn to light.

Our main charge was Oscie, a poodle with a cartoon face and pink skin glowing through his white curls. We were also tasked with feeding two parakeets who lived in a cage hanging on the patio. Our first morning alone, Oscie woke us up by hacking and barfing next to the bed. Such is the glamour of housesitting. But Oscie's puking turned out to be a one-off, and he became a fun companion who lived for snuggling and walks.

Taking him out meant facing the elevator several times a day, not my favorite mode of transportation. I used to have paralyzing claustrophobia, but it diminished with the help of hypnotherapy. Funny how I could travel the world virtually fear-free but stepping into an elevator made my breath clench. I learned that avoiding tight spaces intensified my aversion so I deliberately put myself in the backs of cars, crowded vans, and middle airplane seats, acclimating and calming myself with various techniques—to the point I rarely felt claustrophobia's grasp anymore. Except on elevators. My avoidance method was taking the stairs, but twenty-eight floors was a bit much. I figured living in this building for a month would provide me the opportunity to dust off lingering particles of enclosure anxiety, but being encapsulated in a vertical, moving coffin never became fun. *This*, I thought, *must be the wisdom of no escape Buddhists keep talking about.*

With use of their car we ventured out, eating street food and buying fresh coconut milk made at the local market by women in head scarves. We explored nearby George Town, Penang's capital city, a UNESCO World Heritage site. The first British Settlement in Southeast Asia, George Town attained its independence in 1957 and this history is reflected in its eclectic British and Asian architecture. Walking past temples and colonial-style houses, down streets lined with busy stores and restaurants, we eyed murals everywhere, my favorite being two kids painted atop a real bike affixed to the wall. We trod slowly, though, and didn't last too long outdoors in the hot and sticky October days.

When we walked Oscie in the neighborhood we'd sometimes luck out and see families of monkeys bouncing in the trees. On our beach strolls we'd spy otters floating on their backs and people jet-skiing by. Sadly, we were warned not to take a dip in the waves because of pollution. However, the condo complex had an Olympic sized pool where Dave and I swam every day, often being the only ones there. Oddly, the sprawling facility had a ghost-town feeling because many units weren't occupied. Ralph said that was because Chinese buyers came in and swooped up the relatively inexpensive real estate but didn't reside there.

In November the American midterm elections were coming up, and I received my overseas ballot but needed a fax machine to send it. I posted on a Penang expat Facebook group, asking if anyone could help. Someone suggested I download a fax app on my phone, which I hadn't thought about, and it worked perfectly. Soon I received a private message from a woman named Ellen indicating she'd seen my message and found me on Facebook, only to realize I was a writer from Northern California who'd taught at San Jose State, and that we had friends in common. She explained she and her husband Paul had both taught at Chico State University and had recently retired and moved to Penang and would love to connect with us. I wrote back and explained we were housesitting—and when I mentioned we'd recently done a gig in the Chico area in Forest Ranch, she wrote back that, incredibly, Forest Ranch was the very town they'd lived in for eighteen years!

We figured it was fated we'd meet, so we got together for dinner at an Indochinese fusion restaurant, and as we talked, the connections became even more incredible. Like me, she got her PhD at the University of Washington—and like me, Paul taught creative writing. We discovered we knew more people in common than we'd initially thought. When they mentioned they'd worked in refugee camps in Malaysia, I said our friends Karen and Widi (whom we'd met up with in Hoi An, Vietnam during a school break in China) had done the same in a Vietnamese refugee camp in Sumatra. Ellen said her friends had as well—and sure enough, when I messaged Karen, she knew them. The web of interconnection meant not only a small world but, for a moment, a pocket-sized universe, too.

After dinner, whirling from all the synchronicity, we walked through Avatar Secret Garden, a phantasmagorical attraction created by millions of purple and orange LED lights draped over hulking trees. The centerpiece was a rambling banyan tree with a tangle of roots and shadowy trunk seemingly illuminated by stars. Between the limbs, I spotted a perfect full moon, a golden coin on velvet, and felt I could almost touch the whole cosmos with a single finger.

Chapter Twenty

A Real Gem

Winter 2018

The shaking bed woke me from a deep sleep.

"Dave. Dave! Did you feel that?"

"Wha...huh?"

"An earthquake! Didn't you feel it?"

I jumped up and flipped on the light. Dave rolled over and threw his arm over his eyes.

"It was not a little one!" I rooted in my suitcase for a sundress and pulled it on. "Do you think there could be a tsunami?"

We were on the Indonesian island of Nusa Lembongan, off the coast of Bali, on the bottom floor of a budget two-story seaside resort. Images from YouTube videos of the 2004 tsunami that killed more than 200,000 people in Southeast Asia assaulted my mind's eye, the ocean rushing forth and gobbling up trees and buildings and human lives. And just last week, when we were in Penang, we'd eaten at a seaside restaurant owned by the parents of the "Malaysian miracle baby" who had been sleeping on a mattress and was swept out to sea by that tsunami...and swept back in, still asleep.

"Tsunamis are rare," Dave said, getting up and throwing on his clothes. "Especially big ones."

I hoped Dave was right but wasn't convinced. We were so close to the ocean I doubted scrambling to the roof would be high enough to escape a mountainous wave. We heard a commotion and went out to the porch of our cottage where rain was sheeting down, thunder growling and lightning blasting across the sky. Four Brazilians in their early twenties had come running from their room, drawn to our lit-up window. They stood trembling and terrified beneath the overhang, saying they'd never felt an earthquake before. Putting aside our own concerns, we soothed them, explaining as Californians we'd experienced many and that while there may be aftershocks, they shouldn't worry. One young woman, shaking and crying, latched on to Dave. Earlier in the day at the pool they had been drunk and loud, getting on my nerves. But now, I felt tenderness for them and kicked myself for not seeing earlier they were just kids having fun.

"Hey, don't worry about this, but we need to make sure everything's okay as far as a tsunami warning," I said casually, trying not to freak them out more. Dave and I went out to the front desk to see if the Wi-Fi was working, the duckling Brazilians trailing after us. A crack of lightning illuminated the black sea. I wondered if we should hop onto the motorbike to make a run for the hills—but in this downpour in the dark that would be treacherous. Besides, we couldn't leave the kids behind, could we?

An older woman who worked at the hotel was hunched on a stool, facing the ocean. A sarong draped over her hefty body, she rested her elbows on her knees—a Balinese version of my grandmother. I'd thought she couldn't speak English, but as she peered at the waves she said over and over, an incantation, "Water normal, water normal."

I approached her. "No tsunami?"

"Water normal." She smiled and patted my arm.

I thanked her, assured if anyone would know if a tsunami was coming, a woman who grew up on this island would. I checked my phone and was briefly able to get online and located a report: It had been a 5.4 quake, the epicenter only a few miles away.

The next morning the sky was clear, the sea transparent and calm, no evidence of last night's calamity. A boat picked up Dave for a day of diving with manta rays, and I walked down the beach for a yoga class. Later, our friends Susanna and Doug arrived from their home in Ubud, as we'd arranged in Baja when they'd rented my sister's casita. We spent days together riding around the island on motor scooters, eyeing small temples and a cemetery with markers shaded by colorful parasols, a tradition to keep the hot, tropical sun off the dead in their temporary place until they could be properly cremated. We rode across a Crayola-yellow bridge to nearby Nusa Ceningan, for its calming views of turquoise coves. One day the four of us boarded a snorkel boat and swam amongst the bright fish near watery caves, and each night before dinner we watched the sun dip into the horizon, spilling its purple and orange inks onto the ocean palette.

The time came to say goodbye to this tropical region we loved. The last day of November Dave and I bought two packs of cigarettes in a small store in Bali, then flew to Melbourne. Romi, whom we'd met at the Thailand writing retreat, had requested the smokes because they were expensive in Australia. We were happy to present them as a gift, especially since she was welcoming us into her apartment for a few nights. She guided us around Melbourne, her hometown, along the city streets with their lively café culture and the waterfront where kiteboarders whizzed across the blue surface of Port Phillip Bay. I developed a sore throat and a head cold, though, and spent the rest of the time burrowed on her couch while she and Dave went out for more exploring.

Fortunately, when it was time to hop on the train, I was feeling better. On the two-hour ride, vast open spaces drifted by, meadows and hills pocked with oak trees reminiscent of Northern California's foothills. We were headed northwest to the Victorian gold rush town of Ballarat, in the central highlands of Victoria, for a five-week housesit.

Our host Liz was headed to the UK to meet her newborn grandchild. A kind and generous soul, she had asked us in advance for a list of foods we liked and stocked the fridge. Her house was a modest and comfortable two-bedroom in a suburban neighborhood, walking distance to the mall and a sprawling park. In December, it was summer down under—Australians associate Christmas with blue skies and barbecue—and we were thrilled to find juicy peaches, nectarines, and apricots. However, for the first few weeks it was unseasonably rainy and cold. Having come from Southeast Asia, I didn't have enough warm clothes so at an Op Shop, a second-hand store that provides "op"portunities for people who need jobs, I bought a couple of long-sleeved shirts and of course couldn't pass up browsing the shelves of used books.

Gem, the dog in our care, was about the size of a purse. A black and white Papillon mix with butterfly ears, she followed me everywhere, snuggling up to me on the couch, perching on the dining room chair next to mine, trailing after me into the bathroom. The immediate affection was mutual. Each day, rain or shine, we walked her, most often to Lake Wendouree. The lake, four miles in circumference, was surrounded by walking trails and inhabited by thousands of birds: black swans and their downy cygnets, sacred ibises, kookaburras, all kinds of coots and ducks, songbirds, and pairs of electric-green lorikeets roosting in the trees. Examining the birds' markings in Dave's photos, we identified them in Liz's *Readers Digest Complete Book of Australian Birds*.

One day we drove up into the foothills to a place famous for mineral baths. We spent two hours in the Hepburn Bathhouse and Spa, immersed in pools and eucalyptus steam rooms. Back near the house, we occasionally walked through the mall and, after all our time on a small island, I was walloped by the bright convenience. At a bakery we bought lemon and apricot "slices," what we'd call a "bar," and I ordered a "flat white," what we'd call coffee with milk, no foam. Dave smiled at me over our treats and said, "Being retired is like being a kid on vacation, except you have a credit card and can drive."

My cold was gone, but I had a lingering cough. I was grateful I didn't have to go to work this way, that I'd stepped off the conveyor belt of constantly trying to attain more and more and more. I was reading Paul Monette's AIDS memoir, *Borrowed Time,* and came across this fitting line: "The walking away was very important; that was the whole point of the life of the high Bohemian, dabbling in bourgeois pleasures without getting caught." I liked the idea of enjoying the world's things without owning them.

We both read a lot while the winds whipped outside. Dave called *84 Charring Cross Road* addictive and so when he finished it, I dove in and was charmed, wondering how Helen Hanff could be nostalgic but not sappy. Dave pulled off Liz's shelves a number of thrillers, a genre I can't get into. But in our time there, I read memoirs for a contest I was judging, two Paul Monette books, Michelle Obama's memoir, *Architecture of a Novel, 84 Charring Cross Road* and its follow-up, and two Somerset Maughams. With my degrees in literature, how I'd never before read him was astounding. I was especially taken with the masterful storytelling of *The Razor's Edge,* about a man who decides to live differently from what society expects and ends up on a spiritual journey. I related to the expansion that happens when you live unconventionally and wondered how both Dave and I would be different if we'd stayed put in Santa Cruz. One thing I knew for sure: we wouldn't have such a vast web of connection with people everywhere, which made me feel that the wide world was becoming our home.

When we'd been in Bali over a year before, I'd met an Australian woman named Deanne at a café, and we'd dived into some deep territory as we'd talked about our lives. We'd stayed in touch and now she and her husband Buck came to visit us in Ballarat. We spent twenty-four hours together, relishing food, conversation, and music. They are professional musicians, so Dave and I were in melodious heaven as we sprawled in the living room while they played guitars and sang an array of folk/rock/country originals and covers. I plucked along on my ukulele but soon abandoned it to pure listening, Gem coiled on my lap.

Buck told quite a story about what got him into music: In his twenties, he was snorting a lot of coke and working for a car dealer who was also his drug dealer. Only in his thirties, the guy died from a heart attack, and around that time Buck had heard on the radio Bob Dylan, backed by Tom Petty and the Heartbreakers, was playing a show in Sydney. He didn't know Dylan's music, only that he was "that famous guy from the 1960s." On a whim, Buck went to the show, and his revelation was, "I want to do *that.*" Two weeks later he bought a guitar, packed up his belongings, and hitchhiked out of town. He traveled across the country for six years, busking. Eventually he settled in Sydney and to this day makes most of his money from music. I'm fascinated by the origin stories of people who lead alternative lives.

When they left it was as though a delightful storm had passed, the living room calm and quiet. Gem sat at my side while Dave and I dove back into our books. It struck me home might be the place where we can entertain then retreat into our cave, to fall silent and rest. That could be a cottage on a Balinese island or a grand house in Seattle, or anywhere we happened to be.

With only a week left in Oz, we planned to head back to Baja by way of California, where we needed to take care of a few odds and ends. We'd had a video call with a homeowner for a sit in a flat in San Francisco but turned it down for two reasons: she wanted us to sleep in a double bed, not the queen in the main bedroom; and after some probing we came to understand her cat was incontinent and so old it might die on our watch. We'd applied for a few other housesits and figured something would fall into place. I tried not to check my messages obsessively, reminding myself "waiting" robs me of living.

As the hours before I had to say goodbye to Gem wound down, I basked in my time with her. On the couch she curled up in the crook of my knees, a soft bundle. I memorized the design of dots on her nose, ran my fingers through her butterfly ears, stared into her golden-brown eyes. I gave her treats and brushed her, indulging and torturing myself. Leaving her would be like yanking out a tooth.

It took seventeen hours to fly from Australia to California, with a stopover in Tokyo so short we didn't even deboard. It was strange to touch down in Japan, a place both of us had spent time in our previous lives: I'd taught in Yokohama and Dave had traveled to Japan often over ten years for his corporate job. We made a vow to come back together sometime.

At Chambliss' in San Jose, we faced an ever-dwindling but persistent pile of our things stacked in an unfinished room in the back of his house. Dave decided it was the moment to divest himself of his corporate work clothes, and so he donated dress shirts, ties, and suits to a men's shelter, which would be used when the guys went out on job interviews. One man's ending, another's beginning. Dave also handed over a tux, and the guy at the desk said he himself would wear it every year when he emceed their fundraiser.

We had to make a decision about our bikes that we'd ridden many miles along ocean cliffs in Santa Cruz, and taken on a ski lift in Big Bear to ride down the fire roads, and pedaled up a mountain in Zion National Park to watch the sunrise, and cruised around Portland. They were not the right bikes for Baja, and we didn't want them cluttering up our friend's house, so what to do with them? That question had been on our mind when we were talking to Debbie and Tony who happened to mention they wanted to buy bikes. Dave and I blurted out, "We have bikes for you!"

We were caught up in a flow of giving and receiving: When a friend discovered we needed to rent a car during our month in California, she loaned us her extra one. The day we gave our snow tires to a stranger, another friend offered us free passes to the Monterey Bay Aquarium, and yet another invited me to a concert because she had an extra ticket. This obtaining and letting go felt like breathing, like the movement of the tides, a similar vibe to all the strangers who let us stay in their homes in exchange for caring for their pets.

We scored a housesit in the East Bay, in Walnut Creek, where we hung out with a galumph of a golden retriever named Jasper, whom I adored, but my heart still ached for Gem. The homeowner had told us the guest room was comfortable, but the bed was a too-short futon that was akin to sleeping on a tilted rock. I felt like a kid whose parents had left their door shut, not wanting their teens to have sex on their comfortable platform bed. They hadn't explicitly told us we couldn't use their room, but the closed door sent a signal. I didn't want to ask because I wasn't going to take no for an answer. I needed a good night's sleep. So I washed the sheets and we slept in the verboten bed, and that night I dreamt I got busted for muling drugs. Clearly my unconscious was working through my issues with authority. Before we left, we did our usual thorough housecleaning, and I worried so much about making the room look untouched I decided keeping it a secret was silly. I wrote a note to the hosts welcoming them home and explaining we'd slept in their bed and why. I worried they'd ding us on our review, but to my relief they wrote a glowing one and also sent us a message apologizing.

Before all that, though, we'd found a book on their shelves about the region's history and opened it up to a page headed with Dave's last name, Rhine, and featuring Dave's great-grandfather! For years Dave had told me his ancestors co-founded the Bay Area town of Clayton. We were only thirty minutes away, so spurred by the book, we drove to the town whose centerpiece was a historical society and museum in a white-and-green Victorian farmhouse. The house had been a private home and later used as a bunkhouse for employees of a cattle ranch before being bought by the city. Interestingly, it was a nomadic house; it had been moved in 1910 from its original location using wooden rollers and a horse, and in the 1970s it was relocated onto Main Street.

Climbing up the steps onto the museum's wooden porch, we opened the door to a room filled with people chatting, holding teacups, and snacking on cookies. Turned out we'd stepped into the middle of the Camelia Tea, an annual event honoring the descendants of the town's pioneer families. Talk about synchronicity. When Dave stuck on a nametag inscribed with his last name "Rhine," people exclaimed like he was a celebrity. We toured the restored home filled with artifacts and pictures, many featuring his ancestors. It was mind-blowing to think how his family, Jews fleeing persecution in Germany, led to this very moment where we stood before their images in a museum. I imagined they would have wanted such prosperity for their descendants. Call it synchronicity, call it kismet, call it wonder—the label mattered less than the feeling of how eons mysteriously and miraculously intertwined.

166

Chapter Twenty-One

Size of a Lemon

Spring 2019

Back in Mexico after six months in Thailand, Malaysia, and California, our friends asked, "How was your vacation?" That question startled me. Travel wasn't our *vacation*—which comes from the Latin for *being unoccupied*. We weren't taking a break but exploring the world. Travel was our *vocation*, our *calling* as world citizens. Nevertheless, our Baja friends saw us as having come back home, and it was beginning to feel more that way to me, too—even though we were on visitor visas limiting our stay to 180 days.

It felt wonderful to do morning yoga on the rooftop patio beneath a smudge of daytime moon, birds flitting by, the ocean a shimmer in the distance. I was happy to hike the hills and walk the beaches, and to sit at my desk and write. Soon, though, I fell ill. As in Australia, I developed a sore throat and cough, and like in Thailand, I had a painful and dizzying ear infection. Clearly something was off-balance and it was time to stop self-treating these issues as I had on the road, so I made an appointment with an Ear, Nose, and Throat doctor in Cabo San Lucas.

In his office, Dr. Landeros greeted me with the customary kiss on each cheek and invited Dave and me to take a seat. He asked about my life, what I did for a living, what kinds of stress I might be under, what my diet was like, and what I did for exercise, questions a doctor in the U.S. had never posed. After I explained my symptoms, he peered into my ears and throat and said I had developed surfer's ear, a growth of bone inside the ear canal from so much swimming, making me prone to infections. He said he'd prescribe antibiotics but that I needed to avoid cold water, use ear plugs while swimming, and apply eardrops afterward. He felt around on my neck and paused.

"How long have you had this?" he asked.

He guided my hand to the left side of my throat where, my heart quivering, I fingered a rocky lump. "I have no idea."

He held up a hand mirror and told me to tilt my head back. A foreign object pushed at my skin from the inside. I never looked at my reflection this way. If I had, would I have noticed the bulge months before? Or years?

"Don't worry," he said, apparently reading the tension on my face. "We will take an ultrasound to see."

My knees got watery and the room wobbled. I had a growth in my throat. Was that why I hadn't been able to shake being sick?

He walked us to the next building where he handed me over to another physician, who, to my surprise, drew me into a back room and performed the ultrasound right then. Dr. Landeros and Dave watched a wall screen projecting my internal image; the doctor explained I had a mass in my thyroid. As freaked out as I was, a contrast didn't escape me: with ultrasounds I had in the U.S., the technician remained stoic and silent, with results arriving in a week or two.

"It's large," Dr. Landeros admitted. "About the size of a lemon."

My palm tingled as I imagined cradling the density and circumference of a lemon. What I felt on my neck had been the tip of the "fruit." I recalled lying in a hotel bed in Vietnam a few years ago, and when I'd tried to swallow a panicky feeling took over as my throat froze. Occasionally that sensation had returned. No wonder.

Through the haze of my thoughts, I registered Dr. Landeros was talking, reassuring me most thyroid nodules are benign, but I needed a needle biopsy to be sure. I nodded numbly, thinking about how my brain surgeon had said the same thing six years ago, predicting the walnut-sized tumor in my head was benign and wouldn't kill me. She was right. The post-surgery pathology report indeed determined it wasn't cancer. And three months later we'd traveled to India and Sri Lanka, my surgeon's advice ringing in my ears: *Forget this ever happened. Move on with your life.*

Would I be so lucky a second time? I took a deep breath. *Don't catastrophize, Kate.* But I couldn't help it. Silly me to think after brain surgery at age fifty I'd triumphed over the single medical challenge of my life.

"Don't worry," Dr. Landeros reassured me. "You're in good hands. But I do recommend you stop consuming caffeine and dairy, both of which can impact the thyroid."

Back home, I threw away the half-and-half and quit coffee on the spot. This affected Dave not at all because he drank only tea, and he hadn't had dairy in years since he was lactose intolerant. I knew little about the thyroid, so I consulted Dr. Google to learn it's a butterfly-shaped gland housed below the Adam's apple that controls many of the body's important functions by secreting hormones. I imagined one wing of my butterfly pinned down by a lemon and unable to fly.

The next day I lay on a gurney, shivering like I was immersed in ice water. The nurse brought a warm blanket, but nothing could allay my trembling, not even Dave at my side. Using an ultrasound as a guide, the physician inserted a long needle into the mass in my neck and swirled it around. I squeezed Dave's hand, imagining myself a stone statue. I feared breathing too hard might cause the needle to slip into a vital artery.

The test results would take about a week. Over the next few days, I checked my email incessantly. Then one day as we rode in the car headed to the store, I glanced at my phone to see a message from the hospital. I clicked it open to my diagnosis: *papillary carcinoma.*

"Dave," I said, as he steered us down the bumpy dirt road. "I have cancer."

Staring out the window, he reached over and took my hand. A hurricane whipped around in my mind. I would need surgery. Cancer treatment. Should I do it here in Mexico? I thought my insurance would cover me wherever we were, but I wasn't sure. We had a housesit in Hawai'i set to start in two months. This was my second major illness in a few short years. Was this the end of the nomadic life I loved so much? My mind stuttered to a stop, not daring to plunge into the abyss.

Returning to the casita, I texted Dr. Landeros for an appointment—yes, he'd given me his cell number—and he offered to see me the next morning. He explained the surgery and said they'd have to extract a few lymph nodes to ascertain if the cancer had spread. If the malignancy was advanced, I'd need to undergo radioactive iodine (RAI) treatment to destroy any remaining thyroid tissue since removing a thyroid is akin to skinning raw chicken, not necessarily possible to scrape off every single fragment. He explained his three-man team would perform the procedure with "care" and "love," which made me want to hug him.

That afternoon I Googled RAI therapy and discovered afterward you remain radioactive and must avoid contact with others for a week: no sharing of a bed, kitchen, or bathroom. It made me wonder if sometimes people behind me in line at the grocery store were radioactive. Even worse, possible side effects included salivary gland malfunction, loss of taste or smell, dry mouth, loss of hair, chronic pink eye. I read 61.1% of patients report moderate to severe long-term side effects. I wondered how therapeutic such treatment truly was, that it might be worse than the tumor. I'd seen friends thrive from cancer treatments, but I'd also seen others suffer tremendously and even die from harsh therapies. I decided I needed a second opinion.

I talked to a doctor friend in the U.S. who agreed with the treatment plan. However, she said it would be better for me to work with a surgical oncologist and an endocrinologist, not an ENT. If my tumor was benign, I wouldn't have flinched at having the surgery in Mexico because I thought their medical system to be so humane. But now I decided to go to California. Part of me yearned to go *home.* I was surprised by this desire. I'd grown up there and had a network of friends and family. A history. I never questioned my understanding of the culture in the San Francisco Bay Area, nor struggled with language, as I did at times in Mexico. What I wanted was ease.

This decision launched me into the opposite of ease, as on the phone from my desk in the casita I was plunged into the morass of the U.S.'s medical bureaucracy. I was transferred from one department to the next, asked a million questions, told to fill out a stack of online forms in different formats, call x person, wait for y person to call me back. I wondered how people who were uneducated, or had no insurance, or were working full time with kids, or were so ill they could barely sit up handled all of this. Finally I was connected with an intake coordinator and after several more rounds of calls and emails, I was informed my records had to be translated from Spanish into English. I tried to remain calm and be grateful I'd retired with a medical insurance package, but I nearly crumbled at one more requirement. Instead, I bucked up and posted on Facebook that I needed someone to translate a medical document. Minutes later someone responded that her bilingual R.N. friend could do it. She did so the next day and wouldn't take payment so I sent her a gift card, gratified for my network.

I tried to breathe and take each moment as it came, knowing stress was cancer fertilizer. Dave talked me through guided healing meditations and performed reiki energy healing on my throat. Inspired by Susanna whose stage-four colon cancer had healed, I decided to shift my diet to whole-food plant-based—vegan without processed foods to bolster healing. I made smoothies with celery, spinach, papaya, spirulina. I cooked pots of vegetable soup and steamed artichokes, dipping them in aioli made from blending cashews and garlic.

I knew nature was a palliative, so we took quad rides along the dirt roads to the edge of the beach. One day a rock jutting from the water came alive with hundreds of crabs scampering around. Thousands of little lives. It seemed my life wasn't any more significant than theirs.

That night I shot up from a hard sleep in the dark, my head swimming, chills shaking my body, my tongue a wad of cotton in my mouth. Dave lightly snored at my side. Panic seized me; I thought I was having a stroke or a heart attack. Switching on my light, I leaned back against the pillows, taking deep breaths, exhausted but not able to sleep. When Dave's eyes opened, I said I might need to go to the E.R. I wrapped myself in my bathrobe, wobbled to the couch and slumped, my head in my hands. Dave asked me what was going on. I explained the chills, the shaking, the feeling that ten cats were piled on my chest. I believed I saw fear in his eyes. And exhaustion.

He said he would take me if that's what I wanted.

Miserably I thought about the hour drive and wondered if people in the E.R. spoke English. I decided to return to bed, and soon my sister Ann and her partner Gary came by bearing papayas and bananas from their garden. Ann sat on the bed with me and when I explained how I felt, she asked if I thought it was anxiety.

I didn't think so. I'd had a panic attack once before, and at the time I knew my mind was creating it. I explained to Ann that this felt real. Physical. Like my body was out of whack.

"Sounds like a panic attack to me," she said.

But would a panic attack wake me at random in the middle of the night? Having my sister there comforted me, reminding me of the time, after our father had died, when we'd bought our mother a new mattress. When it was delivered, all three sisters and my mom piled on, feeling the absence of our father but also our interwoven strength.

While Ann and I talked, Dave and Gary went up to the rooftop patio for a tai chi session. I worried about how once again Dave was being thrust into the role of taking care of me. I remembered him helping me bathe because my right arm wasn't working after brain surgery, and rushing to the pharmacy for stool softeners when I developed a bowel impaction. When he'd vowed *for better or for worse*, no way could he have imagined I'd need brain surgery after only a year of marriage...and now this.

A neighbor came by and offered me a Xanax. I figured Dave must have told him what was going on. I decided what the hell and took it—and in minutes I started to feel relief. Ann told me I was relaxing before her eyes.

As much as I'd been holding it together, apparently deep down my unconscious was wrestling with disaster. Clearly, the mind could mess with the body, and I couldn't always control it with my meditative breathing and woo-woo stuff.

When Ann and Gary left, I told Dave I was feeling better. He dropped to a chair, wiping tears from his eyes. I went to him and held him, silently sorry for what I was putting him through. I knew his back was hurting, that he was feeling the weight of our world on his shoulders. I was trying not to be too needy so as to not add to his burdens, even though I just wanted to wrap myself up in him and stare into his blue-green eyes because I dreaded the idea of leaving this planet without him.

Once a palm reader in Hong Kong grabbed my hand and blurted out I was going to die at eighty. If he was right, this cancer wouldn't be the end of me. If he was right, I'd live another twenty-five years. If he was right, I had before me merely twenty-four springs and summers, twenty-four falls and winters. I clenched inside at the thought that my remaining seasons were countable. But I'd take them.

Over the next few days, we made our plane reservations to return to the States and talked to Chambliss about landing at his place. Incredibly, my friend Kevin, who'd read my posts on Facebook, offered us his apartment minutes from Stanford. "I won't be there," he said. "Use it as much as you need."

A Baja amiga performed magnetic therapy on me, which had me feeling light and free. Another gave me a rosary from Eastern Europe. Our next-door neighbor came by with essential oils. And the next day she and another neighbor stopped at the hospital in Cabo to pick up the CD of my ultrasound that I had to bring to California. In thanks, I baked them flourless peanut butter cookies and then Dave said, "Let's go to the pool." We soaked in the jacuzzi, plunged into the cold pool water, took outdoor showers. Baja christened, we returned to the casita, where he picked up a book and I played my ukulele. Living wasn't stopping yet.

Unsure if the airline allowed passengers to carry plasma in luggage, I tucked my biopsy slides into my suitcase—the nomad bringing her very blood back to the place of her birth. I left the Bay Area to live the life I wanted to live, and illness kept forcing me to return. Healthy and in our early fifties when we set out on the road, we hadn't thought much about what we'd do in case of medical emergencies. We assumed we'd handle things as they happened, and we had. The brain surgery had reinforced that retiring early to see the world had been a wonderful decision because maybe I had less time than I hoped. However, I'd not considered we'd have another significant medical emergency to face before I hit sixty. For a moment my confidence in our choices wobbled—but I asked myself if I'd rather be sitting in one spot, scrutinizing my health, living a limited life for fear of something going wrong. The answer was a hard no.

When we arrived at Chambliss', I melted into his hug, thankful for all the times he welcomed us into his home. My heart must have grown three sizes because of everyone's generosity: Laurie came by with bags of groceries, filling the fridge with a rainbow of produce. Lisa sent me a flowing yellow scarf imprinted with sparkly butterflies. Tony guided me in a past-life regression healing session, and when I dropped down deep, I saw myself handed a gold scepter by an Egyptian sun-worshipping priestess. In a way she was me, but I also stood apart, watching her. Dressed in gold, she was dazzling, and a magnetizing beauty emanated from her. She spoke to me telepathically, not with words but with energy, conveying I should never forget how powerful I am.

At my consult with Stanford surgeon Dr. Lin, she recommended a full thyroidectomy, given the tumor's size, cancerous nature, and the fact that another nodule, though miniscule, was buried in the other "butterfly wing." Alternatively, she could remove half, but the other side would need to be monitored regularly. I was thrilled with the idea of not being on thyroid

173

medication for the rest of my life until she said people often still require the pills when half a thyroid can't compensate. Also, I was turned off by the idea of needing regular ultrasounds, keeping me in a constant state of worry.

I asked her what she'd do in my situation, and she said she'd take it all out. I concurred. I noticed she had small hands, which I prayed would serve me well when I was sprawled on the gurney having my throat slit open. When I asked about the picture on the wall of two cute kids, she said she had five-year-old twins.

"If you can handle that, surgery is probably a snap," I cracked, and she laughed.

I clung to the fact that she told me thyroid cancer is one of the "most curable" types—and RAI, if I needed it, was simple: swallow some pills and sequester.

Easy for her to say, I thought, sitting there all young and pretty and accomplished behind the armor of her medical pedigree. I'd scrolled thyroid surgery Facebook groups and learned the "61.1% of patients" with side effects were real people who suffered. I didn't want permanent dry mouth. To never again be able to smell a newly-picked tomato. To have perpetual pink eye. If I could waive radiation, I'd kiss the germ-ridden ground.

Surgery took four hours, and when I rose out of anesthesia's mists, I tried to squeak out a question but couldn't speak. Dr. Lin assured me my voice would return. She said I needed only one night in the hospital and she'd call me in a few days, as soon as the pathology report came in.

While waiting for the call, I tried to adjust to the correct amount of levothyroxine, the hormone replacement I'd have to take for the rest of my life. When I swallowed the first pill, my heart nearly bolted from my chest and my skin crawled with unseen, burrowing bugs. The endocrinologist gave me side-eye when I explained how I was feeling, like she was a mother thinking her kid was exaggerating. Nevertheless she reduced my dosage. Still, my body felt like it wasn't connected right. As though my limbs had been removed and haphazardly plastered back on. The image of my butterfly having flown had helped me soften the idea of this surgery, but reality thundered back.

The only external evidence of the surgery was a band-aid on my throat, and although I could eat, it was awkward to swallow and stressful to talk too much. I couldn't sing, but I played my uke in Kevin's living room and worked on an editing job at his kitchen table. Still, it wasn't easy to focus. I kept waiting for the phone to ring with the pronouncement of my destiny. Had the cancer spread? Would I need radiation or other cancer treatments? What was happening in the dark alcoves of my body?

I tried to remember to not fear death, to recall the fleeting gift I'd been given during my seizure years before, when Gabriele had appeared in my dream: *Don't be afraid of dying; the veil between the worlds is thinner and more beautiful than you can imagine.*

A week passed. And a second one. I called Dr. Lin's office several times, and was told the pathology was taking longer than usual. I tried to suss out from the nurse's tone if the delay was good or bad, but in a flat voice she merely reconfirmed that the doctor would call me the minute the results came in. I recalled the Egyptian sun-worshipping priestess who had assured me of my strength. Thinking of her, my skin lightly tingled until I cynically rolled my eyes at the cliché of a life regression taking me to her rather than, say, a ditch digger. No matter, I was bolstered by my memory of her.

Finally, one afternoon when I was sitting on the couch trying not very successfully to read the paper, my cell phone rang. I saw it was a Stanford number and fumbled to answer.

"Kate. It's Dr. Lin. Your results have come in."

I grabbed a pen from the coffee table, my pulse thumping in my ears.

Her next words made my breath hitch: "I have good news. Your tumor is benign."

The room swayed. Was this a dream? I didn't have cancer? *Your tumor* but not *my tumor* anymore. It sat in a lab somewhere, or had been strewn into a garbage can. A piece of me I would be leaving behind when I jumped on the next plane out of here.

She explained the needle biopsy results had not been wrong but that I had "Niftip," a noninvasive follicular thyroid neoplasm with papillary-like features—a type of tumor formerly called cancer that had been downgraded two years ago by the American Medical Association.

"It's no longer deemed a carcinoma," she went on, "because it has never been shown to spread beyond its capsule. That's why the pathology took so long because the whole capsule had to be examined. If your tumor had been discovered a few years ago, you would have had to undergo RAI. But now it's not necessary."

I thought of Dostoyevsky in front of the firing squad whose blindfold was whipped off and he was told, "You've been given a reprieve. Go home." Did he retreat to his modest green and white wooden house that still stands on a riverbank in St. Petersburg? For me, at this moment, home was Kevin's apartment. Or maybe home was Dave, I thought, as I fell into his hug and the past fearful six weeks crashed to a halt. My head on his shoulder, I cried tears of relief and shock, my raw throat constricting.

Two tumors, two surgeries, no cancer. Knowing so many people who've had cancer, I almost felt guilty with such luck. Then again, maybe it wasn't fortunate to have had a non-cancerous organ removed. But I

175

reminded myself of the lemon, that it had begun to obstruct my swallowing. It had needed to come out.

Afterward, searching old pictures for ones with my head flung back, I identified the bulge in my throat, completely oblivious to something inside me that could have undone my life. It had been in me much longer than two years—and if it had been found earlier, I would have undergone unnecessary cancer treatment. I researched it and discovered according to *JAMA Internal Medicine*, up to one-quarter of patients likely have.

Days later, we landed at Hilo International Airport for the four-month housesit to care for a "poi" or mixed-breed dog named Snickers. Walking out into the sultry air I recognized our hosts, Rich and Babette, from our video call, a couple a decade beyond our years. They draped fragrant leis around our necks, welcoming us in the aloha spirit.

Babette caught sight of the band-aid on my throat. "What happened?"

"Well, we didn't want to worry you—not for a minute did we think we would cancel the sit on you—", I swallowed my half-truth, "but I had surgery to remove my thyroid."

Babette tilted her head, at the same angle that would have alerted me to my tumor in a mirror, and placed her fingers at her throat next to a faded scar. Goosebumps budded on my skin, my body telling me what my mind had not yet grasped.

"I had mine out too," she said. "Thirty years ago."

A woman I just met but whose life I'd be living for the next four months—sleeping in her bed, walking her dog, picking mangoes from her trees—had been through it too. She said she rarely thought about it anymore. I recalled my brain surgeon's words: *Forget this ever happened and move on with your life.*

It's good advice. But not completely attainable.

Because my scars—the two-inch line running horizontally across my throat and the indentation in my skull hidden in my blonde hair now streaked with gray—will forever be reminders that I have a countable number of springs and summers left to travel with Dave. Maybe twenty-four, maybe not.

Chapter Twenty-Two

Island Style

Summer-Fall 2019

What fortune that right as we were focusing on eating primarily fresh fruits and vegetables, we were plopped onto a property located in the south of Hawai'i's Big Island where we could harvest papayas, mangoes, avocadoes, pineapples, and bananas. And in a thriving garden we could pick potatoes, carrots, peas, lettuce, and tomatoes. Sitting on a rural subdivision's end lot, the house had a view of tropical greenery with a slice of green-gray ocean in the distance. Every day we walked Snickers around the hilly, shaggy golf course owned by the community. We rarely saw golfers because summer was low season; many of the homeowners lived elsewhere and came only in winter to escape cold weather. At night, rampaging wild pigs dug up the turf so we had to watch our step for holes and pig poo.

I was glad to have four months to focus on healing, and yet a bittersweet feeling filled me. While beyond grateful the thyroid tumor was benign, I mourned the loss of my butterfly, a vital part of my body's regulatory system. It felt like rocks were lodged in my throat, and it tightened when I swallowed. I couldn't project my voice and couldn't sing. Skin-crawling feelings in my feet and thighs and scalp—probably due to my body adjusting to synthetic hormones—mimicked a low-grade anxiety. Would I ever feel normal again? Or was this my new normal? Although thankful my missing organ could be compensated for by taking medication, rather than having to undergo something like dialysis, I struggled with the fact that for the rest of my life I'd have to swallow a pill every morning and wait an hour before I could eat. Being reliant on Big Pharma made me feel vulnerable. What if at some point, for some reason, I couldn't get ahold of the pills? That thought felt like being trapped on an elevator. I invoked my spiritual teachers, thinking of *facing reality without freaking out.* It helped to think of Babette, who'd said she rarely thought anymore about not having a thyroid. Still, my ego was clinging to the notion that I didn't need pharmaceuticals and that I was a fast healer, an identity I formed after brain surgery.

I recalled a night in the ICU after brain surgery. Oddly, a memory of being on the surgical table had come to me, even though I'd been under sedation. My spirit/soul/essence had wanted to escape my body during the violence of my head being drilled open—and my body had ordered, as one might to a dog, *Stay!* And then more calmly, *Stick around, you just might learn something.* I'd laughed out loud in my hospital bed at this fantastical remembrance. I'd thought it odd my body was teaching my soul, because I'd imagined the spirit as the wise part of me. But now I realized my spirit couldn't experience this life, this time-space reality, without my body, which had its own wisdom. Of course Walt Whitman knew this when he wrote: *I have said that the soul is not more than the body, And I have said that the body is not more than the soul*

Now, when I listened to my body, it was telling me to take long baths and naps, massage the scar lightly, breathe deeply, stretch a little, take gentle walks, read good books, listen to music, laugh…and write.

I had the perfect writing spot, a lanai stretching out from the back of the house. Sometimes when I looked up from my keyboard I'd see a rainbow arcing across the horizon. I had temporarily put aside my book about travel to work on a new project, co-authoring a novel called *Revolutionary Kiss* with my friend Janelle. We tackled alternate chapters, and it was motivating to get quick feedback. I looked forward to receiving her pages. Inspiring each other, we were writing at a fast clip. Janelle had recently retired from teaching. At five-foot-two, she had boundless energy and could perform feats of astounding physicality, like spending an uncanny number of hours at a time working on remodeling a house. Her vitality fed her survival instincts while dealing with her own health issues and the tragic loss of an adult daughter. A history buff, she'd penned several historical novels over the years that I'd read in manuscript form, and I admired the way she could make a whole world come alive on the page. We decided to work together on a historical romance set during the French Revolution, an era she knew well. Why romance? We thought having a pre-formulated plot would be good guidance for an attempt at writing together. Besides, Janelle had already written in the genre, as had my mother whose books I edited.

After my neck stiffened from too much time at the computer, I made my way to the back yard where Dave puttered around, pulling weeds and otherwise creating beauty. As I picked silky lettuce from the vegetable beds, he set off down the road, Snickers at his heels, to bring bananas to the neighbors since the trees produced more than we could eat. The previous night, a warm and drizzly evening, we'd sat on the neighbors' lanai for a music jam. I'd brought my uke and joined more than a dozen other people who were singing and playing guitars, bass, keyboards, harmonica, percussion, and banjo. We couldn't believe we'd lucked into neighbors who did this every few weeks. The gathering had been so wonderful that my sadness about not being able to sing abated.

I came back inside, filled the kitchen sink with water then dunked in the lettuce. It had to be thoroughly washed because snails in Hawai'i that slink across produce can spread something lovely called "rat lung disease" which in extreme cases can lead to paralysis and even death—a case where being a vegan is not healthier after all! Next I threw a load of towels in the washing machine, then focused on cooking, putting beans that had soaked overnight into the crockpot, and adding chopped greens, garlic, onion, fresh turmeric, ginger, and tomatoes. I thought about how much Dave and I enjoyed domestic life and wondered why we tended to other people's gardens, walked other people's dogs, and cooked in other people's kitchens. I thought maybe we should face the costly and time-consuming application for permanent residency in Mexico and get our own dog (I wanted a twin of Gem), garden in our community plot, and when we wanted to travel have a housesitter of our own care for our place. On the other hand, we could sell the casita and buy a small property elsewhere (where?) with a yard where we could plant our own vegetable garden and fruit trees.

As my mind wandered around these ideas, I noticed each possibility brought a flurry of feelings, a weird mix of longing and boredom, a crazy tension between a desire for home and a yearning to fly. When I got out of my head and came back to the now, I realized I was already living the answer, that traveling while enjoying other people's houses and pets, punctuated by alighting in Baja for months at a time, was a balance I loved. Short of duplicating myself or entering some magical sanctum where I could live two lives simultaneously—a traveler and a homebody—the life we'd fallen into was a good fit. Truth was, if I had a Gem of my own, I would struggle with leaving her, even with a trustworthy housesitter, for months at a time. Maybe one day the scales would tip and I'd decide to fashion a life around having my own dog, but truth was, even when it was heartbreaking to say goodbye to a dog I'd fallen in love with, part of me was glad to hand the responsibility back to the owner.

Once I'd asked Dave if he could live *here*, or *here*, or *here*, naming some places we'd visited. He'd said, "I'm okay pretty much anywhere." I have been in relationships with people who don't know how to be happy or satisfied, and it goes without saying it's much better to live with someone who is essentially at peace with life. Whereas I tend toward multitasking, when Dave is reading, he's reading. When he's gardening, he's gardening. When he's eating, he's eating. Sure, there are times he's not quite as Zen. He can get irritable, especially when driving, which brings out his Dr. Jekyll— who takes as a personal affront each tailgater, speeder, and slowpoke. But the point is that while he loves to travel, he doesn't have a pull to be *somewhere else* all the time. I can tend toward agitation which likely has to do with spending too much time maneuvering in my mind what's to come, trying to control the future. That's why I'm drawn to Buddhist teachings that remind me to *be here now*. Meditation is my medication.

I'm not saying Dave is complacent. He enjoys researching and planning our travels and adventures. Mostly, though, he's milking whatever moment he's in, whether he's studying Spanish, doing the dishes, or hiking up a hillside. People ask me, since Dave's retired, what he does all day. I'm loathe to answer because I don't want to affirm the idea that our value lies in what we *do*. Let me just say he's no Gatsbyesque Daisy Buchanan lounging around on a hot day, the curtains billowing through the room, lazily proclaiming: "Let's do something. What *do* people do?" If he's not engaged in an activity, he's okay gazing out the window at the birds. I will say when he returned from distributing bananas that afternoon, he left in the car to drive around and take pictures, and I liked that he was following his creative impulses.

When I started to feel up to it, we explored the area, hiking around South Point, the U.S.'s southernmost spot, scrambling across lava rocks with Snickers at our heels, the waves banging against the cliffs below. A thirty-minute drive took us to Hawai'i Volcanoes National Park, where we followed a trail that wove through broad expanses of grassland, and then another that led us down steep, lush tropical terrain to a sulfur-scented lava lake crater, Kilauea Iki, that was like walking across the moon.

We went to the wild Puna coast to visit our friend Lynn, encountering roads blocked by lava that had flowed through the previous year, gobbling up 700 homes while making new land—evidence of the destructive and creative power of Kilauea (one of the most active volcanoes in the world) and Pele, the goddess of fire. Lynn took us to visit one of her friends who'd built a house with bamboo he himself had felled. It was a work of art with woven ceilings, golden bamboo pillars and, pane-less windows open to the plumeria-scented air. A sensuous countertop bar linking the kitchen and living room had been crafted from one long piece of monkey pod wood. When I asked about it, he said during the 1990 lava flow in Kaimu, his friends had gone to the site with an Alaskan sawmill and made slabs out of felled trees.

We had reached our seventh-year wedding anniversary and so we went to 'Anaeho'omalu Bay for lunch at Lava Lava Beach Club, the place we got married surrounded by forty friends and family. Honu, green sea turtles, dozed on the sand in the spot where we'd said our vows at sunset.

Our friend Stacey hadn't been able to attend the wedding but now she flew in from California for a visit, and together we snorkeled in the clear waters at Honaunau Bay and visited Pu'uhonua o Hōnaunau National Historic Park, the "Place of Refuge" and former royal grounds. When ancient Hawai'ians broke *kapu*, or sacred laws, they could escape the punishment of death if they evaded captors and made it to this hallowed place to be absolved. Fierce ki'i, wooden images of scowling gods, stood guard at the sacred temple. I felt the mysteries of time's passage in the hand-hewn royal canoes, thatched houses, and ancient fishponds.

Another day we drove into the town of Hilo and walked through lush Lili'uokalani Park along the ocean, featuring a Japanese garden with willows draping over ponds, arched bridges, and gnarled banyan tree roots. Earlier, in the same park, Dave and I had stumbled into King Kamehameha Day celebrations that honor the man who is credited with uniting the Hawai'ian Islands in 1810. On a stage bursting with vivid flower arrangements, groups of men and women, young and old, danced versions of hula to beating drums, their hips and hands conveying the ancient stories.

The next week, my former colleague Persis and her partner Dean happened to be on the island so we spent a day together at Punalu'u Black Sand Beach asking Dean, a birder, the name of every bird we saw. Also, Dave's sister Sue and brother-in-law Dan stayed with us for a week, cementing the fact that if we built it (i.e., went to cool places), people would come. It was fun to invite people into "our house," wherever we happened to be, as though we were billionaires with homes all over the world.

One day we picked up a hitchhiker who had her thumb out and packages at her feet. Entering the car, she filled the air with the pungency of someone who hadn't bathed in weeks. I rolled down my window. When she smiled and thanked us for picking her up, I noticed scab marks pocked her face.

"Is this Babette's car?" she asked, revealing she knew our hosts. She told us for the past two-and-a-half years she'd been living in a tent on a piece of land she owned. It had running water, she said, and an outdoor bathtub but no hot water. "That's okay," she said, "I don't need hot water." She claimed she was comfortable in her tent, except she hated all the noise of weed whackers—"everyone's always cutting back the elephant grass"— and tractors: "everyone's building." She said she didn't want to build and didn't have the money for it anyway. Before she lived here, she had been in New Hampshire. I didn't pry but was burning to know why she moved. I also wondered what was going on with her face: picking at scabs because of a drug addiction? But she wasn't skinny or agitated. It seemed to me she was wearing something about life on her face. She told us we could drop her off on the corner, but Dave said he'd take her to her property down a rutted road. When he stopped, she stepped out, thanking us, and we never saw her again. I imagined a parallel universe where I was living by myself in a tent on a piece of property due to some romanticized vision I had about living on the land. Or my own potential addictions could have carried me away. I shivered myself back to the present, Dave at my side. I might love to wander but I want a real roof over my head.

When it came time to leave the Big Island, we boarded an eight-seater plane for Maui after a worker climbed a ladder to pour fuel into the wing. Sitting behind the pilot we could see him busy at the instrument panel. I was grateful for the hypnotherapy I'd done to allay my claustrophobia because squeezing into this craft would have panicked me in the past. Now, I actually enjoyed lifting off and watching the Earth recede.

The host of our housesit picked us up at the airport and took us to dinner. He was kind but there was a mournful aura about him, his eyes those of a gentle dog who'd been scolded. His home was tucked in a suburban neighborhood of upcountry, the part of Maui featuring farms, gardens, and ranches on the western slopes of Haleakala, a dormant caldera. We approached the front door through an entry framed by tropical plants, a koi pond, and a serene Buddha head sculpture. Inside, the home was clean, modern, and bright, a sprawling living space filled with white leather furniture and a dining room table inlaid with mother of pearl. The kitchen was stocked with luxury appliances. He mentioned his wife was currently at their condo in Honolulu and they would be meeting up on the mainland for their trip to visit family. Eyeing my ukulele, he mentioned he used to play and showed me two beautiful ukes and binders of music stashed in a closet. I wondered why he didn't play anymore and what was making him—a man living many people's dream life—so sad.

He took us to the back lanai with comfy patio furniture and, at a small table, a single office chair on wheels where he said he spent most of his time. The patio looked out over the fourteenth tee of Pukalani golf course and beyond to the seascape. This golf course was well groomed and had an electrified fence to keep the pigs away. I pictured him sitting as the golfers came and went, and asked him if he golfed. "Well, that was the idea when we bought the place," he replied. "But no." I noticed the hot tub and said how happy I was we could enjoy the view while taking a soak, and he said, "Sure thing but the tub needs to be flushed first." Another luxury he didn't use. Dave said no problem, he could do it, and I knew he would since we reveled in a good jacuzzi.

He showed us how to feed the three outdoor cats, one a white Siamese with piercing blue eyes, another with tiger stripes, and the third a spotted feline that resembled an ocelot and hissed at us. He told us the cats would show up each day for the two feedings and were elusive but might warm up. As it turned out, the cats kept their distance, although the striped one would stretch out on a patio chair, tracking us with his green-gold stare, and eventually allowed us to pet him.

Before the host left the next day, he handed us the keys to his luxury minivan and, in an apologetic tone said it would be best if we didn't drive the Tesla parked in the garage. That was fine with us. I'd be a nervous wreck if we were driving someone's $100,000 vehicle. As it was, to my horror a week later I scraped the side of the minivan when pulling out of a tight parking space and ordered touch-up paint online which thankfully covered the scratch.

Some days we took long walks and swam at Baldwin Beach Park, an uncrowded and shady stretch of sand populated mostly by locals. Once we hiked at Waihou Spring Forest Reserve whose well-worn trail wound through assorted timber species planted over the years to reforest an old grazing land. At Maluaka Beach, we met up with Christine and Kenny, whom we'd seen on our last trip to Maui and with whom we'd taken the challenging ocean swim. They were their same vibrant, athletic selves. We spread blankets and towels under a shade tree and talked all afternoon, now and then snorkeling in the calm bay.

Daphena and Steve, friends from California, overlapped with us by coming to Kihei on the south shore, the sunniest and driest end of the island. For nearly forty years, Steve had a timeshare here. I'm fascinated how some people love returning to a single place over and over, a ritual not part of my genetic code. Near their condo, we dipped into Kamaole Beach for a snorkel with the most turtles I'd ever seen in one spot. Together we hiked Keoneʻōʻio Bay, also known as La Perouse Bay after a French explorer. Tucked in a rounded peninsula, it's the site of Maui's most recent volcanic activity, about 500 years ago. We got to this wild and remote place driving down a dirt road. Hiking across crunchy black lava lining the aqua waters, it felt like we were on an isolated planet adrift in the cosmos.

Later we met up at Maui Coffee Attic. I immediately felt at home in this café since upstairs hanging on the walls were a variety of ukuleles and downstairs held another of my favorite things: shelves with hundreds of books. A stage and chairs were set up for a rock and blues band about to play. Also joining us was Karen, a woman I'd befriended after meeting her son two years before on Why Nam beach in Thailand. He and I had struck up a conversation and upon learning I was a traveling writer he enthused, "You have to meet my mom! You have so much in common." He'd pulled out his phone and connected us right there on Facebook. I soon learned she'd lived in thirty-one different places all over the world.

Dave and I had visited her cottage in the upcountry hippie town of Makawao where she gave me a signed copy of her novel *Hot Tickets, A Week on Maui*. In a short few days I lapped up the story, a smart, funny, and at times poignant love letter to Maui and to friendships between women. As we all boogied to the band on an island in one of the most remote archipelagos in the world, I thought about how wherever we went, we found our tribe.

Intrigued by one of the lesser visited islands, Moloka'i, Dave and I rented an Airbnb for a week and boarded another small plane. On the flight, out the window a double rainbow appeared—not an arc, but a complete circle we hovered above. A magical talisman, it followed us the whole way.

We'd ordered a "rent a wreck" that awaited us in the airport parking lot, the keys stashed beneath the ratty mat. It had no A/C, but we didn't mind rolling down the windows for island breeze in lieu of paying three times more for a rental from Hertz. As we drove west on the two-lane road at the forty-five-mile-per-hour speed limit across open grassland it became clear the residents of Moloka'i had succeeded in resisting private developers' attempts to increase tourism. I imagined these unpopulated sweeping hills, an aqua crest of sea in the distance, to be what most of Hawai'i had looked like decades ago.

Soon we reached Kaluako'i Resort, a collection of condos overlooking the ocean, with manicured lawns populated by wild turkeys. Our bright rental with walls painted in orange and yellow had a loft bedroom and a westward facing lanai, where we savored the sunset each evening and, at night, the distant twinkling lights of Oahu. While soaking in the communal pool, we could see surfers ride the waves. From there we could walk to Papohaku Beach, a three-mile expanse of white sand we had all to ourselves. Oddly, on the adjacent grounds sat a ghost town of a resort that had gone bankrupt in the 1970s. We wandered through someone's ruined dream, eyeing broken stairs leading to stained doors latched with rusty locks, and windows covered with plywood—an eerie, powerful statement about the unlikely failure of capitalist exploitation of this island.

Seeking food, we drove to the main town called Kaunakakai that had the island's only gas station and a couple of dusty grocery stores behind wooden storefronts. We bought an oddball assortment of overpriced canned and frozen foods, and picked out fruit and veg from a wilting selection. Fortunately, back on the street we turned the corner and discovered a farmer's market. The stalls burst with island-grown produce and flowers and locally made art. Two young girls draped in leis performed hula on the sidewalk. I wandered into a cozy gift-and-bookstore and discovered *Without Reservations: The Travels of an Independent Woman* by Alice Steinbach. As I read it during our time on the island, I appreciated that Steinbach's stories were attentive appreciations of wandering, not necessarily centered around mishaps like much travel writing. She conjured up stories of how travel changes the traveler, and her words about slow travel resonated: "The feeling of connection comes from seizing the actual world … [not] rushing from place to place, always looking ahead to the next thing while the moment in front of me slipped away."

The island's protection from development became even more apparent as we boarded the only for-hire boat on the island and snorkeled over a pristine reef alive with pulsing jellyfish and humuhumunukunukuāpua'a, Hawai'i's state fish with its gold body and light blue mustache. Everywhere it felt like we were exploring an untouched antediluvian land. When we drove east, following the ups and downs of the rocky shoreline to Halawa Valley, we hiked alone along natural lush trails with pearly waterfalls draping down emerald mountains in the distance. We rambled through a forest area where trees had shed a carpet of multicolored leaves, emerging at a secluded bay where we swam. As I floated in the calm water, I half expected a dinosaur to emerge from the canopy.

The main reason for my interest in this island, though, was sojourning north to 3,000-foot sea cliffs, some of the tallest in the world. At an overlook, we peered down at Kalaupapa Peninsula, the sunlit and shadowed former leper colony and now a national historic park. In the mid-1800s those infected with the disease were shipped to the bay and forced to sail on longboats to this desolate enclave; anyone who refused was dumped off the boats and lucky if they made it to the shore alive. Maybe not so lucky, though, because the peninsula had no infrastructure and people perished from exposure to the elements and lack of food.

Eventually, the Catholic priest Father Damien settled there with his ministry and began building houses and a hospital. Damien, who helped humanize those with the disfiguring ailment, was canonized. More than 8,000 people died there, including Damien himself who eventually got infected. He was succeeded by Mother Marianne Cope who remained at the colony until her death at age 80 in 1918. Although a cure for leprosy (now called Hansen's Disease) was discovered in the 1940s, mandatory isolation was enforced until 1969. I knew much of this because, growing up, my mom explained how at Catholic nursing school she'd dreamed of working at Kalaupapa, to be the Florence Nightingale of the lepers. In the early 1950s, when she graduated, she indeed got her first job in Hawai'i but in a hospital on the Big Island, before Hawai'i was a U.S. state. As a kid, I was enthralled with black and white pictures of my mother wearing a pineapple print mumu and zoris, what she called flip-flops. She didn't make it to Moloka'i until a trip there with my father in the 1970s.

From the overlook, the sanctuary was so distant I saw only a mass of tropical greenery, no buildings where a handful of patients who, although cured, still lived with the ravages of the disease and voluntarily remained there. I'd been anticipating hiking down the steep cliffs on the trail and returning via mule, the only way to access the peninsula other than flying in and landing on its narrow runway. However, a recent landslide had destroyed the trail, and the flight was expensive so I decided to raincheck it. Besides, I hadn't wanted to pop over there on a plane but journey down slowly, letting the magnitude of history settle into my scarred body.

As my eyes swept over the point where the land met the endless sea, I thought of all the people who had lived and died there, and how my parents likely had stood in this very spot, how my childhood had disappeared—a home gone missing—how worlds came and went.

Chapter Twenty-Three

When We Can Hug Again

Winter/Spring/Summer/Fall 2020

At Anza-Borrego Desert State Park, I sank into a camping chair next to Dave. The campfire crackled in a circle of stones below a melon moon. Sammie and Lulu, a bonded pair of brother and sister dachshunds, were intertwined on their doggy bed, making it hard to tell where one pup ended and the other began. They were wiped out from the excitement of the two-hour drive followed by an early evening walk on the trails warm from the desert sun.

We had come to California after Hawai'i to visit friends and hunker down until renters vacated our casita. We were doing a two-month housesit in Carlsbad, northeast of San Diego. The homeowner, a woman in her sixties name Dewey, had given us the keys to her car and her RV. A former race car driver and a prolific quilter, Dewey was headed to South America. We were to feed the dogs twice a day and administer ear drops twice a week. She asked us to bring in the mail and eat the oranges and grapefruits we picked from the trees in the back yard—and to take the dogs camping if we were so inclined since they loved it.

The RV was fully outfitted with everything we needed: towels, sheets, dishes. She'd shown us how to run its systems and gave us the phone number to reserve a space at the state park via her friends Ken and Harriet, the volunteer camp hosts. They worked there during winter to escape Iowa's freeze, doing such duties as helping at the entrance, keeping the grounds clean, and being present for questions and problems. Their second home, the fancy fifth wheel trailer, had a barbecue, meat smoker, coffee roaster, ice maker, and satellite dish.

Even though we were California natives, Dave and I had never been to this area, the largest state park in California, nearly 590,000 acres that includes one-fifth of San Diego county. We spent three days hiking along desert washes and around toppling rock formations. The landscape was populated with cacti, palms, and the rare elephant tree that stores water in its gray trunk and limbs. We walked through Palm Canyon to an oasis tucked away in a rocky V-shaped gorge, crowded with thick shaggy palms like a towering circle of Chewbaccas from *Star Wars*. Eight species of migratory birds use the oasis, which is fed by underground springs, as a watering stop while traveling through the desert. It struck me that Ken and Harriet were like these birds, a migratory couple who travelled between their homes using an RV instead of wings. Maybe we were migrating animals, too, since our unfurling pattern was to leave Baja and come back again.

While housesitting for Dewey, we spent time with our friends Tony and Shannon in San Diego. That's when we first heard about a virus with the sci-fi name of Covid-19 that was spreading around the world. Tony, director of occupational safety at an international manufacturer, gave us a packet of face masks and encouraged us to wear them on the plane. I thanked him but silently wondered if he was overreacting.

In Japan and China when I'd seen people wearing masks in stores or on public transport, I knew it meant they were sick and didn't want to spread their germs. My father, too, had sometimes wore a medical mask in public because he had a chronic lung ailment that made him vulnerable to viruses. Since we weren't sick or immunocompromised, wearing masks didn't seem necessary so I tucked them in my suitcase.

Instead of heading straight to Baja, we flew to Oaxaca for a week. Mexico was a big country that we wanted to see more of. A UNESCO World Heritage Site, Oaxaca is a colonial city with a bustling zocalo (main square) populated by people strolling and sitting at the outdoor cafes sipping rich Oaxacan chocolate. The antiquity of the colonial buildings struck quite a contrast to Baja, which didn't become a Mexican state until 1952 and, with its desert landscape, is thought of by mainlanders as the under-developed outback. Along the city streets, the sun illuminated buildings painted in bright colors, the mercados bulged with produce, and booths sold beaded jewelry and purses. We explored art galleries and churches. Art adorned the buildings, from expressive murals to graffiti-style splashes. In Templo de Santo Domingo de Guzman a restoration team of three women, up high on a scaffold, was busy brightening up a mural above the altar.

In the zocolo, we lucked upon festival dancers, women with red flowers crowning their hair; they were dressed in white blouses and long colorful skirts that swirled with their movements. The men, bells ringing on their ankles with each step, wore masks with exaggerated human faces. As a band played, couples stepped onto the plaza to dance languid *danzón*, like an underwater tango.

One day we explored sites outside of the city, including the ruins at Monte Albán, a UNESCO Heritage site, which had been inhabited over a period of 1,500 years by the Zapotecs who built terraces, dams, canals, and pyramids. Among the ruins, the ceremonial center still stands tall atop khaki-colored mountains that rise out of the valley. We walked up the pyramid's steep steps to the top of a ridge, and standing there overlooking the ruins, my mind overlaid bustling Oaxaca City on top of this ghostly scene and wondered how in the future people might view the ruins of our cities and imagine what our lives had been like.

Once Monte Albán had begun to decay, another site, Mitla, functioned as the center of political and religious power for the Zapotecs. There we walked along the ruins of domes and crumbling stone walls surrounded by cactus. The architecture wasn't as grand as Monte Albán's and didn't have its extensive views; it is characterized as having been built for pragmatic residential living rather than for magnificence, sort of like Reno compared to Vegas. But I liked walking along the courtyards and peering into the long narrow rooms of the one-story rectangular buildings, envisioning the ancients' daily lives.

We spent another day at the petrified waterfalls of Hierve el Agua, in the mountains between Sierra Mixe and Sierra Norte de Oaxaca. Formed for thousands of years by the runoff of water with high mineral content, these *cascadas petrificadas* look like white water sliding down the mountain but are stone, a visual illusion. After snapping pictures of a petrified fall that draped down nearly 200 feet, we walked along an area with iron-scented mineral pools. Their color was unreal, crystal clear and turquoise, creating a feeling of an infinite water mirror. I'd seen a lot of water features in my life, but nothing like this place, and I was reminded how much the world has to offer. Traveling expanded my vision; there was always more to this miraculous planet.

Back in the city as we ate breakfast in a café, I overheard the couple next to us talking about their travels. We struck up a conversation, and it turned out they had left New Jersey more than a year before to become full-time travelers who also did a lot of housesitting. In their forties, they had reached FIRE—Financially Independent Retired Early. I didn't dig into how, but there are many ways people do this, including strong investments, living frugally, not going into debt, real estate, and inheritance. Although they'd been to more than twenty countries, they had no interest in collecting passport stamps but preferred slow travel. I recognized them as fellow wanderers. As we talked, we discovered we knew nomads in common and that the Airbnb they were renting was right next to our hotel. We took out our phones to add each other on social media and agreed to meet for dinner.

That afternoon I perused JoAnna's Facebook page and discovered that in addition to posting about their explorations, she wrote about their daughter Devin, who had died at age fourteen. My heart plummeted. You never knew what lived behind people's stories and smiles. Later, JoAnna told me they always loved travel, as did their daughter, but her loss prompted them to live on the road. Through their lifestyle, they honored her, especially while taking care of pets since she had loved dogs. To have lost a child is unfathomable to me, and JoAnna said the grief is never-ending. I flashed on the sad Maui man, wondering if he'd suffered such a loss.

Our dinner conversation took a lighter turn when we talked about all the ways we don't mindlessly consume, something that makes our lifestyles possible. Dave and I mentioned how instead of going to salons, we trim each other's hair. When Joanna said she badly needed a haircut, Dave offered his services. Bouts of laughter later, we convened in our hotel room and Dave trimmed her soft, dark hair. JoAnna said we were destined to meet. It felt that way, given how we'd shared so much intimacy when twenty-four hours earlier we'd been strangers. I thought about how there was a certain vulnerability to being on the road that seemed to open us up to others. No wonder our web of connection kept expanding.

When we landed back at our casita, new threads of the web were spun. Through an online group, we discovered Doug and Johanne, a couple close to our ages who were housesitting near us in Baja, in north Todos Santos. We gathered on the rooftop patio of the home they were caring for, overlooking the Pacific Ocean where whales breeched and spouted on the horizon. As we talked, I agreed with Doug that there was an instant connection among us, what he called the "brother/sisterhood of housesitters."

They had given up busy careers in Vancouver, Canada and left everything behind to become home-free by choice. Their goal was freedom, escaping the nine-to-five. Full-time global nomads, they now own only what fits into two suitcases and two carry-ons. As of this writing, they are on their sixty-eighth housesit spanning fifteen countries. They've cared for 118 dogs, 78 cats, plus alpacas, donkeys, chickens, bees, birds, rabbits, and turtles. Lovers of the water, they've had gigs on eleven islands, and they prefer remote and off-the-grid locations. I admire their adventurousness and their contributions to communities they stay in. For instance, in Portugal they walked dogs at the rescue shelters, in Thailand they volunteered with Trash Heroes to reduce litter, and in Panama they brought supplies to a small village school and spent a day with the kids.

Like us, they didn't know they were going to become housesitters when they pulled the plug on their conventional lives. As Doug put it, it was a "leap and the net will appear situation." When he mentioned he had written a book, I immediately bought it. I could hear his jovial voice as I read *A Tale of Two Geckos: We Transformed Our Lives and So Can You!*, which he called "not so much a how-to book as a why-not?"

I was glad we'd met them before we learned that our San Diego friend Tony had not been exaggerating by handing us a packet of face masks. The news we were reading online was frightening: a global pandemic had struck, and people were suffering and dying. The governor of Baja Sur announced that everyone must shelter in place. The beaches were closed down, and only one family member at a time was permitted to go grocery shopping. No one was allowed to gather in groups for any reason. The announcement ended with this poignant line: "The time will come when we can hug again."

Dave and I were thankful to be at the casita when the Stay at Home orders were announced. Many sitters had their gigs canceled, leaving them to scramble for places to live. The world closing down put the kibosh on our plans to travel and housesit in Europe, but we truly had nothing to complain about in our cozy little house where we could sit in the garden or on the rooftop patio, peering at the waves in the distance. We did wonder, though, if this would be the end of our traveling lifestyle as we knew it. Shakespeare lived his entire life in the shadow of the Bubonic Plague, which waxed and waned over the years. But 400 years later, surely science would come to our rescue.

I thought about how hard quarantine would be on people who live alone. With schools and job sites around the world closed, I couldn't imagine how people would be able to continue to make a living. And if they were able to go to work, what would they do with their kids who weren't in school? As I read stories of elderly people imprisoned in nursing facilities that weren't allowing visitors, it tore me up imagining what it would have been like for my mother who lived the last years of her life in assisted living. The stories of people dying alone in the hospital, no loved ones allowed at their side, were devastating. That could have been the case for my father. As much as I missed my parents, I was grateful they didn't have to live through this era.

Days began to blend together. I continued working on the French Revolution novel, sinking into the dreamy living-two-lives feeling. Still, I would have gone stir crazy if not for my access to the outdoors. I might not have been able to walk the beach, but I could hike the hills. It was eerie looking down on deserted Cerritos Beach and passing not another person or car or quad for miles. I ambled by skeletons of half-built homes, construction having come to a dead stop, and realized this would be the last time I would see this area sparsely populated. The building boom had paused but it would no doubt restart with a vengeance at some point. Atop a hill, I lingered to catch my breath and in the expanse of fields one guy and his horse plowed a furrow. Creatures that I'd rarely seen before appeared: roadrunners darted across my path, rabbits bounded amongst cacti, horny toads sunned on flat rocks. I wondered if this was what would happen after an apocalypse—nature breathing a sigh of relief at the extinction of the human species.

In quarantine, the internet took on fresh importance. It was bittersweet watching friends in isolation sharing their creativity. One played his guitar and sang a new song each day. Another, in her pjs in bed, YouTubed herself telling hilarious, heart-warming stories. People offered up what they were cooking, painting, writing—and I developed an online course called "Inspired Writing," connecting writers from all over the world. Dave and I attended two online weddings, something we never could have imagined a short few months earlier. For Dave's birthday, I assembled a collection of video clips of friends wishing him Happy Birthday. We both got a little teary seeing everyone's faces. Three of my good friends and I started meeting bimonthly on Zoom, and I realized that, ironically, we were talking more regularly than we ever had before. Our neighbors organized a "Dance on Your Rooftop" party, streaming music through a Zoom session where we waved at each other on our screens and from our rooftops. These experiences fed a pandemic hunger to feel connected.

We also wanted to help Mexicans who relied on daily work to feed their families. We donated to a local organization that distributed free food, and Dave got involved, packing bundles into trucks and delivering them to the church.

Our six-month visas close to expiring, we made our way to Cabo for a free extension being offered by the government. Standing in line in the nondescript government building, every person's face encased in a mask, felt Orwellian. By this point, some restrictions had been loosened. Beaches opened for limited hours, and restaurants began serving food outdoors. Our small community had created a bubble and at times we relaxed our use of masks. Decision fatigue set in as we questioned every move we made: Wear a mask while talking to a neighbor in the yard? Swim at the pool around other people? Go into this store, or that one? These were small worries compared to what many had to face, yet I found myself aching for ordinary life...and wondering if normalcy would ever return.

And then the news reported a vaccination becoming available and we cheered, imagining freedom from the plague. Excited we could see the tunnel's end, we decided to take a few housesits in the States, hoping we could get vaccinated since the shots would not be available in Mexico for a while.

Three weeks before leaving, I was taking a walk to the beach when a big truck approached, hogging up the narrow dirt lane. I stepped up onto the berm, and as soon as it passed, I slipped and my foot and flimsy flip-flop flew different directions, my body slamming to the ground. Stunned, I sat up and numbness transformed into stabbing pain in my left foot and ankle. I tried to move but that leg was useless, except to send jolts of agony up my body. Crying, I looked around for assistance—only to see a few lonely cacti and a half-built house. I screeched out for help. Suddenly a pickup truck approached. It stopped and three strangers hustled out, two surfer dudes in swim trunks and a tan young woman with tangled hair. She hovered over me, lightly placing one hand on my leg and another on my shoulder, immediately alleviating my nausea.

"Are you a healer?" I asked.

She smiled and said no, but one of the guys said, "She just might be."

The guys helped me stand on one leg and hobble into the truck as I told them where to take me. No one was wearing masks, and for a moment I thought getting Covid would add insult to ankle injury. The bumpy ride sent fiery stabs into my leg.

"This hurts worse than my brain surgery and thyroid surgery," I said, trying to distract myself.

"Wow, I just had a tumor removed from my chest two months ago." The driver pulled down the neck of his tee-shirt to display his scar. "I still have morphine pills they gave me. I have no idea why I brought them today, but I guess you were the reason." I wasn't so far gone I couldn't appreciate the synchronicity—and to be reminded that we all suffer, and we are here to help one another. When we got to the complex, the guys helped me hop on my right leg into our house. Dave and his friend Art, who were doing yoga, jumped up from their mats. I sank to the couch and swallowed a morphine pill, thanking the strangers as they left. They were like angels, descending to help me then melting back into the ether.

Art, a former college basketball player, immediately elevated my leg and reminded me to breathe. "Accept the pain and let it flow by," he said as Dave gently placed a pack of frozen corn on my ankle and foot. Art asked if I could wiggle my toes. Yes. A good sign. But the whole area was purpling and swelling. He talked about similar injuries he'd had, as I shifted on the couch to try to eke out an ounce of comfort.

Art said it would be better if I got to bed, but moving to the bedroom seemed insurmountable. He said he'd carry me, and I balked, knowing I'm not feather-light. Ignoring me, he scooped me up. My eyes pricked with tears, from pain and from his kindness.

A neighbor brought me herbal tea and essential oils, and another gave us an ace bandage. I was glad for our community, even if that meant forfeiting quiet and isolation in the resort's close quarters. The web of connection wove through our lives in innumerable ways.

Once again our future plans hung in the balance because of my health. We were supposed to drive to Southern California for a housesit in three weeks. I had a hard time imagining sitting in a car for that long, my ankle and foot throbbing. I could barely get around on a knee scooter, a loaner from another neighbor. What if the doctor in Cabo recommended surgery?

In the past months, I'd turned the corner from the thyroid debacle and had been gaining strength hill hiking. This fall was a demoralizing setback. I tried to focus on the fact that the body knows how to heal. I also reminded myself we'd faced a lot of surprises and unknowns in our nomadic lives, and everything always worked out one way or another. To help myself relax, I created a mantra: *love* on the in-breath and *healing* on the out-breath, a soothing practice that helped me drift off to sleep.

Later, x-rays determined I had a bad sprain. While such a sprain could take longer to heal than a break, it also meant no surgery. The doctor told me to start walking in a therapeutic boot. Wearing the thing made me feel half robot, but I figured I could make the long car ride with it strapped to my leg. Good thing, too, because Dave couldn't fit the knee scooter in the car.

My fifties had been so turbulent: brain surgery, thyroid surgery, surgery on my thigh to remove a squamous cell growth, and now being hobbled by my own inappropriate footwear. This brought to mind my father, who at age fifty was diagnosed with a rare lung disease. Doctors told him he'd likely live only two to three more years, and he was forced to retire on disability. While he was still able, he and my mother traveled to Europe and Hawai'i. He had to haul along his slant board so that twice a day he could lie down, his head low and feet high, to drain his lungs. Then Mom would pound on his back, sides, and chest so he could cough up mucus, since his lungs no longer had the ability to do so on their own. When I visited my parents, I gave Mom a break and performed Dad's therapy. Eventually he had to go on oxygen and travel became impossible. Still, he'd visit friends, go shopping, or attend his men's social group slinging a portable oxygen tank over his shoulder.

He was in and out of the hospital many times for numerous complications, but at home, each day he got up, did his therapy, showered, dressed, drank coffee, read the paper, ate meals. He loved having visitors and never tired of socializing, even when he had to catch his breath while chatting. He also never stopped driving, and after he died I found morphine in his car's glove compartment. Driving on that drug was probably illegal, but he was stubborn about living.

When I asked him if he wondered why he got a lung disease, even though he'd never smoked, he said, "I'm more likely to think *why not me?* Things happen to everyone, and I'm not immune." He outlived the doctors' predictions by twenty-five years, dying at age seventy-eight. Thinking of him, and also the suffering going on in the worldwide pandemic, I could shake off moments of feeling sorry for myself.

In *Still Here: Embracing Aging, Changing, and Dying,* Ram Dass talks about how if we live long enough, we will all face physical changes. This, he says, is an opportunity to learn we are "more than our bodies and our minds."

Clearly, this decade was sending me this message. It was also telling me, in the voice of my father: *Kathleen, you're mortal. Live the life you truly want to live because you don't have all the time in the world.*

Chapter Twenty-Four

Travel is the Bridge

Winter 2021

I punch in the code, and the door unlocks. We let ourselves into the suburban mini-mansion and pass through the front room, a space intended to be a sitting room—but instead of couches and a coffee table, a desk with a big flat screen computer takes up the space. A shelf crammed with hiking gear spans one wall. This décor reveals that an outdoor adventure blogger lives here. Likewise, his wife is a travel blogger and an online influencer, posing in glamorous locales in elegant clothes. Known for traversing the world with their baby and their Persian cat, they have thousands of followers on social media. They are a kind of couple unknown a decade ago: travelers who make their living online.

When I'd looked at their professional websites, I felt like an amateur. I have no YouTube channel and I don't "monetize" my blog (I was behind the curve in even knowing what that word meant). Many housesitting nomads keep spreadsheets detailing every sit, every pet they care for, every cent they save or spend. I'm a different breed, one who had to get a tutor to pass statistics. I prefer stories to numbers, personal travelogues to "how to" articles. I don't count countries, and the fact that there are many places we haven't been adds to my imposter syndrome…or at least a sense that I'm old-fashioned. Even writing a book that will appear in paperback, not solely as an ebook, seems archaic in traveling circles. But of course as Theodore Roosevelt said, "Comparison is the thief of joy"—and life isn't a competition.

We pass the staircase and enter the kitchen with spacious walk-in pantry to the right and, straight ahead, a dining room. Next to the dinner table sits a cage the size of a doghouse for Bun Bun, the fuzzy butterscotch-colored rabbit with long floppy ears. She is smaller than I'd imagined she'd be when I'd seen her in pictures—and, as I approach she slips into a hidey hole in the corner of the hutch. On our Skype call, the homeowners had told us she was shy. I make a mental note to lure her out later with a lettuce leaf.

To our right a sunken living room spreads out with a gas fireplace and a window displaying a view of the back yard. Tucked in the corner is a blue couch that later we'll reposition to face the fireplace and the view. We intended to move it back, but when I shared a picture with them and asked if they liked the couch's new spot, they appreciated the *feng shui* and requested we leave it. (We joked that we should add "home decorators" to our housesitter profile.) Out the window, beyond the lawn near a stand of trees, looms a heated chicken coop that holds three chickens we'll need to feed. Gathering eggs and cleaning poop is also on the agenda.

In the distance, the Oquirrh Mountains float blue-gray on the horizon. We are surrounded by mountains here in Sandy, Utah: the Oquirrh to the west and the 160-mile Wasatch Range to the east—our reason for being here, so we can ski. And, we hope, get vaccinated.

So that we didn't have to meet in person during these pandemic times, we'd done a house tour by video. Housesitters and homeowners not meeting face-to-face has become more common. Initially the pandemic nearly put an end to housesitting. But now U.S. housesitters are dipping toes back into domestic waters, as well as other countries that are allowing entry, such as Mexico. In fact, that's where this international couple (he's from the U.S., and she's Eastern European) is headed, to the Yucatan to give birth to their second child into a world of dual citizenship.

Prior to driving to Utah, we'd done a sit in Southern California, our first during the pandemic. We'd masked, and the hosts had opened the windows and doors for fresh air. After they oriented us to the house, yard, and cat, Dave and I headed downstairs to the self-contained mother-in-law unit for the night. When the hosts left in the morning for their flight, we came upstairs. It was a smart way to go, but I felt Covid had robbed us of an opportunity to befriend new people.

The pandemic did more than that, though. It brought divisiveness to the forefront. We had been scheduled for a housesit in Colorado but when in an email I'd suggested a masked turnover, the homeowner erupted, "I will not wear a mask in my own home!" He claimed no one in his community wore masks and that they weren't required in the businesses in his town. My subsequent research showed that while the area was politically conservative there was a county mandate in place requiring masks in public. I wondered if all his neighbors spurned the mask requirement or if there was a rift in his community.

The politicization of the pandemic and the polarization of the masses in the U.S. was scary and sad. That was a benefit to living in other countries: as an outsider, I wasn't immersed in their political scene and could disengage from such fury. That said, I knew I'd been part of the problem, firing shots at people I disagreed with, mocking the other side as fools— conveniently ignoring that some of my cousins were of the MAGA ilk. I didn't like how dogma stirred up my hate for the faceless "other" and so I'd tried to extricate myself from the storm. This host's animosity shook me, and we mutually agreed to cancel the sit. It had become personal, a wall of hostility built by media and politicians that benefitted from stoking enmity. I felt helpless to do anything about it.

But life wasn't letting me off the hook. I was presented with another chance to face these issues at a gig a year later when Dave and I walked into a housesit, stepping onto a "Make America Great Again" welcome mat, the telltale red hats perched on a bookshelf. My stomach clenched. I thought of the Buddhist nun Pema Chodron's insistence that everyone was our teacher—that in fact, I should thank these people for appearing in my life so I could learn more about my habitual tendency to close down when I'm "hooked" or triggered. The goal was to relax in that moment and stay open. I thought if they were going to talk politics, I'd try to listen calmly and respond with my truth without expecting change. Could I do that without becoming embattled? I thought about how much easier it was for me to give people the benefit of the doubt in other countries.

However, once we crossed their threshold, the focus of our time together wasn't politics, it was introducing us to their two hilarious French bulldogs. With the pups' scrunched-up faces and throat-breathing, it was like hanging out with Yoda and ET. The home was beautiful and the hosts exceedingly friendly, inviting us to eat anything we wanted in their well-stocked kitchen and introducing us to their neighbors. While they were away, a gift arrived in the mail for me, a silk pillowcase with a note saying it would make my skin feel great and give me a better night's sleep. I was dazed by her thoughtfulness juxtaposed with how we saw the world through completely different lenses. I could never understand her point of view when it came to politics, and I'm sure she couldn't mine. I'd been certain "my side" was compassionate and hers malicious. But clearly that wasn't necessarily the case. We are more than our political beliefs. And there are complex reasons we develop those beliefs in the first place. I realize I speak from a place of privilege: although I'm queer I appear straight, and I'm white, educated, middle class, and able bodied. But there's got to be a way for us to come together as human beings beyond the fractiousness—and being invited by strangers to their town to live in their home, take care of their beloved pets, sleep in their beds, and befriend their neighbors seems like a good way to try. As Rumi said, "Travel is the bridge between you and everything."

And now, four months after falling in Mexico, I am skiing at Brighton in Utah, my ankle supported in a custom ski boot. It has been three years since we've been skiing, and at first I was nervous when, disembarking from the lift I stared down the mountain that confronted me with its verticality. I didn't learn to ski until my late forties and am envious of the ease displayed by those who learned young. I remind myself to breathe, to lift on the turns, and to hum the Eagles' "Take it Easy" to soothe my mind. Soon I am reminded why I love the sport, the sensation of sailing by meringues of snow and emerald trees. Skiing is an opportunity to face my fears and to feel how I fly when I let go.

Later, back at the house, after showering and eating dinner, I snuggle next to Dave under a blanket on the couch in front of the fire, the skin on my face pleasantly tight from exposure to the elements. This is a lovely version of life. I cherish our snowy days followed by evenings warming up with hot tea, cooking and filling the kitchen with savory scents. Our stinky tasks of cleaning out the chicken and rabbit cages aren't fun, but they are a fair price to pay for living here for free. Nothing becomes drudgery because I know it is temporary. Reminding myself that we'll be moving on helps keep life fresh.

As we lean into this wintry Utah life, I don't yet know what lies ahead: that in a few months we'll be housesitting again in Hawai'i in a neighborhood that had been nearly demolished by lava flow, and that there I'll meet a woman in her seventies and help her get her first book published. Or that when we return to the mainland we'll ride bikes around the rim of the Grand Canyon, hike Carlsbad Caverns and Rocky Mountain National Park, visit our niece at her university in Tennessee, and be deeply moved by the struggle for human equality at the Birmingham Civil Rights Institute, housesitting along the way. At one housesit for a young couple in Colorado, there will be no table, so we'll go to a yard sale to buy one, leaving it for them as a gift. Eventually we'll drive back to Baja then hop over to housesit in Lake Chapala, Mexico, followed by more than two months in Panama. All of this will unfold as we build itineraries around housesitting opportunities that pop up on the websites, each one like a Christmas box to open.

Here in Utah I also don't yet know that even though we'll get triply vaccinated, we'll contract Covid while in Panama and, fortunately, weather it like the flu. We'll also both face other medical issues that we'll treat as we go. These bodies are imperfect and don't come with warranties. They are a reminder of our impermanence—and the conduit through which we touch life.

The message about life's transitory nature slammed us hard when we received a phone call that Mark, our Thailand friend, had died at his house in Alameda. He'd reluctantly come to California for health care and couldn't wait to get back to Koh Phangan, his now-home, the place he'd been searching for his whole life. I hated that he hadn't made it back to the island. I wished he'd slipped into the mystic while dancing at Eden or while spinning records at an island party.

I took comfort in remembering that for years he'd sought a scene where people could express their zaniness, their creativity, their essence, away from the watchful eyes of The Man—and finally he'd found it. He'd veered from cynical critic to ecstatic creator, inviting the embrace of community.

Mark had reminded me that going against the mainstream had risks but also great rewards. I considered myself a person who lived outside the coloring-book lines, but knowing Mark pushed me to see where convention still held me in its grip, especially when it came to people-pleasing and caring what others thought of me. He was a walking example of Michel Foucault's dictum that while the powers that be may assert themselves into our lives, "we are freer than we think."

I believe the best way to memorialize him is for Dave and me to continue seizing our own version of freedom. Often we will be walking on a secluded beach or along a tree-lined ridge, or we'll be hanging out with a young hippie crowd, or we'll be soaking in live music and Dave will say, "Mark would have loved this."

Sometimes I think the seed was planted for the way I live now when at age ten I read *Harriet the Spy* over and over. I couldn't get enough of the way she freely rode her bike all over the city and snooped on people, writing about them in her notebook—a traveling storyteller.

Maybe I'm wired to be lured by the siren's call of living—and reading and writing about—many different lives. Perhaps my wanderlust is fueled by antediluvian desire. When I came across the following words by Lisa St. Aubin de Teran, it seemed I'd found *home* amongst my ancestors: "I find it strangely comforting to think that the earliest form of human life was nomadic, walkabouts—that instinctive urge to take off and roam."

Yes, that's what it feels like, an innate itch that can only be scratched by following my instincts to wander. That's when the world is home—especially when we connect with people along the way.

However, the other day, I did catch myself saying to a friend in Baja that we were coming *home* soon. At times I'll hear myself call California *home*. And when we're housesitting I'll sometimes refer to the hosts' place as *home*. And yet I know at another level, home will always be the vast, still place inside of me that I take with me wherever I go.

Housesitting Tips

Dave and I have credited housesitting with providing us a way to see the world which we could never have achieved otherwise. However, be advised it is an unpaid job and there is a difference between being a housesitter and a houseguest. Here are some suggestions to get started:

Sign up for one or more of the many housesitting websites. We use TrustedHousesitters (for a discount link, see my website below) and have also used HouseSittersAmerica. TrustedHousesitters is based out of the UK but dozens of new gigs appear daily all over the world. Applications are cut off after five, so if you're actively looking for a gig, check the website often because the best ones disappear quickly. Other popular international sites include: Normador, HouseCarers, HouseSitMatch, and MindMyHouse. Regional housesitting websites include: HousesitMexico HouseSittersUK, AussieHouseSitters, KiwiHousesitters, HouseSittersAmerica, and HouseSittersCanada. *Note:* All these sites promote free housesitting, where no money changes hands. There are people who charge for house/pet sitting services, but that's a different approach not dealt with here.

Use alternative ways to find out about housesitting opportunities. Telling family and friends about your availability to housesit, and posting on social media, can lead to referrals. Also, there are Facebook groups for expats and travelers and housesitters in almost every town and region of the world, a good way to see what's offered and to post your availability. Through our connections, we now belong to two private Facebook groups where experienced sitters post referrals to gigs they've heard about but can't do.

Create a great profile. Most hosts are primarily concerned about the care of their pets, so highlight your love for and experience with animals. Also include what will make you a good caretaker of properties. Do you love to garden? Are you neat and clean? Do you have knowledge of pools and spas? Look at others' profiles to get ideas, which you can do on most websites before signing up.

Make your application stand out. Focus on the animals and use their names. Make it clear you've read and considered the hosts' requirements by referring to the important points, especially the pets' needs. Say a few things about yourself to personalize the message, and if you have a website or public social media account, include a link so hosts can be assured you're legit. Mention why you'd like to go to that location and how you'd get there. Make sure you include how they can contact you and when you're available to video chat. Asking a question or two is a good way to engage the owners, but save the rest of your questions for the video call.

Prepare for the chat. The purpose of the phone call/video chat is to discover if it's the right fit for both parties. Create a list of questions you have but don't launch right into them. Relax and enjoy meeting new people and organically thread in your questions, such as: Do you like to overlap with the sitters? If so, when would you like us to arrive and leave? If not, how will we get into the house? Where do the animals sleep? How do they get along with other people and animals? Have they ever gotten into fights or bitten anyone? How do they adjust to new people? Are the dogs good on leads, and how often do they need to be walked? Have you had other sitters in the past—and how did that go? Where are the closest neighbors/family members? Will I have access to the whole house? What size bed will I be sleeping in? Will there be room for our things in a closet? The fridge? Are there quirks about the house I should be aware of? *If you're driving:* Where can I park my car? *If you're flying in/taking public transportation:* Is there a vehicle available for my use? If not, where are the nearest grocery stores? How would you like me to handle getting the pets to a vet in an emergency?

Start out local. The best way to start is by doing short gigs in your area. The shorter sits are less competitive, and you're more likely to be chosen if you're local. This way you can accumulate reviews before you apply for international housesits.

Read House Sitting Magazine (housesittingmagazine.com) for a wealth of stories and tips.

For a discount link to TrustedHousesitters, and for more about our experiences traveling and housesitting, visit my website: www.kateevanswriter.com

Application that got us a gig in Lake Chapala, Jalisco, Mexico:

Hi Nancy and Rolf,

Dave and I would love to come care for Chloe and your home. We've done 40+ sits in the past eight years and are big-time dog lovers. We will walk with her, cuddle with her, and chat with her. Dave's nickname is Dr. Doolittle since he really does talk to animals! We're comfortable administering medications, and in fact I'm also on a thyroid pill, so Chloe and I will be thyroid buddies. :)

We're clean and organized, and are always very communicative with homeowners and are good at dealing with issues as they arise. Our home is in Baja California Sur so we'd fly to you from Cabo. I (Kate) speak enough Spanish to communicate as needed. I'm a writer and will be working on a book, so Chloe will never be lonely. Dave is retired from Business Development, and I am retired from teaching university English.

During housesits we love to spend time with the animals, read, do home yoga, cook, practice Spanish, and play the ukulele (well, I play, Dave sings along). We also enjoy walking, especially with a dog, and of course exploring the area.

We've traveled extensively in Mexico but have never been to the Chapala area and have heard great things about it. We're non-smokers, light drinkers, and are fully vaccinated. Feel free to visit my website and blog (www.kateevanswriter.com). I write about our lifestyle, but please note that I ask homeowners for permission if I want to post about the sit or any pictures of the property.

If you'd like to chat, we are available via phone (xxx-xxx-xxxx), Skype (*handle*), WhatsApp, or Zoom. We're currently in the States in the Pacific Standard time zone.

We have two questions:

1. How much overlap do you like with the sitters...hours or days?

2. Is a car necessary to get around? *[This listing had not indicated use of a car, but this question led to the owners allowing us to use theirs.]*

Let us know if you have any questions.

Cheers, Kate & Dave

Acknowledgements

Cathleen Miller, bless you for reading fresh pages week after week, giving me astute feedback, and cheering me on. Without you, I might still be wallowing.

Dave Rhine, for listening to every word with your incisive reader's mind. Your ability to detect repetitions, redundancies, and bad moves is evidence of your superpowers.

Angela Yarber—you believed in this book from the start. What luck we met in Hawai'i.

The following people answered my questions and/or read all or part of the manuscript to offer feedback, and I'm immensely grateful: Angela Yarber, Ann Knight, Anna Carvlin, Anne Jennings Paris, April Hirschman, Au-Co Tran, Babette Morrow, Barbara Kent, Chris Englert, Crystal Benner, Daisy Luu, Deanne Dale, Dewey Debutts, Doug Dyer, Ellen Kahan Eggers, Heather Diamond, Janelle Melvin, Janice Stanwood, Jim Stanwood, JoAnna Prescott McClendon, Johanne Sauve, Karen Lynch, Karen Sumaryono, Kelly Harrison, Laurie Heckathorn Morgan, Leah Carey, Leah Griesman, Lisa Estus, L.L. Kirchner, Nadia Al-Alawi, Nancy Larrew, Patricia Harrelson, Paul Buckberry, Paul Ridge, Paul Robert Mullen, Sarah Seymour, Shelley Mann Hite, Spike Wong, Susanna Bachman, Suzanne Rico, and Suzanne Roberts.

Gracias Alice Anderson for your feedback on my query letter.

Janet Fitch, our time in Baja made this book and its title much juicier.

Thank you to Deborah Eistetter for providing me with historical information about the Clayton Historical Society & Museum.

To all my friends, old and new, nomads and stay-at-homers: You are what this living thing is all about.

Deep gratitude to all the hosts who invited us into their homes.

Some details and wording in Chapter 14 were drawn from a Facebook post written by Mark Phinney and used with the blessings of his cousin Jill Gutierrez Wilde.

Portions of Chapter 21 appeared in an altered form in *HuffPost* as "Diagnosed with Cancer, I Had Surgery and Then a Big Surprise."

Excerpt from "Hell is the Highway" by Tim Bluhm reprinted with permission.

Excerpt from "Colliding" written by Kyle Hollingsworth and performed by The String Cheese Incident reprinted with permission. (Thank you to Beth Palmer for your assistance in this.)

Finally, to my parents, Don and Arlene—gone, but still here.